School Leadership

School Leadership:
Beyond Education Management

An Essay in Policy Scholarship

Gerald Grace

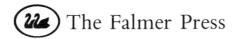 The Falmer Press

(A member of the Taylor & Francis Group)
London • Washington, D.C.

UK   The Falmer Press, 4 John Street, London WC1N 2ET
USA   The Falmer Press, Taylor & Francis Inc., 1900 Frost Road, Suite 101, Bristol, PA 19007

First published in 1995

A catalogue record for this book is available from the British Library

Library of Congress Cataloging-in-Publication Data are available on request

ISBN 0 7507 0414 4 cased
ISBN 0 7507 0415 2 paper

Jacket design by Caroline Archer

Typeset in 10/12pt Bembo by
Graphicraft Typesetters Ltd., Hong Kong.

Printed in Great Britain by Burgess Science Press, Basingstoke on paper which has a specified pH value on final paper manufacture of not less than 7.5 and is therefore 'acid free'.

Contents

Preface and Acknowledgments

Writing a book is an individual and solitary experience. Having something to say in a book is the result of collective and social experiences of support, dialogue, interaction and learning from other people. My greatest debt of obligation is to the eighty-eight headteachers who have been my co-researchers in this attempt to obtain a greater understanding of school leadership. With so many other pressures upon their time and thought it is a continuing tribute to the ethic of public service professional commitment that they 'made time' to help with this work. I hope that the result, as represented by this book, will not only interest them, and their colleagues, but have practical and professional relevance for their work.

The research, upon which this book is based, could not have been accomplished without the support of my colleagues in the University of Durham and in the University of Durham School of Education. The University gave crucial assistance in the form of research grants and the awarding of research leave. I thank those who provided the necessary institutional support and resources to make this inquiry possible, especially the Vice-Chancellor, Professor E.A.V. Ebsworth. My colleagues in the School of Education covered for my teaching and supervision responsibilities during the period of my research leave and I am very grateful to them. Particular thanks must go to Linda Burton, Mike Fleming, John McGuiness, Richard Smith and Linda Thompson, and to Susan Metcalf, my secretary, and Joyce Adams and her colleagues in the Education Library who kept me supplied with the materials and sources necessary for the project.

I learned much from my colleagues both in New Zealand and in Durham during my periods as Chairperson of the Department/School of Education about the dynamics and dilemmas of practical institutional responsibility, and reflecting upon these experiences has helped to shape this book in particular ways.

The Institute of Continuing and Professional Education at the University of Sussex provided a place for me to think and write. I am grateful to the Director, Dr Carolyn Miller, and to Professor Tony Becher for their assistance in obtaining for me the status of Visiting Fellow in 1993–94, and for the study facilities which helped me to be a reflective practitioner.

During the years in which this book has been in formation I have learned from the academic and theoretical work of Basil Bernstein that it is necessary

to try to go beyond the surface appearances of social and educational phenomena to make visible the deep structuring of that phenomena. For me, much of
that deep structuring is the living force of historical cultural practice, still
operative in contemporary educational settings.

It will be clear to the reader that my analysis has also been significantly
and positively influenced by the work of Michael Apple, Stephen Ball, Richard
Bates, Jillian Blackmore, Tony Bryk, Roger Dale, Rosemary Deem, Brian
Fay, William Foster, Thomas Greenfield, Amy Gutmann, Christopher
Hodgkinson, Richard Johnson and the Education Group writers, Marilyn
Joyce, Jenny Ozga, Fazal Rizvi, Charol Shakeshaft, Brian Simon, John Smyth,
Patricia White and Michael Young.

My thinking about the issues involved in the study of school leadership
has benefited from discussions with Mike Byram, Frank Coffield and David
Galloway, and from feedback on early draft material received from William
Taylor, Tony Edwards, Colin Lacey and Jeannie Lum. I am grateful also to
the participants in the American Educational Research Association (AERA)
Conference at New Orleans in April 1994 for positive and stimulating input
to the project. The papers and arguments presented at that conference, in
particular by Patricia Broadfoot, Paul Croll, Valerie Hall, Andrew Pollard and
Robert Chase (National Education Association, Washington) have shaped the
analysis in important ways.

Valuable assistance has been received on the wider comparative aspects
of this research, especially on emergent European experience, from Dr Sjoerd
Karsten (Amsterdam) and from Dr Lourdes Montero (Universidade de Santiago
de Compostela), and the writing of the book has been made easier by the
hospitable encouragement of Malcolm Clarkson of The Falmer Press.

It would be wrong, of course, not to acknowledge the influence of those
whose approaches to school leadership and governance are either explicitly or
implicitly criticized in this book. Among such writers, the work of John
Chubb and Terry Moe has probably been most influential in public debate in
various settings. While acknowledging that their analysis of school governance and their prescriptions for its future are radical, this present work argues
that they are radically limited and misconceived. The proposition that the
constitutional, democratic governance of schools has been tried and has failed,
and the proposition that educational salvation will be found in the application
of market forces in education, cannot be sustained on the evidence of this
book.

My experiences in New Zealand were deeply formative of much that
appears in this book. It was there that I realized that education could not be
a commodity in the market place and it was there also that I realized that
active democratic involvement in school governance and educational decision
making was a real and practical possibility.

My struggle with these ideas has been sustained by the encouragement
and help of my family. June Grace has not only translated script to text with
great efficiency but, more importantly, has critically evaluated and shaped

what has finally been said. Claire Grace has warned against theory winning over practice. Helena Grace has had a significant effect upon the writing of Chapter 10 on women and educational leadership. Dominic Grace has made me think about what the 'field applications' of this project might be in various cultural and social settings.

Finally, the solitary writer must take responsibility for the final text. However, I hope that I have made it clear that this study of school leadership is the outcome of a collective enterprise.

Gerald Grace
August 1994

Introduction

The study of the culture and politics of educational leadership[1] is currently emerging as a major field of social and educational inquiry. As a particular sector of this academic and research enterprise, the study of school leadership is attracting much more attention internationally. In a field previously dominated by studies of educational organization, administration and management and described by Greenfield and Ribbins (1993, pp.164–65) as 'unnecessarily bland and boring', the culture of school leadership, true to its nature, is reasserting itself. Texts such as John Smyth's (1989) *Critical Perspectives on Educational Leadership* point to the possibilities for the construction of new directions in leadership studies which are informed by historical, cultural, socio-political and critical analysis. Reviewing recent work on leadership, Beare, Caldwell and Millikan (1993) conclude that:

> There is now a far richer body of knowledge winning the confidence of scholars and practitioners alike. This has been achieved with more expansive, multidisciplinary study of organizations and leaders . . . Leaders, aspiring leaders and others with an interest in leadership can now proceed with much greater confidence than was the case a decade before. (p.141)

What has caused this renaissance of interest and activity in the study of educational leadership? The answers to this question are as complex and as contradictory as the phenomenon of leadership itself. The existence of various forms of crisis in many societies—legitimation crisis, moral crisis, economic crisis and social and political uncertainties—generate the conditions in which salvationist leadership is looked for.

Hargreaves (1994) points to the effects of the post-modern paradoxes where 'globalization can lead to ethnocentrism, decentralization to more centralization, flatter organizational structures to concealed hierarchical control' (p.47). He notes that 'the main educational response to this social crisis has been to resurrect old cultural certainties' (p.54). Contemporary interest therefore in 'strong', 'outstanding' or 'visionary' educational and school leadership can be interpreted as a partial return to old cultural certainties. Schools need strong leadership.

Reinforcing old cultural certainties about the need for strong school leadership are new ideological certainties that educational salvation is to be found in the application of market forces to schooling culture. Related to Chubb and Moe's (1992) view that 'the whole world is being swept by a realization that markets have tremendous advantages over central control and bureaucracy' (p.46), new constructs of educational leaders as market leaders and as school entrepreneurs are growing in prominence and power.

There are, therefore, paradoxes and contradictions in the constructs of school leadership currently held by different interest and ideological groups as they respond to various aspects of the post-modern crisis.[2] The ideal salvation-ist leader may be a traditional scholar, an expert professional, an organizational executive, a moral teacher or an educational entrepreneur. While contradictions exist as to the nature of the leadership required, the form remains strongly individualistic. Despite a weak rhetoric of shared governance or partnership in leadership, the political and ideological cultures of many societies continue to legitimate the 'need' for strong individual school leadership.

For those who wish to resist the assertion that strong and effective school leadership is inevitably the property of one person (or of a small, elite group) and therefore a continuing manifestation of necessary social hierarchy, the critical study of educational leadership becomes essential. If, as writers such as Smyth (1989), Foster (1989), Rizvi (1989), Blackmore (1989) and Bates (1992) suggest, educational leadership can be a shared, transforming, empowering and democratic enterprise, how is this to be achieved?

The question of what educational and school leadership could and should be is at the centre of political, ideological and educational debate in many contexts. Traditionalists—pedagogic, moral and cultural—are interested in school leadership and have traditional views about it. New Right marketeers in education are confident about what sort of leadership the 'new freedom' requires. Democrats and community educators, feminists and critical theorists construct scenarios for alternative forms in which educational leadership can be expressed. School boards, school governors, principals, headteachers, teachers, parents, community members and pupils (or students) all have their own constructs of what 'proper' school leadership should be. For all these reasons it is widely recognized that it is necessary to go beyond the study of education management to gain a greater understanding of what education leadership is, or might be.

This book is a contribution to that end. In describing it as an essay in policy scholarship, I am using 'essay' to imply 'an attempt' and 'policy scholar-ship' to imply a mode of analysis which goes beyond policy science. Policy science, a concept first used by Brian Fay in his influential book *Social Theory and Political Practice* (1975), is a form of social and educational analysis which attempts to extract a social phenomenon from its relational context in order to subject it to close analysis. Following the models of natural science from which it is derived, it is relatively uninterested in the history or cultural an-tecedents of the phenomenon under investigation. The concern of a policy science approach is to understand present phenomena (in particular, present *crisis* phenomena) in order to formulate a rational and scientific prescription for action and future policy.

When applied to the study of education leadership, for instance, a policy science approach tends to exclude consideration of wider contextual relations by its sharply focused concern with the specifics of a particular set of leadership behaviours. This approach is seductive in its concreteness, its apparently value-free and objective scientific stance and in its obvious relation to policy formation. Policy science research has a high appeal to governments, state agencies and research foundations because it promises to 'deliver the goods' in a technical and usable form. As Chapter 1 of this book argues, Education Management Studies is a corpus of research and writing informed by a policy science approach, which is attempting to deliver, among other things, an *effective leadership package* which can be applied in a range of educational settings.

The perspectives of policy science are, however, very limited. What tends to be excluded in policy science research is the relation of surface social phenomena to the deep structure of historical, cultural, political, ideological and value issues. Many contemporary problems or crises in education are, in themselves, the surface manifestations of deeper historical, structural and ideological contradictions in education policy. There can be no fundamental appreciation of these problems and no effective policy resolution of them, unless they are properly contextualized by detailed scholarship.

Policy scholarship resists the tendency of policy science to abstract problems from their relational settings by insisting that the problem can only be understood in the complexity of those relations.[3] In particular, it represents a view that a social-historical approach to research can illuminate the cultural and ideological struggles in which schooling is located. By these means it can make visible the regulative principles which have constituted the nature of leadership at different historical periods and it can demonstrate the constraining effects of wider social, economic and political relations.[4]

Whereas policy science excludes ideological and value conflicts as 'externalities'[5] beyond its legitimate remit (producing what Greenfield, 1993, p.141 calls 'neutered science'), policy scholarship, in its necessary engagement with history, demonstrates that such conflicts and dilemmas have always been central to the experience of schooling. Policy scholarship brings back into the analysis of school leadership an historical and a contemporary sense of the ideological, power and value relations which shape and pattern school leadership in particular historical periods and in various cultural settings.

The term 'scholarship' can be used in various ways. It can stand for detailed but narrow preoccupations. It can stand for archaic, cultural pretentiousness. In the concept of policy scholarship it is used in neither of these senses. The aspiration to scholarship which is relevant here is a commitment to locate the matter under investigation in its historical, theoretical, cultural and socio-political setting and a commitment to integrate these wider relational features with contemporary fieldwork data. In this sense, policy scholarship is used as an essay in wider and deeper understanding.

In the chapters which follow, some attempt has been made to realize these principles in the study of English school leadership, with special reference to the changing position of the headteacher.[6] It is hoped that such a study will have both national and international relevance. English schooling culture is in a process of radical transformation. At the centre of these transformations is the position of the headteacher and questions to do with how headteachers, as school leaders, are responding to radical change. But the transformations of English schooling culture have their situational variants in many other cultural and national settings. The issues addressed by this book are some of the central issues which are being considered by education policy makers across the world. Such issues have their specific historical and cultural formation and are approached in each setting with a distinctive cultural repertoire, but it may be claimed that wherever there are school principals, school headteachers, school leaders, boards, governors or trustees, the power relations and the moral and professional dilemmas examined in this book will be recognized.[7]

Notes and References

1 Educational leadership is a term often used to describe leadership in a wide range of settings e.g., national and local education policy formation, community and adult education, higher education, etc. School leadership generally refers to leadership in a specific institutional setting i.e., an educational institution for children or young people. However, these distinctions are not strictly observed because difficulties arise when it is necessary to refer to educational leadership (relating to curriculum and pedagogy) in a school setting.
2 For a critical examination of notions of post-modern crisis see Harvey (1989).
3 In a political or policy-making culture in which rapid transformations are being looked for, such scholarly observations are regarded as unhelpful.
4 This is also regarded as unhelpful.
5 For a discussion of this in relation to economic science (as a branch of policy science) see Grace (1995).
6 The term 'English school leadership' has been used throughout to distinguish English schooling culture from the different traditions of Welsh and Scottish schooling culture.
7 It is hoped that, following recognition, culturally specific research and discussion will be stimulated.

Chapter 1

School Leadership Studies: Beyond Education Management*

As part of the rising dominance of market culture in education during the 1980s it is important to note the remarkable growth of Education Management Studies (EMS) within the wider field of Education Studies. As education has been recontextualized in the market place, with explicit assertions that 'education shares the main characteristics of other commodities traded in the market place',[1] the growth of EMS has been a predictable cultural outcome. Education-as-a-commodity requires to be 'packaged', delivered' and 'marketed' as efficiently as possible and Education Management Studies has risen to a position of potential dominance in order to facilitate these developments. Not only have texts on various aspects of education management begun to be a significant sector of educational publishing but, more pervasively, the language, assumptions and ideology of management has begun to dominate the language, consciousness and action of many of those working within the education sector.[2]

Within these broader developments, the study of school leadership runs the risk of being reduced to a branch of EMS, to a set of technical considerations about the school as a production-function centre, a devolved budget centre,[3] or a value-adding centre. Within this culture of enterprise education, a new discourse is generated in which school boards, trustees or governors become 'stake-holders' or 'players' and principals or headteachers become chief executives, market analysts and public relations specialists. Thus constituted, school leadership becomes a suitable subject for MBAs in Education and a useful addition to the portfolios of courses and conferences offered by a growing educational consultancy industry.

To resist these reductionist tendencies in many societies, which may be called the commodification of school leadership, it is essential to place the study and analysis of school leadership in its socio-historical context and in the context of the moral and political economy of schooling. We need to have studies of school leadership which are historically located and which are brought into a relationship with wider political, cultural, economic and ideological movements in society. The argument of this book is that school leadership is

* This chapter is a development of a paper first published in the *British Journal of Educational Studies*, Vol.XXXXI, No.4, December 1993. The author and the publishers thank Blackwell Publishers for permission to reproduce some extracts from this paper.

a suitable topic for analysis from the perspectives of policy scholarship rather than from the reductionist frameworks of policy science or education management science.[4]

From the perspectives of policy scholarship, school leadership is a cultural, sociological and historical subject for study and not simply a technical one. It is also an important topic for comparative study but whereas the perspective of Education Management minimizes specific cultural and historical relations and universalizes technical 'solutions', policy scholarship is sensitive to the different cultural forms in which schooling and various concepts of leadership have been shaped. The tendency to suppose that there is a science of education management which can be generalized in an unproblematic way across different societies has resulted in a field of study described by Smyth (1989, p.3) as 'superficial and fundamentally flawed'. In calling for a reformulation of the field, leading writers such as Greenfield (1986) and Bates (1992) have argued that there is a crucial school leadership–culture relation and a school leadership–values relation which can only be understood by reference to the historical and cultural particularities of specific societies. In other words, a policy science of school leadership is not sufficient but a comparative cultural analysis of school leadership will demand considerable study. To generate such a comparative cultural resource for greater insight into school leadership requires initial policy scholarship studies where the phenomenon of leadership is analyzed in depth in particular societies. Once an adequate corpus of such studies exists it will then be possible for second stage critical analysis to review the field and to look for the possibilities of cross-cultural applications and of reciprocal learning. The attempt must be to try to construct a cross-cultural scholarship of school leadership which is historically and sociologically informed and which goes beyond the technical primers of Education Management Studies. This is not to say that technical primers are without value. That they meet evident professional needs for those in leadership positions in schools is clear. The cultural, social, moral and political significance of school leadership, however, tends not to be the focus of the technical primer. To understand that requires more extensive study.

It is as a contribution to the first stage of this more extensive scholarly enterprise that this book is offered. What it will attempt to do is to illuminate some of the conceptual and substantive issues related to the study of school leadership in one particular cultural and social formation i.e. England. This chapter will outline a possible agenda for the study of school leadership and it will outline an initial socio-historical framework for understanding this phenomenon in England. Some conceptual distinctions between leadership and management will subsequently be addressed, again within a socio-historical setting. The following chapters will elaborate this initial synopsis by reference to more detailed evidence and insights derived from recent literature and contemporary research inquiry. Some attempt will be made in conclusion to consider possible lessons which may be learned from research and practice in other contexts of school leadership.

Agenda for the Study of School Leadership in England

The work of Bernstein (1977 and 1990) provides an important theoretical framework for the understanding of school leadership in England. Whatever the specific focus of his work, Bernstein has always insisted that the analysis of cultural and pedagogic practice and discourse cannot take place in abstraction from the historical and social structural features of particular societies. From this perspective, the origins of power and control in educational systems reside in the basic class structure of society. Thus Bernstein (1977) has argued with particular reference to English schooling that:

> Class structure and relationships constitute and regulate both the distribution of power and principles of control, that is, constitute and regulate the relationships between categories, the hierarchical form of their constitution and regulate the realisation of the categories—that is, the principles of control. (p.181)

Class relations are an important manifestation of power relations but Bernstein (1990) recognized a wider network of power relations which affects the schooling process:

> Education is a relay for power relations external to it. . . . The educational system's pedagogic communication is simply a relay for something other than itself. Pedagogic communication in the school . . . is the relay for class relations, the relay for gender relations, the relay for religious relations, for regional relations. Pedagogic communication is a relay for patterns of dominance external to itself. (pp.168–9)

If school leadership is itself seen to be a form of pedagogic communication and an important constituent of the hidden curriculum of English schooling, then it has to be understood within a network of power relations, both within the school and within the society in which it is located. An agenda for the study of school leadership derived from this theoretical position would involve the following academic and research programme:

a) Examining the founding conceptions of school leadership in English provided schooling[5] and in independent schooling[6] as manifested in the nineteenth century. In particular, such an analysis would have to show the constitution of power relations from both an organizational and a wider social structural perspective.

b) Clarifying the constitution of school leadership and school management as a shared responsibility of governors and managers (class leadership) and of headteachers (pedagogical leadership) in the nineteenth century.

c) Tracing the changing power relations between 'the governors as leadership' and 'the headteacher as leadership' related to wider social,

7

ideological and political developments in English society in the twentieth century.

d) With particular reference to English 'state' schooling,[7] to analyze the modern constitution of leadership in relation to some of its major regulative principles, i.e., principles of moral leadership, principles of professional leadership and principles of market leadership in education.

e) With particular reference to the role of the headteacher, to examine the ways in which the salience of these principles has changed over time as a result of wider cultural and ideological change in English society.

f) Understanding how those currently acting as headteachers in the state system are responding to the radical changes in the nature of school leadership arising from the education legislation of the 1980s.[8]

g) Making explicit the implications of changes in school leadership in relation to equal opportunities commitments, particularly questions to do with the representation of women and of ethnic community groups in school leadership positions.

h) Following through the implications of Bernstein's assertion that education is also a 'relay for religious relations', by considering whether or not the leadership of schools of religious foundation presents particular challenges to headteachers in an era when market culture in education is rising to dominance.

This academic and research programme amounts to more than can be attempted in this study. However, a number of these issues will be examined in detail in the following chapters. For the present, an outline socio-historical framework, with particular reference to the role of the headteacher in English schooling will be developed as a way of placing this influential form of pedagogic communication in context.

Constituting School Leadership: A Socio-Historical Framework of Analysis

Leadership, Class and Hierarchy

Bernstein's (1977) assertion that 'class structure and relationships constitute and regulate both the distribution of power and principles of control' (p.181) can be seen to be manifest in the power and control mechanisms of English popular schooling from its origins. The leadership of the popular, elementary and working-class system of schooling was vested historically in middle-class managers and governors. From the nineteenth to the early twentieth century such groups constituted in general an active and significant school leadership class.[9]

Among the various motives for the provision of popular schooling by church and state, issues of social control and of class-cultural transformation[10] at a time of rapid social and economic change were very important. Given this particular 'mission' for English provided schooling, it is not surprising that the importance of the controlling and monitoring functions of middle-class school managers was constantly stressed. As HMI Allen put it in 1845:

> There must be constantly at hand the unbought services of someone, either clergyman, esquire or members of their families, who, keeping the most important ends constantly in view, will be capable, both by education and intelligence, to give that counsel and infuse that spirit which cannot be looked for from our present race of teachers. (Quoted in Tropp, 1959, p.27.)

In an hierarchical and class-stratified society such as England, whole institutional leadership could not be expected from or entrusted to a headteacher who, however carefully selected and trained, would be in origin working class or petty bourgeoise at best. Institutional leadership, which involved setting the goals, ethos and values of the school; establishing its 'mission'; allocating resources available; and determining the mode of organization necessary to achieve this mission—all of this was a function of class position in English society, not of professional status. School leadership in this sense could not be trusted to a mere elementary school headteacher, male or female.[11]

What could be entrusted to a headteacher and indeed expected of a headteacher was pedagogical leadership and moral leadership, although even here such leadership functions were to be under close surveillance and inspection. Pedagogical leadership involved the headteacher in being an exemplar of efficient and effective whole class teaching to the requirements of a prescribed curriculum and an organizer of the deployment of other teachers who were, in this sense, literally assistant teachers to the headteacher.

Moral leadership involved being a personal exemplar of certain religious and moral values in schooling and of being the chief agent for their transmission in the schooling process. The notion of school leadership as moral leadership was a dominant construct across the whole range of English schooling incorporating working-class elementary schools, middle-class grammar schools and upper-class public schools. The moral order of all schools was seen to be closely related to the moral order and the social order of the wider society. In nineteenth- and early twentieth-century England one of the most important functions of schools at each social class level was to provide appropriate moral socialization relevant to the class destinations of its pupils i.e., to understand the moral consequences of 'knowing one's place' in the social structure. Headteachers at all levels of the schooling system had a particular responsibility to ensure that this was accomplished effectively by the pedagogic arrangements of the school and by the amplification of its moral and cultural codes.

School leadership as moral leadership was seen to be a bulwark against anarchy both within the school as an organization and in the wider society. In English provided schooling, headteachers were regarded as key subaltern agents in the maintenance of moral and political hegemony and this was re- garded by managers and governors as their most important responsibility. The 'disciplined' and 'moral' school was the desired goal and whether a school achieved that status or not was seen to be directly related to the personal qualities of the headteacher. A model example of the headteacher as a trans- forming force was reported to the Newcastle Commissioners in 1861 in these terms:

> There could hardly be a more striking sight to the understanding eye than the interior of the school in which I have seen 600 children present at one time, all under the most perfect command, moving with the rapidity and precision of a machine and learning as though they were learning for their lives. It is difficult to overrate the greatness of the work which Mr James Wrigley, to whose intelligence and unflinching energy the success of the school is entirely due, is effecting in the town. (Newcastle Commission Report, 1861, Vol.2, pp.222–3)

In English upper-class schooling, school leadership as moral leadership was also pre-eminent as the influence of Dr Arnold of Rugby and of 'his sense of pastoral mission' (Baron, 1970, p.185) spread in the public school system.

In all schooling systems, headteachers as school leaders were defined by their moral qualities and their capacity for giving moral leadership. Such leadership in the elementary school sector was, however, always given under class-cultural surveillance whereas in the grammar school and public school sectors of English education, the moral leadership of 'headmasters' was exercised in conditions of greater cultural autonomy. The 'headmaster tradition' of the public schools had been the successful creation of influential leaders such as Arnold of Rugby and Thring of Uppingham and was consolidated by pro- fessional organizations such as the Headmasters Conference (1869) and the Headmasters Association (1890).[12] The headmaster tradition as a cultural and organizational strategy worked to empower headteachers *vis-à-vis* the formal authority of the governing body. At its most influential, the mystique of headship was constituted by personal charisma, moral, and frequently religious, authority, impressive scholarship, the capacity to 'master' all other members of the school, indefatigable energy and a sense of mission or vocation in the role. The headmaster tradition as a cultural and ideological construct was a resource which could empower even those headteachers who failed to realize all of its characteristics. Norwood, in 1909, gave expression to this ideology in dramatic form:

> The headmaster is an autocrat of autocrats and the very mention of the title conjures up in the minds of most people a figure before which they trembled in their youth. . . . The headmaster, in most

English schools, certainly holds a position of absolute power for which no analogy can be found in any other profession whatever, a position further of authority and in influence far surpassing all that is exercised by those of the same rank in other countries. (Quoted in Baron, 1970, p.183)

The 'headmaster tradition' of school leadership, although formed in the exclusive contexts of upper-class education in England, can be seen to have had significant cultural and pedagogic mediations in other sectors of English schooling.[13] Its construct of school leadership and its culture of headship as personal, powerful, controlling, moralizing and patriarchal has become an important constituent in the subsequent discourse and practice of school headship especially in the secondary school sector.

As Norwood observed in 1909, such associations of the role, including its cultural autonomy, have been historically specific to English society. This is where the perspectives of policy scholarship which insist that contemporary school leadership cannot be understood without reference to its historical and cultural formation have to be taken into account. The cult of the public school headmaster in England may have transformed over time as the class structure of which it was a part has been transformed, but these phenomena, it can be claimed, are still potent features in the constitution of English society and schooling. Insofar as the cult and mystique of public school headship was recontextualized within English state schooling, it assisted in processes of greater cultural and professional autonomy for state school headteachers. In that sense, the relative empowerment of public school headmasters and (subsequently) headmistresses became a source for the relative empowerment of other headteachers.

School Leadership and Social Democracy[14]

The removal of explicit class-cultural control in English state schooling from the 1940s onwards in what has come to be called the social democratic period, marked a significant transformation in the direction of greater cultural and pedagogic autonomy for all schools but particularly for those in the working-class, elementary tradition. While attention has been given to the consequences of these changes for curriculum autonomy and for the relative pedagogical autonomy of teachers in English schools, the consequences for school leadership have received less attention, and yet this was a period of fundamental change in power relations.

From a socio-historical perspective, crucial changes in the constitution of school leadership in state schooling can be discerned from the 1940s to the 1970s. They may be summed up as the institutional and professional empowerment of the position of the headteacher relative to that of school managers and governors. While formal institutional leadership remained as the prerogative of school managers and governors during this period, in practice what may be called operative school leadership or manifest school leadership was to a large extent ceded to the headteacher. The extent and nature of this delegation of institutional leadership varied by category of school (being more developed in secondary than in primary schools) and also regionally by local education authority (LEA) jurisdictions (where some authorities exercised, via the governors, strong political leadership) but as a general tendency, delegated institutional leadership occurred in English schooling. The position of the headteacher as school leader was enhanced and empowered at this time as never before in state schooling. In many schools, headteachers became influential in advising and guiding the managing body on all sectors of the school's operations and while it was not unknown in this period for governors to refuse the headteacher's advice, it became increasingly exceptional for this to happen.

Headteachers in English state schooling, especially in the secondary sector, were able to establish a measure of ideological and professional dominance over other local agents in the schooling process. This dominance, at the local site level, was encapsulated by the use of 'my school' in headteacher discourse at this time. When headteachers of this period used the expression 'my school' they were articulating a degree of manifest school leadership which was exceptional both historically and comparatively.[15] In the 1940s and 1950s, in conditions of greater cultural autonomy in English state schooling, headteachers were able to assert the potentialities of their role for strong leadership. Freed from close central state surveillance in the professional aspects of their work, such headteachers were able to acquire something of the aura, respect and power of the headteachers of the great English public schools. In other words, a mediated and lower key version of the ideology of the 'headmaster tradition' could be recontextualized in state schools by those headteachers who had the confidence and personality to do so.[16] The extension of the 'headmaster tradition' to English state schooling can be interpreted as a form of class-cultural reproduction. Given the influence of the English public school system as a model for education, the amplification of its constructs of school leadership in the wider system is hardly surprising.

However, the changing nature of school leadership in England by the mid-twentieth century cannot be so simply explained. In the emergence of the culture of the headteacher as *the* school leader, a complex of cultural and historical elements was involved. The public school tradition gave obvious legitimation to the notion but the emergent hegemony of headteachers was assisted by other factors having to do with class relations and professional autonomy in state schooling. A crucial feature of the potential empowerment of headteachers, especially in working-class localities, was a change in the class and power relations of formal school leadership in the social democratic period. The class relations of an earlier period had been clear and explicit. The managing and governing body of a school had a class composition which ensured appropriate class-cultural leadership. The leadership of schooling was the property of those whose business it was to give leadership in all aspects of social, cultural and political life. In this class relation, even the headteacher of a provided school was a 'servant' of the managers. By the 1940s and 1950s these class relations had changed significantly. In a more democratic and participative political culture, the membership of school managing and governing bodies had become socially comprehensive and heterogeneous. The respectable citizens and elected politicians who constituted school governing bodies at this period were in a changed class relation to headteachers in state schooling. Where those members were middle-class professionals they perceived the headteacher as a member of their class, *albeit* in a variable status relation depending upon the social status of the school. Where those members were working-class citizens they perceived the headteacher, especially the graduate secondary school headteacher, as having superior cultural and occupational status. In short, the class relations of school leadership in English state schooling were significantly transformed by the social democratic changes of the 1940s, 1950s and 1960s. The effect of these changes was, in practice, an empowerment of the position of headteacher. Headteachers were no longer in a servant relation to the governing body. In class terms they were now in a relation of equality with many of the governors and even in a position of cultural and occupational superiority to some elected members.

As the class relations of school leadership changed, so too did the relations of cultural autonomy and the relations of professionalism. Arising from political, economic and social crises of the 1920s, the autonomy of English state schooling in curriculum, assessment and pedagogic approaches steadily increased and by the 1960s the autonomy of English schools from external prescriptive agencies was considerable. What had arisen in fact from a political and ideological crisis in the 1920s—a crisis of conservative hegemony—had become incorporated and propagated as an official part of the cultural freedom and pluralism of the modern English state.[17] English schooling had acquired a relatively large degree of cultural and pedagogic autonomy, not only from the central agencies of the state but also from the local agencies of the state, particularly in the secondary school sector.[18] Headteachers were the beneficiaries of this extensive cultural autonomy. While formal responsibility for curriculum, assessment and modes of teaching and learning was delegated to managing and governing bodies of schools, in practice this was delegated again to the headteacher, who became the responsible agent to report to the governors on these matters. The power of headteachers to be cultural leaders and pedagogic innovators during this period was great. It was a feature of the position of headteacher which attracted many ambitious and creative teachers to apply for school leadership at this time.[19]

The relatively autonomous relations of English schooling meant that by the 1960s and early 1970s headteachers had the potential to enact various constructs of cultural leadership in 'their' schools.[20] In Bernstein's terms, a headteacher might be an agent of cultural reproduction (renewing and defending traditional academic standards) or an agent of cultural interruption (bringing innovation and progressive methods into the school) or an agent of cultural transformation (attempting radical reorientation of the cultural and social purpose of the school).[21] Whereas in nineteenth- and early twentieth-century schooling in England the headteacher was little more than the cultural monitor for a pedagogic code prescribed by others, the headteacher of a state school in the 1960s could be the creator of a new pedagogic code or at least a major influence in its formation and implementation. The position of headteacher had considerable innovative potential for those who wished to activate change.

While headteachers benefited from the relative autonomy of English schooling by the 1960s, they also benefited from the growth in status and influence of professionalism and expertness. The social democratic period in English social and cultural life was also a period of the near hegemony of the professionals.[22] The ideology of professionalism proclaimed the powerful conjunction of knowledge and skills, demonstrable meritocratic excellence, expertness and specialized understanding, with dedication and moral commitment to notions of individual and public good. Headteachers as leading professionals were able to exploit to the full this ideology in their relations both with parents and with governing bodies. Professionalism was a powerful form in which autonomy could be claimed and practised. The headteacher advised the governors as the formal school leaders from a position of considerable strength as the manifest school leader and as the acknowledged leading professional in the school.

Insofar as professionalism subsumed moral commitments as well as instrumental expertise, headteachers were able to use the moral authority of their role to advance and propagate particular values to constitute the ethos of a school. These might be traditional Christian values, innovative Christian values, or relatively secular values to do with community, cooperation, fraternity and solidarity. The limits of headteacher autonomy always became explicit however wherever radical value change was attempted i.e., the transformation of values and ethos rather than their modification. Such attempted transformation had potential political and social consequences which could not be countenanced even in the period of high autonomy in English schooling. The terminated careers of Michael Duane at Risinghill in the late 1960s and of Terry Ellis at William Tyndale School in the late 1970s witness to the limits of headteacher autonomy. These two headteachers tested the strength of 'the headteacher as school leader' literally to breaking point.[23]

In general, however, the era of social democracy in English schooling from the 1940s to the late 1970s was a high point in the changing profile of headteachers as leaders. For a complex of political, cultural and social structural reasons, the position of headteacher had been strengthened although the extent to which these possibilities were realized depended upon the style, personality and confidence of individual headteachers and the strength of operative leadership which they encountered from their governing bodies or from the local education authority. The headteacher as school leader was never without real constraints during this period but the scope for a headteacher to be 'in command' was greater in this period than at any time before or since. It will probably be looked back upon as the golden age of English headship.[24]

Kogan *et al.* (1984) have given a summary of the power relations of this period in school leadership:

> The orthodox view of school decision-making is that it is controlled by the headteacher. This view of his (*sic*) authority has persisted in the public view and was frequently mentioned by governors in our research. Bacon's (1978) research showed that it still was the most important position in the school and could wield great power. The position of headteacher is vested with a high degree of both formal authority and possession of power. The Articles of Government give the headteacher responsibility for the internal running of the school but this is only couched in general terms. The headteacher does in fact have control over the internal organisation, management and discipline of the school. He (*sic*) has the power to define his own role and to a large extent the structure of the school. (p.59)

While the powers of headteachers (male and female) at this time were undoubtedly great, the dangers of constructing a golden age ideology have to be resisted. Headship as school leadership had real constraints as well as real powers even within the period of high schooling autonomy. In reviewing this period of English headship, Musgrove (1971) argued that headteachers were empowered in the cultural, professional and pedagogical sectors of their work of school leadership but underpowered in managerial autonomy. It was Musgrove's thesis that serious institutional autonomy had to involve discretionary powers over financial, material and staff resources and that such powers were not possessed by the majority of state school headteachers:

> because they have no voice in the major issues which concern their schools. In the maintained schools they have no say in matters of finance and resources and recruitment of personnel. They must take the children allocated to them and often the staff. (p.70)

In an analysis which was to anticipate educational and political debates of the 1980s about the importance of delegated budgets in schools, Musgrove was arguing in the early 1970s that 'financial control is at the heart of managerial power' and that 'headteachers should have more power' (p.72).

The extension of managerial powers of this type to headteachers in state schooling would have constituted a radical change in the social democratic balance of power in the education system. The social democratic settlement of schooling[25] from the 1940s to the 1970s was based upon an implicit understanding that cultural and professional autonomy was largely vested in the headteacher as leading professional, while financial, resource and staffing decisions were largely vested in local democracy, through the agency of the local education authority. Headteachers were, in effect, the administrators of resource decisions and of the bureaucratic procedures enacted by local government. Depending upon the political and ideological nature of that local government, the extent of its resources and the mode of operation of its bureaucracy, headteachers were more or less constrained in managerial autonomy. The culture of social democracy in English schooling gave legitimacy to the notion of professional autonomy but at the same time it gave legitimacy to the notion that the control of resource management was the responsibility of local democracy. For some headteachers, the exercise of this local democracy in schooling was experienced as enabling and supportive. For others, it was experienced as a bureaucratic impediment upon the operation of the school.

The authority of the headteacher as school leader for most of the social democratic period was premised upon notions of professional leadership and of administrative leadership but not, in any fundamental way, upon managerial leadership and managerial capacity. However, the structural and organizational changes of secondary schooling in the 1960s and 1970s and particularly the development of large comprehensive schools had important consequences for the culture and practice of school leadership. The size and organizational complexity of such schools gave an impetus to the development of a management culture in schooling. Hall *et al.* (1986) have noted that:

> The 1970s saw the emergence of more prescriptive writings (e.g., Allen 1968, Barry and Tye 1972, Poster 1976) on how traditional conceptions of headship needed to change and allow for the acquisition of management skills. These advocated that headship should be based, at least in part, on managerial technique and training, rather than depend on personal mystique or professional teaching expertise. (p.3)

In accordance with dominant managerial theories of the time considerable emphasis both in the literature and in official reports was given to the notion of quality leadership working in a context of consultation, participation and power sharing. The report, *Ten Good Schools: A Secondary School Enquiry* (HMI/DES, 1977) argued for the potency of the headteacher as school leader, providing that leadership was given in a style appropriate for modern managerial culture:

> Emphasis is laid on consultation, team work and participation but without exception the most important single factor in the success of these schools is the quality of leadership of the head . . . (Effective leaders) . . . appreciate the need for specific educational aims, both social and intellectual, and have the capacity to communicate these to staff, pupils and parents, to win their assent and to put their own policies into practice . . . They are conscious of the corruption of power and though ready to take final responsibility they have made power sharing the keynote of their organisation and administration. Such leadership is crucial for success.

Where greater consultation and participation of other members of the school was a reality, then the individual power of the headteacher as school leader was necessarily constrained. However, there is little evidence available to assess the extent and the nature of participative school management and governance in the 1970s. It may be that the rhetoric of participative management at this time was stronger than its actual practice.

While new models of democratic school headship were developed, the continuing influence of the 'headmaster tradition' should not be underestimated. Official reports and policy statements were marked by contradictions between a predilection for strong and effective leaders in schools and a formal commitment to the values of consultation and participation in decision making. It seems likely that one of the ways in which this contradiction was resolved was by a reconstitution of the headmaster tradition *within* the new consultative approaches to school leadership. In other words, that the headmaster tradition was recontextualized within modern management culture rather than being abolished. From this perspective, headteachers could continue to give strong and effective leadership by their management of the culture and logistics of meetings, whether with staff or with parents. In this way, consultation and participation could simply be new mechanisms in which the power and leadership of the head was not only realized but given a new 'democratic' legitimacy in a consultative age.[26] It is instructive at this point to note the ideological sub-text of the influential HMI Report of 1977 in its description of quality leadership:

> (Effective leaders) . . . appreciate the need for specific educational aims . . . and have the capacity to communicate these to staff, pupils and parents, *to win their assent and to put their own policies into practice* . . . (my emphasis)

A better description of the operation of headteacher hegemony could hardly be given!

This is not to suggest, however, that headteachers in this period were largely engaged in cynical manipulation of their colleagues or of parents. It is to suggest that the changing nature of school headship in the 1970s was a complex phenomenon constituted by various forms and styles of educational leadership. These forms and styles encompassed those who continued to operate on the principles of the 'headmaster tradition' regardless of educational and social change; those who recontextualized that tradition within new consultative procedures; those who were genuinely committed to real consultation in the school and to new forms of leadership; and, those who wished to make a radical break from the whole notion of leadership in either its historical or its modern management forms.[27] Each position embodied a different conception of how the power relations within the school should be exercized. The social democratic settlement in English state schooling thus facilitated significant institutional pluralism with the result that a variety of academic and pedagogic cultures developed in state schooling, especially in the 1960s and 1970s. It also facilitated the development of various power cultures related to the ways in which headteachers conceptualized the notion of school leadership. It was such institutional variety of both educational and power cultures in state schooling which was radically challenged by the school reforms of the 1980s and early 1990s.

Leadership, Accountability and the Market Place

Chitty (1992) has succinctly summarized the educational changes of the 1980s in English schooling in these terms:

> Conservative reform of the education system in the 1980s was embodied chiefly in the Education Reform Act 1988. This landmark piece of legislation represented the first substantial challenge to the system constructed at the end of World War Two, introducing to it such concepts as a national curriculum, local management of schools, grant-maintained status and city technology colleges. It has significantly altered the education system of England and Wales. (p.31)

The complex and often contradictory influences of New Right ideologies upon the radical restructuring of English schooling have been examined in detail by writers such as Griggs (1989), Ball (1990), and Education Group II (1991). All commentators have observed the contradictions arising from policies which constitute greater central state control of cultural and professional issues (e.g., the introduction of a national curriculum and a national code of assessment) and policies which appear to facilitate decentralization and greater institutional autonomy (e.g., by the introduction of delegated budgets and of local management of schools).

Other contradictions have arisen from an imperative to return schooling to traditional academic values and standards, alongside an imperative to stimulate enterprise education and develop a competitive market culture both within schools and between schools. The writers of Education Group II (1991, p.xi) refer to the 'formative power of New Right ideas and policies' in contemporary English schooling and claim that '1988 is animated by the spirit of Education Ltd, Education-as-a-Business Corporation: commercial in outlook, hierarchical in organisation. . . .' (p.ix). They go on to argue that:

> One way of understanding changes since the mid-1970s is as the reduction of educational autonomies . . . to make the institutional superstructures, including the education system, conform more tightly to the requirements of the market society . . . 'Accountability' is the way this project is pursued. Schools should be accountable to parents for the education of their children. (p.75)

Greater accountability of state schooling to parents (or 'consumers') has been a salient characteristic of the reforms of the 1980s. This strategy has involved an incremental depowering of local education authorities and an apparent empowering of those at the school level i.e., parents, governors and head-teachers. Governing bodies, in particular, are seen to be an important agency through which greater accountability to the constituency of parents can be achieved.

The era of the dominance of New Right ideologies has brought about significant change in the nature of school leadership in England. The ideological and legislative changes of the 1980s have fundamentally affected the power relations of school leadership. In particular, school governing bodies have been empowered or, looked at historically, re-empowered, to act as operative school leaders. Ribbins (1989) notes that:

> A close examination of the legislation suggests that although both governors and headteachers have been allocated significant new powers and duties, these have not been equally apportioned. Governors seem to have 'benefited' more than headteachers. (p.194)

In the new era of strong accountability it does seem likely that contemporary headteachers will not enjoy the relative position of dominance and autonomy which many of them possessed in an earlier period. The fact that many governing bodies have not yet realized the full extent of their operative powers does not alter, in a material sense, the changed power differential.

The re-empowerment and reconstruction of school governing bodies in the 1980s has been part of a wider political strategy to reduce the sphere of autonomy possessed by professionals working in English schooling. The education reforms of the 1980s have been propagated and legitimated by a rhetoric stressing greater parental, community and business involvement in the running of schools. This has also been accompanied by a rhetoric stressing the need for more effective mechanisms of monitoring the use of resources in education in relation to measured outcomes.

The return of operative institutional leadership (at least, potentially) to school governors can be represented, and is officially represented, as a victory for democratic accountability over professional vested interest and 'irresponsible' autonomy. However, it could also be represented as an attempt to reconstitute the class-cultural control of an earlier period of English schooling. While the language of school reform may be radical, it would hardly be surprising, in the present political context, if its intentions were, in fact, conservative. Empowering school governors, *vis-à-vis* headteachers, could be a strategy for restoring the power and influence of 'the natural leaders' of society, *albeit* legitimated in the discourse and procedures of democratic accountability.[28]

The analysis of Education Group II (1991) has suggested that New Right reform in education is premised upon a particular construct, i.e., 'parentdom

. . . as a conservative social category' (p.76). To the extent that this assertion is true, it might also be argued that empowerment of governing bodies is similarly premised upon a notion that the majority of school governors will in practice constitute 'a conservative social category'. Thus social and educational conservatism as realized in parental and governor power would become a most effective check against the progressive ideologies of teachers and headteachers, and a significant curtailment of 'irresponsible' autonomy. However, all the consequences of empowering parents and governors cannot be foreseen and the assumptions of universal conservatism seem improbable. It is possible that the empowerment of school governors could give legitimation to the particular interests of a whole range of social, cultural, ethnic or religious groups in the conduct of schooling. In some cases this might lead school governors to test their leadership role to the breaking point, as some headteachers did in the 1960s and 1970s.[29] Such conflicts can be expected to be particularly sharp and constitutionally difficult where the agenda of the governors is markedly at odds with that of the headteacher or where the governors may accuse the headteacher of acting in professionally inappropriate ways. As Ribbins (1989) argues, 'the bracketing together of governors and headteachers as managers of the school' (p.194) assumes the existence of high levels of consensus on policy and practice in education. In other words, there are potentially radical and unpredictable outcomes of governor empowerment as well as conservative and consensual ones.

Given the heightened importance of governing bodies in the exercise of leadership in English schooling, detailed research into their constitution and modes of operation is now required—research along the lines of the ESRC-funded project at Lancaster University, 'The Reform of School Governing Bodies: A sociological investigation', directed by Rosemary Deem and Kevin Brehony. Such research will need to focus upon questions such as: (1) Who are the school governors now? (2) How does the experience of school governorship affect retention in, and recruitment of, the governing body? (3) In what ways are governors asserting operative school leadership and what are their relationships with headteachers and teachers? (4) What is happening to gender and ethnic representation on governing bodies?

It seems clear that as a result of the education reforms of the 1980s, headteachers as school leaders have to negotiate a new relationship with governors as school leaders. In terms of institutional leadership, the position of the headteacher is less certain and secure than it was. It is also more problematic in two of the other dimensions of leadership, that of pedagogical or cultural leadership and that of moral leadership.

The greatest loss of autonomy for the position of the headteacher has occurred in the cultural sector of school life. The headteacher as curriculum or pedagogic innovator, so much favoured in the 1960s and 1970s, is now faced by the constraints of a national curriculum and a national system of assessment and recording. At the same time, potentially more active involvement of governors and of parents in these issues can be expected. The capacity of headteachers to give relatively autonomous cultural and professional leadership, one of the more attractive features of this occupational position, has now been severely constrained. It could be argued that the cultural position of the headteacher in English state schooling has been returned to that which characterized nineteenth-century headteachers i.e., monitoring the effective delivery of a prescribed cultural code. While this may be acceptable and indeed welcomed by headteachers of conservative disposition, those interested in cultural and pedagogic innovation face a more constrained future and a potentially serious loss of job satisfaction in the role.

Moral leadership also presents many contradictory elements for contemporary headteachers. While 'mission statements' are being constructed for English state schools it is being increasingly understood that the 'mission' which counts is success in a competitive market situation for schooling. A process of ideological transformation is occurring in contemporary English society in which education is regarded as a commodity; the school as a value-adding production unit; the headteacher as chief executive and managing director; the parents as consumers; and the ultimate aim of the whole enterprise to achieve a maximum value-added product which keeps a school as near to the top of the league table of success as is possible. In short, the market relations of schooling have emerged as the dominant preoccupation of the 1980s and 1990s. School survival and job survival depend upon being successful in the market, just as business survival depends upon a successful market relation. Contemporary headteachers are therefore expected to 'market the school', to 'deliver the curriculum' and to 'satisfy the consumers'. Expectations for innovation in the role of the headteacher have now moved substantially from the cultural and pedagogic sector to the marketing, financial and presentational sectors of schooling. Indeed the very term 'headteacher' is now often regarded as an anachronism for a position where the critical relation is with an external market rather than with a direct classroom or pupil relation.[30]

The contradictions for moral leadership in the role are that moral worth is now to be found in a reinvigorated version of the Protestant ethic i.e., justification through individual demonstrable merit. The moral economy of schooling is in danger of losing other commitments (where they existed) to community, collegiality, social justice and the public good. None of these considerations is thought to be measurably productive of success in the educational market place as currently constituted. Headteachers who take such values seriously as part of the educational process seem likely to face much sharper dilemmas in trying to resolve the contradictions. Schooling culture is becoming dominated by the culture of individual success (at both pupil and school level) and by explicit, measurable outcomes of this success. At the same time, schools are expected to make statements of wider social and moral concern, and to stress the importance of citizenship and of ethical responsibilities. It was a particular irony that a Catholic Secretary of State for Education was the chief agent for the propagation of an aggressive form of the Protestant ethic in schooling in the early 1990s.

School Leadership and the Wider Socio-Political Framework

In elaborating changes in the constitution of school leadership in England, I have necessarily been drawn into observations relating these changes to wider features of the changing socio-political structure of English society. I will try to summarize these now in outline form.

It is apparent from socio-historical analysis that school leadership in English state schooling has a complex relation with ideological and structural features of the wider society and not one of historically fixed correspondence. In the nineteenth and early twentieth centuries, in the *period of explicit class-cultural control of provided schooling*, the position of headteacher was clearly subordinate to that of the school managers and governors. The power relations were class relations and school leadership was very much the property of the 'natural leaders' of society. However, even in this period of high constraint and of explicit control, headteachers, or more precisely English 'headmasters', were beginning to acquire over time the attributes of operative school leadership. The cultural, patriarchal and hierarchical features of English society all assisted the rise of the headmaster as school leader. The mediated effects of the public school headmaster tradition contributed to a steady empowerment of the position of headteachers in grammar schools and much more gradually to headteachers in elementary schools and their successors. In this relative empowerment over time, the class origin of headteachers was as important as the class origin of the pupils.

In the *social democratic period of English schooling* from the 1940s to the late 1970s, the changing class relations of school leadership, the growth of autonomy in the schooling sector and the strong position of professionalism all contributed towards a continuing empowerment of the position of headteacher as school leader. It is an interesting and contradictory feature of the social democratic period in England that operative school leadership did not become significantly more democratic or community based. The chief beneficiaries of the class and cultural changes of this period were headteachers, particularly, but not exclusively, male graduate headteachers. School leadership in practice was strongly constituted in hierarchical, patriarchal and professionally dominant ways. The dominant position of headteachers in the social democratic period was one sector of what I have called the near-hegemony of professionalism in social, political and cultural life at this time.

This dominance, particularly the dominance of public service professionals, provided a ready target for ideological attack from New Right agencies in the 1970s and 1980s. The social democratic settlement of schooling was vulnerable to attacks about its relative lack of democratic accountability and it was vulnerable to the charge of 'producer capture'. The New Right populist project appropriated very effectively and very skilfully the rhetoric of democratic accountability in schooling and sought to integrate this with the discipline of market accountability—despite the many contradictions which result from this conjunction.[31]

The position of headteacher in this *period of market accountability for schooling* is undergoing radical transformation. Many of the traditional privileges and freedoms of the position are now under review. Many of the features that attracted teachers to apply for the position in the past are seriously curtailed. The power relations of school leadership are shifting away from the leading professional and towards other groups, parents, community members, business and religious interests. On the other hand, the weakening and predicted ultimate disappearance of control from the local state, from the local education authority, appears to give headteachers a new executive freedom—a new form of enterprise and management empowerment. There are, therefore, conflicting and contradictory elements in the constitution of school leadership in this present period of market accountability. Those headteachers who are drawn by the image of managing director, or skilful player of the education market place, will experience the excitement of new roles to be practised—on what is sure to be called 'a new playing field'. Those for whom the professional aspects of headship were especially important, particularly in the cultural, pedagogic and pupil relations sectors, have to face the challenge of adjustment or flight from the field.

All headteachers have to negotiate a new relation with the school governing body. The notion of 'my school' can no longer be maintained. The demands for persuasive advocacy *vis-à-vis* the school governors have increased significantly. Those headteachers who are confident in their advocacy skills will seek to 'manage' their school governors so that as much operative leadership as possible remains in their hands. Their ability to do this in practice will not depend simply upon advocacy skill but also upon the social and political constitution of the governing body. Headteachers now find themselves at the focal point of many of the contradictions contained in New Right ideological positions. The imperatives of authoritative leadership, prescribed curriculum, traditional moral values, democratic accountability and of market accountability present a rich field for potential conflicts in English schooling, and for those charged with leadership responsibilities during the 1990s.[32]

Notes and References

1   See *Government Management: Brief to the in-coming government* Vol.2, Education Issues: New Zealand Treasury, Government Printer, Wellington, 1987, p.33. Quoted in Grace (1989, p.213).
2   As Ball (1990) puts it: 'discourses construct certain possibilities for thought. They order and combine words in particular ways and exclude or displace other combinations . . . A new discursive regime has been established and with it new forms of authority' (p.18).
3   The devolving of finance to schools in the Local Management of Schools (LMS) initiative has introduced the language of 'the budget centre'. For one discussion of its implications see Thomas (1990).
4   For distinctions between policy science and policy scholarship see Grace (1984, 1987 and 1990).

5 'Provided schooling' refers to schooling instituted by the state and by religious agencies in England in the nineteenth and early twentieth centuries before the language of 'state schooling' was used to describe this system.

6 'Independent schooling' refers to private educational institutions for middle-class and upper-class youth and in particular the influential public schools within this category.

7 'State schooling' is the shorthand form used in English educational discourse for the schools provided by local government and by religious agencies i.e., the maintained sector of schooling in receipt of public funds.

8 The results of some empirical inquiries in the north-east of England into how headteachers are responding to contemporary educational change will be reported in later chapters.

9 The notion of a 'leadership class' in Scottish education has been elaborated by Humes (1986). In the case of Scotland such a class is seen to be constituted by senior professionals and bureaucrats. In the case of England there has historically been a much stronger sense of social class leadership.

10 Johnson (1970) has described the class-cultural transformation process in popular schooling in the nineteenth century in these terms:

> . . . an enormously ambitious attempt to determine through the capture of educational means, the patterns of thought, sentiments and behaviour of the working class. Supervised by its trusty teacher, surrounded by its playground wall, the school was to raise a new race of working class people—respectful, cheerful, hard working, loyal, pacific and religious. (p.119)

11 Women headteachers in the nineteenth and early twentieth century had to face not only the ideology of class superiority but also the ideology of male superiority. Their leadership had to be constructed in the most difficult conditions of double oppression.

12 For further discussion of this see 'Aspects of the Headmaster Tradition' in Musgrave (1970, p.183).

13 It must be noted here that the public school tradition was very much the tradition of 'the great headmasters'. Such headmasters could provide a powerful cultural reference point and model for male headmasters in the provided system, see Wilkinson (1964). More research is needed to investigate the gender mediations of this tradition for women graduate headteachers and for the comparable category of Very Superior Women.

14 See *Unpopular Education: Schooling and Social Democracy in England since 1944* Education Group (CCCS) (1981) for a detailed examination of and critique of social democratic approaches to education policy.

15 Kogan *et al.* (1984) noted that 'the British educational system gives headteachers considerable freedom to shape what are seen as their schools in the way they see best. . . .' (p.79).

16 It should be noted here that different forms of confidence and perhaps different personality dispositions are likely to be required for a plurality of leadership styles. The 'headmaster tradition' placed a premium upon high and manifest confidence and a strong and assertive personality.

17 For a discussion of this see Grace (1987).

18 The secondary school sector (grammar and comprehensive) enjoyed, in various degrees, the autonomy arising from specialist subject knowledge. Secondary modern schools whose pupils were not entered for external examinations in the 1940s and 1950s had an unusually high degree of cultural autonomy however without strong subject specialization.

19 My interviews with headteachers have shown the importance of scope for curriculum leadership and innovation in attracting teachers to apply for a headteacher's position in the 1960s and 1970s. The opportunity to have 'an impact upon the curriculum and teaching of a school' was a significant factor in deciding to apply for headship.

20 These possibilities became more fully available to headteachers in primary schools as the 11 plus selective examination was progressively abolished from the 1960s onwards.

21 See Bernstein (1977, p.149).

22 For a discussion of the power and influence of professionals during the social democratic period see Education Group (CCCS) (1981).

23 See 'The Case of William Tyndale' in Dale (1989, p.125).

24 The older headteachers among my interview sample took this view. They looked back to a 'golden age' of autonomy for the headteacher. They believed that the position had now lost much of its attractiveness and that there would be problems in recruiting and retaining headteachers in the future.

25 The notion of an education settlement implies that education is an arena for political and ideological struggle among different interest groups, out of which particular settlements are achieved at different periods. As the Education Group (CCCS) (1981) put it:

> the term 'educational settlement' . . . refers to the balance of forces in and over schooling . . . One way of understanding the history of educational policy is in terms of the succession of crises and settlements. (p.32)

In *Unpopular Education* reference is made to 'the educational settlement of 1944', 'the collapse of the 1960s settlement' and the 'emergent educational settlement of the 1980s'. In essence, a settlement is a relatively established compromise or determination in education policy.

26 For an interesting discussion of these possibilities see Musgrove (1971, pp.68–87).

27 As, for instance, at Countesthorpe College, Leicestershire, see Bernbaum (1973) and Watts (1977).

28 See Galbraith (1992) for an account of the ways in which 'democracy' can legitimate the control of an active electoral minority.

29 The recent struggles between ethnic community governors and other agencies at Stratford School, London, need to be researched in these terms.

30 Headteachers in my fieldwork sample had been told that to be in classrooms was, in effect, a flight from the management realities of the job. This had angered and distressed some headteachers, particularly in junior and infant schools. Women headteachers in these schools were disturbed by the notion that efficient school leadership required a greater distance from classrooms and from children.

31 See the discussion 'Public professionals; villains, victims or victors?' in *Education Limited* (1991, pp.107–12).

32 For an important review of these conflicts see Ball (1994).

Chapter 2

Leadership and Management: Locating the Concepts

The intention of this chapter is to locate concepts of leadership and management in the changing discourse of state schooling in England. Such an undertaking will also involve a necessary engagement with related concepts such as institutional organization and administration. Concepts of leadership and management do not float freely in the discourse of textbooks of educational administration or in the prescriptions of technical primers of school management. Such concepts have a history, a politics and a set of complex and changing cultural and ideological relations with the wider society of which they are a part. Watkins (1989) has argued that leadership, power and management in education settings 'should be looked at as relational concepts developing over lengthy periods of time' (p.30). It is necessary to trace this cultural history. Ball (1990), drawing upon the work of Michel Foucault, has pointed out that discourse constitutes a relationship between power and knowledge and that therefore:

> . . . discourses are about what can be said and thought but also about who can speak, when, where and with what authority. Discourses embody meaning and social relationships, they constitute both subjectivity and power relations. (p.17)

What will be attempted here is an exercise in analyzing the changing discourse of English schooling, as leadership is first constituted in the nineteenth century in moral terms and is reconstructed over time in market relation terms. It will similarly trace the changing discourse of school management as it moves from preoccupations with social control to contemporary forms of market and finance management in education. The chapter focuses upon the structuring of leadership and management discourse in education, located in a socio-historical framework.

One of the serious limitations of educational administration as a field of study has been its restricted analytical frameworks. As Greenfield (1986) has concluded, in his authoritative review of the field, 'the study of educational administration is cast in a narrow mould' (p.134). This narrow mould has emphasized the technical, the operational and the measurable elements of administration and marginalized the historical, political and socio-cultural dimensions of the activity. The discourse and language of educational administration has reflected this absence of comprehensive vision and expression.

One of the purposes of Herbert Simon's founding text, *Administrative Behaviour* (1945), was to establish a vocabulary of administration theory to serve the new science of educational administration. The limitation of this vocabulary, however, was, as Greenfield (1986) notes, that it 'would say nothing that could not be expressed in operational definitions' (p.136). The tendency of this language use in educational administration has been reductionist and this has resulted in oversimplified analysis.

One of the key areas in which this reductionism is most apparent is in the study of leadership and management in education. The concept of leadership, like the concept of culture, is not readily amenable to the check-list analysis of operational features which are favoured by texts of educational administration. Management, on the other hand, is, ironically, a more manageable concept and seems to be amenable to check-list analyses of various types. The concept of management can be more easily commodified than can the more intangible but nevertheless 'real' concept of leadership.[1]

Within the culture of educational administration as science, the effect of this qualitative distinction has been that leadership has been recontextualized as a form or part of management. Educational leadership which had a recognized location in studies before the rise of administrative science, lost its distinct conceptual identity in subsequent studies.[2] In a powerful critique of these tendencies, Foster (1989) asserts that 'the concept of leadership has been chewed up and swallowed down by the needs of modern managerial theory' and that 'what essentially has happened is that the language of leadership has been translated into the needs of bureaucracy,' (p.45). He goes on to argue that 'any discussion of leadership seems to dissolve into a discussion of effective management techniques' (p.48).

The reconstitution of educational leadership as a phenomenon distinct from educational management faces two challenges. The first is to establish, in conceptual terms, what the distinctions between leadership and management might be, because 'if leadership cannot be reduced to management, then it must involve something more than management.'[3] The second is to locate the discourse and practice of educational leadership and management historically so that the changing nature of these concepts over time can become explicit and visible. An example of this form of socio-historical location was given by Callahan (1964) in his analysis of 'Changing Conceptions of the Superintendency in Public Education 1865–1964'. Examining the historical development of American school superintendents, Callahan was able to demonstrate how the concepts and language of leadership changed over time. From early conceptions of the superintendent as 'scholarly educational leader' (1865–1910), the position had been reconceptualized in the early twentieth century as 'business manager' or 'school executive'. The rise of more explicit democratic values in American schooling from the 1930s to the 1950s resulted in a greater emphasis upon the superintendent as 'statesman in a democratic school system'. Finally, the rise of administrative science from the 1950s onwards led to the emergence of the superintendent as 'applied social scientist'. The value of Callahan's analysis is that it demonstrates that the discourse and practice of educational leadership and management is bound up with changes in the social, political and cultural system of the wider society. This is a further manifestation of Bernstein's assertion that 'education is a relay for power relations external to it'.[4]

This chapter will attempt to follow the example of Callahan by tracing the historically changing language of school leadership and management in England. However, whereas the focus of Callahan's analysis was upon the position of the school superintendent, the focus here will be upon the headteacher in English schooling as positioned in a changing discourse.

School Leadership and Management: The Language of Hierarchy and Control

The language of school leadership and management in nineteenth-century English schooling was a form of pedagogic discourse which spoke of hierarchy and control. In a strongly class-stratified society, such as England, leadership could only arise (or be legitimated) as the cultural attribute of class position. At the most general, structural level, leadership in education referred to the political ability of dominant classes in England to enact, design and provide an educational system for the efficient schooling of other classes. In its origins in English provided schooling, educational leadership was a concept firmly located in notions of class hierarchy and of class-cultural control. Leadership was a realization of hierarchy and a responsibility of hierarchy–it was *noblesse oblige*.

The culture of leadership in nineteenth-century England had, in all its manifestations, two crucial sources of legitimation i.e., a secular authority and a sacred authority. The secular authority of leadership arose from its visible and explicit connection with class hierarchy. Leadership was a dynamic expression of class power. The sacred authority of leadership, on the other hand, found its legitimation in the notion that existing hierarchies had been ordained by God. When children in nineteenth-century elementary schools sang the morning hymn 'The rich man at his table, the poor man at the gate, He made them high and lowly and ordered their estate', this ideology was celebrated and renewed. School leadership was a particular mediation of this wider culture of leadership in English society.

In the provided system of schooling for the working class, school leadership had two realizations. As Chapter 1 has argued, institutional and cultural leadership was vested in school governing and managing bodies recruited from appropriate class leaders.[5] Pedagogical and moral leadership was the responsibility of the headteacher, acting under direction. The language of school leadership in both the provided and the independent systems of schooling in nineteenth-century England, equated leadership with hierarchical position (the 'headmaster' must lead by energy and example) and with moral and spiritual responsibility (the 'headmaster' must have a sense of vocation or mission).

Foster's (1989) observation that 'if leadership cannot be reduced to management, then it must involve something more than management' (p.48), would have been answered in the English nineteenth-century schooling system with the assertion that the defining quality of leadership was moral energy and sense of purpose. Moral energy—the dynamic manifestation of moral and spiritual authority and sense of purpose—was the desired characteristic and quality for headteachers in the nineteenth-century schooling system whether their responsibilities were for a working-class elementary school or for a high status public school. Headteachers as school leaders were expected to have a mission to bring the school and its members nearer to the great pedagogic ideal of the time, that of 'godliness and good learning'. This was the essence of educational leadership and it applied to all schools.[6] However, mission could not be enacted without management. Nineteenth-century schools, of all social categories, had much potential for organizational anarchy and if the headmaster was to be in reality the 'master' of all other members of the school then he had to implement a strategy of control for the maintenance of internal social order.

In the context of this historical period, leadership as moral energy and mission was in itself regarded as part of the requirements of management. The authoritative moral leader clearly assisted the control process and in this way concepts of leadership and management were in practice linked. Management, as the imposition of social control in schools, required some form of organizational plan and mode of pedagogic operation, however, in addition to the moral force of leadership. The management of pupils and the management of learning entailed the creation of specific pedagogic regimes. The headteacher who was regarded as a good manager at this time was one who exercized close surveillance and control of both the teachers and the pupils. Management, in the elementary school sector, involved the detailed specification of pedagogic tasks for teachers and pupils and the monitoring of their professional and scholastic performance. In the public school sector, the management of the 'headmaster' could be exercized in relation to the pupils via the prefect system and in relation to the teachers by the use of staff meetings and by direct control of the terms of teacher employment.

School management in this period was largely about the capacity of headteachers to keep other teachers and the pupils in a state of subordination. 'Management' was effective social control in schools. The repertoire of management included the inculcation of respect for (or fear of) the headteacher; the use of close surveillance of teacher and pupil activity; and the ability to use powerful sanctions against insubordinate members of the school. These sanctions could include the physical punishment of pupils and the threat of dismissal for teachers. A well-managed school in the context of this time was one in which everyone knew their place and worked diligently at their prescribed pedagogic task.[7]

Any attempt to locate contemporary meanings of leadership and management in modern English schooling must allow for the continuing influence of what may be called the founding concepts. Such concepts of leadership and management in education extended well into the twentieth century.[8] While they may have been reformulated and recontextualized in later periods of English schooling, it seems unlikely that their power and symbolism is now a spent force. Indeed a plausible argument could be made that much of this historical legacy has been reinvigorated by aspects of contemporary New Right ideology in education which reconstitutes, under new forms, principles of hierarchical ranking, 'needs' for strong leadership and close control and monitoring of teachers and pupils.

Professional Leadership: The Language of Social Democracy

School leadership as manifest moral energy, and school management as social control held a dominant position in the discourse and practice of English schooling until as late as the 1930s. The transforming effects of the Second World War and of the crucial social, political and cultural effects which resulted from it, produced a new climate for leadership in 'modern' Britain.

The project of social democratic Britain from the 1940s to the 1970s was expressed in the phrase 'building a better Britain'. This great enterprise of social reconstruction included plans for greater democracy and social justice, the modernization of the economy and of economic production, the greater development of high quality public services for all citizens and a more participative and consultative public culture. Education, in the social democratic period, was regarded, especially by Labour governments, as the cultural means to effect many of these transformations. Education, it was thought, could be a solvent of the class hierarchies and divisions of the past and it could strengthen democratic culture. Schooling based upon equality of educational opportunity would, it was believed, liberate the reserves of talent, of 'human capital' in the British people and a modern educational system using progressive curricula and progressive methods would provide the high standards of education needed for modern economies.[9]

The ideal type of leadership required in the public services at this time was professionally expert (an example of meritocratic success), committed to innovation (a modernizer), and consultative in operation (a team leader). While this may have been the ideal type for social democratic leadership in modern Britain, its realizations in practice were dependent upon the supply of ideal candidates and the effectiveness of such candidates when dealing with conservative and hierarchical social institutions which were resistant to the reforming culture of the time. English schools had many such conservative and hierarchical features.

The discourse of school leadership and management in English state education was a partial relay for the new messages about the nature of leadership and management in the wider society. It was partial in the sense that important elements of its own conservative history in the 'headmaster tradition' militated against the new developments. A century of the cultural practice of hierarchical and autocratic leadership and of management as the imposition of social control was simply not going to collapse in the face of a new social democratic manifesto for schooling. Nevertheless, official legitimation and resourcing of new patterns of leadership and management were empowering and their effects upon recruitment and succession to office became increasingly apparent, especially by the 1960s.

The epitome of the type of leadership expected from the ideal headteachers of this period was that of modern professionalism. If schools needed to change their curricula (both in content and design), their approaches to teaching and learning, their modes of assessment, and their social relations with pupils and communities, then a headteacher was looked for who could give leadership in cultural change. Such leadership would be grounded upon a personal and professional record of successful innovation and evidence of interpersonal skills and capacity for team working. Modern professionalism was, in some senses, a recontextualized form of the 'moral energy' which defined nineteenth-century school leaders. The ideal 1960s headteacher (both primary and secondary) exhibited a form of moral energy devoted to the cultural renewal of the school, to the reform of its pedagogy and to its internal social relations. Such professional moral energy could co-exist with older forms of moral energy directed to the achievement of 'godliness and good learning' or it might act in place of such values now thought to be anachronistic in a more secular age. Musgrove (1971) provides an evocative description of the headteacher as modern professional at this time:

> He [*sic*] has earned promotion through his reputation as a super-teacher and even because he is famous for a 'system'. He may have written books and addressed professional conferences . . . he will probably have gained a reputation as a 'progressive' and an innovator. There has been a post-war imperative for aspiring teachers not to uphold traditions but to subvert them. This means in brief that the new head will have opposed streaming, corporal punishment, eleven-plus selection, single-sex education, insulation from parents, the prefect system (unless elective), traditional examinations, didactic or even expository class teaching—and above all, he will have paid special attention to 'group work'. In recent years he will have espoused the teacher-group as well as the pupil-group; he will have been a champion of team-teaching. (p.107)

Many appointing committees of this period, in both primary and secondary schools in state education, were looking for such modern professionals to lead the school. To some extent the nineteenth-century notion of school leadership as involving a sense of mission directed primarily to moral ends had become, by the 1960s, a sense of mission directed to cultural and pedagogic reform. Leadership, previously located in a quasi-sacred culture, had been recontextualized within a modern, professionally progressive and more secular culture of schooling.

The relatively high degree of autonomy enjoyed by English state schools in the 1960s permitted much scope for different forms of pedagogic leadership from headteachers. At the same time, the progressive empowerment of headteachers (as described in Chapter 1) permitted the implementation of different forms of internal management. Whereas 'management' in nineteenth-century schooling had referred to strategies for the imposition of social control in schools, the early period of social democratic education generated a new discourse. School 'organization' and school 'administration' constituted such discourse and referred to the responsibilities of headteachers for ensuring that the logistical arrangements of the school and the disposition of its teachers and resources were efficiently undertaken. In addition to being an innovative professional, the good headteacher was expected to be a competent organizer and administrator. Given the relatively small size of many schools in the 1950s and 1960s such organization and administration was not particularly complex and it could be undertaken by a headteacher in addition to direct classroom teaching responsibilities. Writing of this period, Musgrove (1971) observed 'what is remarkable about the contemporary school is that it has grown and remained pre-bureaucratic . . . A large secondary school will commonly have only a secretary, clerical grade, as a full-time bureaucrat.'[10]

The discourse of modern management and bureaucracy was largely absent from the schools. Headteachers were expected to relate to their colleagues within the principles and procedures of modern professionalism rather than that of managerialism. This involved respecting the professional autonomy of specialist subject teachers in secondary schools and the pedagogic autonomy of primary teachers in 'their' classrooms. To a greater or lesser extent the organizational and administrative arrangements of the school could be the subject of shared professional discussion in staff meetings. In many schools a culture of professional and collegial decision making about the internal logistics of both pedagogy and organization was developing by the 1960s, although its operational effectiveness and power depended to an important extent upon the dispositions of the headteacher. While some headteachers retained the role of 'autocrat', more of them adopted the role of 'the consultative headteacher[11] and the more radical among them worked to establish democratic forms of decision making in which the hierarchical position of the headteacher was minimalized.[12]

The absence of a managerial and a bureaucratic culture in English schools for most of the social democratic period was largely a function of the perceived irrelevance of such cultures. The empowerment of professional teachers and headteachers at this time empowered the culture of professionalism itself. The dominant notions of this era were that schools could be effectively organized and administered by a competent group of professionals. With the headteacher as leading professional and with a consultative mode of collegial decision making, a model form of internal school governance would be established. This construct received official legitimation and amplification in the 1977 HMI Report, *Ten Good Schools*, in its commendation of the consultative headteacher.

The discourse which commended the smooth organizational functioning of English schools at this time was that of 'good organization' or 'good administration' realized in modern, professional forms. Professionalism placed the cultural and pedagogic objectives of the school and of its educational and social purposes as the prime consideration of internal governance. In this sense, organizational arrangements and administrative procedures had to be evaluated in professional and educational terms. Organization and administration in this professional culture were not viewed as discrete technical devices but as other forms in which the educational purposes of the school could be realized. There was a reluctance to acknowledge any specialized knowledge required for administration and certainly a scepticism that there could be a science of educational administration. It was known that certain people had 'a gift for administration' and that this had assisted their promotion to headteacher, deputy headteacher or head of department but it was regarded as a second order gift in the main, except perhaps for deputy headteachers.[13]

There was a paradox and a contradiction in English school professionalism as a dominant culture in the social democratic period. On the one hand, it emphasized professional expertise in implementing curriculum reform, new methods of teaching and learning and better interpersonal relations in schooling. On the other hand, the efficient organization and administration of the school as a social institution was not given the same status. There was an interesting conjunction in English schooling of what might be called pedagogic professionalism coexisting with the cult of the gifted amateur in administration. Professionalism was exercised culturally rather than organizationally. Wilkinson (1964), in his study of leadership and the public school tradition in England, has drawn attention to the considerable symbolic power of 'the Amateur Ideal' in English cultural life. The pervasive belief that accomplishments in certain high status cultural forms would lead to competencies in other areas of endeavour was strong in English upper-class schooling:

> Education, for the gentleman, meant general education: only people who were not gentlemen went in for practical, vocational training at secondary school level. (p.64)

The 'amateur ideal' existed also within the world of school organization and administration, even in state education and even within relatively large schools. The idea that headteachers required 'training' to run their schools efficiently had little currency at this time. Efficient administration was expected to arise out of general, professional competence, previous experience and, in the case of secondary schools, the services of a deputy headteacher or 'senior master'. In short, school organization and administration was not taken to be either complex or esoteric. It was a necessary, second-order activity to the prime purpose of educating children and young people.[14]

The culture and discourse of modern management practice in English schooling made its first appearance in the 1960s, arising particularly out of the establishment of large, comprehensive secondary schools. 'Management' was not a concept which was congenial to the majority of headteachers or teachers in an educationally progressive period. The older and nineteenth-century associations of management as the imposition of social control had been widely rejected in a more liberal era. The modern associations of management involving market analysis, input–output calculations, quality control and personnel relations were regarded as inappropriate for schools. Within social democratic culture, schools were not regarded as factories and education was not regarded as a commodity. The associations of industrial or commercial management were alien to the culture of English state schooling in this period.

In analyzing the relations between education and production, Bernstein (1977) argued that European schooling systems, and particularly the English schooling system, had been marked by strong, insulating boundaries ('strong classification') between the culture of production and academic culture. There was an historical sense that academic and educational activity had to be protected from the potentially corrupting and polluting effects of the market place. Such protection required a relatively autonomous space for cultural work. In more abstract terms, Bernstein (1990) has expressed this as follows:

> This refers to the relations between education and production where these relations are viewed as categories of function. If the relation between these two categories is strongly classified, then there is strong insulation between the categories, which creates a space in which each category can differently specialize its generative principles and practices . . . the principles are kept apart and are differently specialized. (p.195)

The strong relative autonomy enjoyed by English state schooling in the 1960s was an important space for generating distinctive principles and practices of education. While such principles could include 'administration', the concept of 'management' was seen to be a practice of another social world beyond the cultural boundaries of schooling. This distancing of the culture and discourse of management in education began to break down in the 1960s. Writing in 1986, Hoyle noted that 'the use of the term management to apply to the coordination of the activities of schools has been in general use for not much more than twenty years' (p.157).

The arrival of modern management culture in English state schooling proceeded in two socio-historical phases. The first phase, which may be called social democratic management, characterized the 1960s, 1970s and early 1980s, especially in secondary education. The second phase, market management, has been emergent in all schools from the mid-1980s and 1990s and forms part of a now dominant market culture in the provision of all public services in England.

The significant restructuring of English secondary schooling arising from the comprehensive school reforms of the 1960s and 1970s weakened the culture of 'separated categories' which had kept modern management practice outside of the world of schooling. As one of the consequences of comprehensive education reform was the creation of large schools (in excess of 1,000 pupils) and the creation of schools on split sites, the relevance of modern management practice to the efficient operation of these new institutions could hardly be denied.[15] The coordination of the activities of large numbers of pupils and teachers; the scheduling of curricula programmes and options; the pastoral care of pupils and the maintenance of good human relations in schooling constituted an imperative for the introduction of managerial systems and a managerial discourse in English secondary schooling. This discourse began to normalize and legitimize concepts such as 'the senior management team', 'middle management', 'management by objectives', 'the management of human relations', etc.

A new literature of education management was created to meet the 'needs' of comprehensive school headteachers.[16] This literature was, in its origins, constituted by educational researchers examining the complexities of organizing the large school and by comprehensive school headteachers who generated primers based upon their own professional experience of running large schools. An influential example of the first type was the work of Morgan and Hall (1982) who characterized the 'managerial tasks of the secondary school head' as involving 'conceptual, i.e., operations management' (e.g., staff deployment); 'leadership and human management' (e.g., staff development) and 'external management' (e.g., accountability to governors and LEA). In this research, distinctions were made between internal school management (professional domain) and external management (public domain) and it was argued that training for headship had become essential. Other influential sources which stimulated the development of modern managerial thinking in education included Glatter (1972), Bush *et al.* (1980), Hegarty (1983) and Buckley (1985).

The management culture of schooling in this period could be, in various ways, symbolic, bureaucratic, consultative, and informed by the insights of personnel management. The symbolic value of management systems and of the discourse of management in comprehensive schools was that it could confer status and legitimacy upon new occupational roles.[17] Whereas the status of the grammar school headteacher had been founded upon a moral and scholarly authority, that of the comprehensive school headteacher could be founded upon modern managerial expertise and system thinking. The symbols of management could operate to preserve and recontextualize the hierarchical position of the headteacher in a large and diverse secondary school. It was in the interests of headteachers in some schools to amplify notions of the managerial complexity of running large educational units and to be seen to be 'expert' in the use of managerial discourse and modern management systems.

Used in this way, management culture could be the ally of the reconstitution of hierarchy, under new forms.[18] Wider features of social democratic culture in England, however, worked against the hierarchical potential of management systems. Although the operation of large comprehensive schools necessarily generated the creation of bureaucratic systems of communication and coordination, such bureaucracy had, ironically, the capacity to facilitate more shared decision making. Writers on bureaucracy from Weber (1947) onward have stressed its contradictory potential to be either a resource for democracy and participation or a resource for authoritarian control. The use of bureaucracy in modern school management can, in this way, be appropriated for very different purposes, both authoritarian and participatory.

In reviewing the available research from the 1960s on the effects of bureaucracy in schools, Musgrove (1971) concluded that:

> . . . bureaucratization has meant more power for all . . . teachers in highly bureaucratic schools had a significantly greater sense of power (than those in less bureaucratic schools). (p.104)

While such conclusions went against the conventional wisdom of the time, which equated bureaucracy with a sense of alienation and powerlessness among teachers in schools, Musgrove argued an interesting thesis that 'the advantages of bureaucracy' had been overlooked. In his view, bureaucracy in schools had the potential to empower the teachers *vis-à-vis* the headteacher:

> The development of bureaucracy over the past century has made us a less servile people. It has helped to make jobs secure and has based appointments and promotions on qualifications rather than personal connections. It has regulated activity through rules; but obedience to rules is probably less humiliating than submission to persons. The whim and caprice of superiors at work have been constrained. The advantages of these bureaucratic advances are nowhere more evident than in education.[19]

Insofar as bureaucratization in English schools involved the dissemination of crucial information to all members of the institution and the public specification of correct procedures, then the capacity of headteachers to enact either the 'headmaster tradition' or 'the expert manager' was open to challenge. If, in institutional terms, knowledge is power, then the dissemination of knowledge by bureaucratic means to all the teachers in a school *potentially* disseminates a measure of power. This is especially so when the wider socio-political culture of a society legitimates a consultative mode of decision making.

With official approval given to conceptions of consultative management in the social democratic period in England, it seems likely that many schools were characterized by a positive alliance of bureaucracy and shared decision making to a greater or lesser extent. However, whether a particular school exemplified the ideal of consultative management and shared decision making depended upon two cultural factors, which may be called the leadership style of the headteacher and the participative style of the teachers. A consultative culture (or its absence) would be an outcome of the interaction of these two features. Hoyle (1986) has pointed out that:

> . . . different leadership styles entail differences in the degree to which heads construct missions alone or in collaboration with members of staff who would have been encouraged to contribute to the negotiation of a mission . . . (p.115)

Analysis of differences in leadership styles can easily collapse into an endless typology of the forms in which a sense of mission and social purpose is realized in a particular style. Various writers have commented critically upon the proliferation of such terms, where leadership style may be described as 'charismatic', 'authoritarian', 'democratic', 'facilitating', 'bureaucratic', 'collegial', 'moral', or even 'warm or cold'. Whereas it is possible to have sympathy with the view of Bennis (1959) that 'never have so many laboured so long to say so little' (p.259), the continuing preoccupation with leadership style signals that it is regarded as a 'real' phenomenon with important consequences for the culture, ethos and functioning of institutions. It certainly seems to be the case that in English schooling at this time, the existence of a culture of consultative management and shared decision making very much depended upon the headteacher's enactment of a particular leadership style.[20]

Shared decision making, however, was not only an outcome of headteacher initiative: the participative style of teachers was also crucial to its realization. Participative style refers to differences in the willingness and capacity of teachers to realize the potential for shared decision making in a particular context. It refers to the relative degree of active involvement by teachers in the whole institutional life of the school, as opposed to their formal endorsement of the principles of participation. Where teachers took seriously the notion that professional collegiality necessarily involved a practice of consultative management and shared decision making and where conditions facilitated its expression, English state schools developed new organizational cultures marked by real participation. However, there was a price to be paid for this in the multiplication of committees and working parties and the generation of agenda, minutes and supporting documentation. Active participation in this sense represented an extension of the historically defined role of the teacher and an increase in time and workload pressures. Where teachers took the view that this was diverting them from their major commitment to quality teaching in 'their' classrooms, then the participative style of such teachers might be formal rather than active i.e., they were more likely to be content to leave whole institutional decisions to the senior management team, subject to appropriate reporting of such decisions. In these circumstances some headteachers enjoyed the legitimations of consultative management and shared decision making without experiencing much real constraint upon their own policies for the school.[21] Overall, however, it can be said that the social democratic period from the 1960s to the early 1980s was characterized by forms of management in English state schooling which attempted to realize notions of professional collegiality, consultative management and shared decision making. Autocratic forms of management were in retreat.

Modern social democratic management was theoretically guided by human relations concern. The ideal-type school management culture of this period was human-relational in the sense that it attempted to generate conditions for good interpersonal relations at both staff and pupil levels. Whereas headteachers in the past had worked to enshrine the principle of hierarchical respect (and a measure of fear and awe) at the centre of school culture, the model headteacher of this period was an agent for the generation and dissemination of principles of rapport.[22] The 'good' school of the social democratic era was one characterized by harmonious staff relations and humane teacher–pupil relations achieved by the application of sensitive personnel management, the introduction of pastoral care systems and a pedagogic regime which placed 'the needs of the child (or young person)' at the centre of its educational and organizational culture. A well-managed school was one in which social control arose not out of authoritarian, imposed and punitive systems but out of the voluntary cooperation of its members, working together as responsible participants in the school regarded as a valued educational community.

The ideology of community education was strong at this time. Schools were exhorted to weaken the historic insulations between themselves and the communities which they served. In Bernstein's (1977) terms, there were strong moves to weaken the classifications in English culture between school life and community life. Part of the social democratic ideal in education policy at this time was a community ideal i.e., the idea that good school–community relations should be established and the idea that the school itself should be a caring and humane community.[23] Where this community commitment in schooling was taken seriously in particular LEAs and regions, the desired headteacher was one who had the 'community in education vision', i.e., who could articulate persuasively the principles of generating community in schooling and who had effective management strategies for its realization.

Weakening the boundaries between school and community was, in a sense, a radical extension of the principles of consultative management. The logic of this development was that parents and community members would be taken into partnership with the headteacher and teachers as professionals, in deciding upon future directions for the school. Community members would, in short, become part of the consultative process in English state schooling. Given the historical strength of the insulations between school and communities in England and given the high value which teachers and headteachers placed upon their professional autonomy at this time, it is not at all surprising that this development was limited in scope. A notion of real community management of schooling came into direct conflict with the interests of headteachers (for professional autonomy) and the interests of school governors, including local politicians (for formal and institutional local control). To consult with teachers in a school about its management was, in terms of the history of English schooling, a significant reform. To consult more widely in the community was too radical a proposition for most headteachers and local councillors, despite a formal social democratic rhetoric which commended it as a practice.[24] The guiding principles of state schooling remained, as the Education Group (1981) has pointed out, those of professional control rather than popular and community involvement.

It was these limitations of social democracy in practice which provided the conditions for New Right ideological attacks upon state education.[25] A strong, populist case could be made that English state schooling was too autonomous, too unaccountable and too insulated from both the social world of the community and the economic realities of the market place. Such conditions, it could be claimed, gave too many opportunities for irresponsible leadership and incompetent management from some headteachers and from some local education authorities. Radical reform was called for and this radicalism would have to bring into place new concepts of leadership and management in education and a changed relationship between the school and the wider society.

School Leadership and Management: The Discourse of the Market

A new discourse of school leadership and management in English schooling has risen to dominance in the 1980s and 1990s. It is the discourse of 'market leadership' and of 'market management', arising from a new culture of schooling which Bernstein (1990) observes to be 'a truly secular form born out of the context of cost-efficient education' (p.86). This transformation of both culture and discourse has arisen from New Right ideological attacks upon the weaknesses of social democratic schooling, followed by rapid implementation of education reforms designed to bring the discipline of market forces into the insulated and protected world of state schooling. The cultural autonomy of English education has been radically changed.

Dale (1989, pp.80–9) points out that the ideological and substantive transformations of education under the influence of 'Thatcherism'[26] have been complex and internally contradictory because the projects of 'the industrial trainers', 'the old Tories', 'the populists', 'the moral entrepreneurs' and 'the privatizers' have each had different goals. While recognizing that there is a complex collection of reform agendas subsumed within the shorthand term 'New Right ideology', writers such as Ball (1990) and Education Group II (1991) have suggested that the dominant imperative has been the institutionalization and legitimation of market forces in education. The language of choice and diversity in education has, in the 1980s and 1990s, been appropriated to serve the interests of advancing a market culture in schooling:

> It's Margaret Thatcher's way of saying that 'I brought consumerism into education'. I don't suggest that she sees schools quite like supermarkets, nevertheless, what she is saying in effect is that just as parents have every right to shop where they think fit, when it comes to buying goods, so they have every right to shop where they think fit, when it comes to their child's education. (David Hart, General Secretary of the National Association of Headteachers: quoted in Ball, 1990, p.63)

At the very centre of this process of transformation of English school culture is the commodification of education. Education, regarded in the nineteenth century as primarily a moral and spiritual enterprise and regarded in the social democratic era as a professionally autonomous cultural service, has been recontextualized in the 1980s as a product in the market place.[27] This commodification process has been accomplished by a series of reforms, such as the introduction of local management of schools (which has established the discourse of the budget centre), the promotion of league tables of school results (which has created a language of 'output', 'value-added' and 'measurable product') and by official discourse which has constituted the curriculum as an entity to be 'delivered' and the parents and pupils as the 'consumers' of the education product.

The strong boundaries and insulations which have historically kept the schooling system and the market place as 'separated categories' have been decisively broken in the 1980s and 1990s. Where conservative traditions in the past resisted the conjunction of the market place with academic and schooling cultures, a new radical Conservatism has seen in market culture the means to revitalize the insulated social worlds of the university and the school. In particular, local management of schools in which a significant part of a school's budget is dependent upon its popularity with parents and therefore of its pupil/resource intake, has been celebrated for breaking the power of the 'state school monopoly' and of the 'local education monopoly'. Indeed, Flew (1991) welcomes a situation where:

> ... to the extent that dissatisfied parents are able to remove their children to a preferred alternative school and if it is also ensured that the funding follows the pupils to the actually preferred schools, then the result will be a system under which all the individual schools are exposed to the incentive and disciplines of the market. They will become constrained to compete to attract and retain pupils ... (this) would constitute an enormous improvement over the present maintained school monopoly. (p.48)

Many writers have observed that the introduction of a free market in public services requires the action of a strong state which 'has initial tasks of destruction: smashing up the old forms of regulation ... trade union organization and the incursions of the public professionals.'[28] A strong Conservative state in England from 1979 to the 1990s has been able to restructure and reconstitute the culture of English schooling with decisive and rapid action. Social democratic consultative procedures have in effect been marginalized during a frantic series of fundamental reforms in education that have been introduced in what can be called the *blitzkreig* mode of educational reform, where the sheer pace and nature of the reform process threatens to overwhelm sources of opposition.

These decisive transformations have been welcomed internationally by those who see greater choice and market accountability as a revitalizing force for schooling. John Chubb and Terry Moe, the authors of the influential text, *Politics, Markets and America's Schools* (1990), have argued that English school reform provides a model for America and for other societies:

> Britain has already broken with tradition and moved boldly towards a choice-based system of public education . . . The whole world is being swept by a realization that markets have tremendous advantages over central control and bureaucracy.[29]

The implications for school leadership and management of these wider cultural changes are, potentially, profound. If school leadership, in the person of the headteacher, was expected to provide and articulate a moral mission in the nineteenth century and a professional and pedagogically progressive mission in the social democratic era, then it seems that contemporary headteachers in England will increasingly be expected to articulate a market mission. Moral relations and professional relations are giving ground before the rise of market relations in English schooling. The institutional survival of contemporary English schools is now dependent upon the capacity of their senior management to maintain and increase the school's 'market share' of pupils, results and resources; to market and project the best possible image for the school; to make alliances and networks with industrial and commercial sponsors; and to show entrepreneurial ingenuity in the market for educational services and products.

Hughes observed in 1985 that leadership in professionally staffed organizations involved both a 'leading professional' dimension and a 'chief executive' dimension. The cumulative reforms of the 1980s and 1990s have given much greater salience to the conception of the headteacher as a chief executive. For those headteachers who wish to resist the leadership/chief executive relation or the leadership/market mission relation, there will be considerable pressures and dilemmas to be faced as market culture extends its influence within the schooling system. While such headteachers may have experienced the effects of education reform as the unwelcome arrival of market capitalism in schooling where 'all that is solid melts into air, all that is holy is profaned',[30] the expectations of parents, teachers and governors are likely to be that the headteachers must give the kind of leadership which the new conditions for schooling require. Where the wider socio-political culture legitimates market accountability and competition and where official discourse in education calls for enterprise education and the renewal of the entrepreneurial spirit, the pressures upon headteachers to conform to the new culture of educational leadership will be great.

The most fundamental obligations of educational leadership involve securing the future of an organization and of its members. Contemporary headteachers in England are now caught up in a quasi-market system which constitutes effective school leadership as entrepreneurial vision and energy. Without such vision and such energy and the capacity to disseminate these to other teachers, the very survival of the school may be at stake. These requirements for school leadership extend across the whole of the educational system. Even the more 'innocent' world of primary education is not exempt from them, as West (1989) points out:

> Heads may well find themselves engaging in entrepreneurial activities and operating more and more across the boundary of their schools than is currently the case. The widening of their chief executive role and subsequent displacement from the core act of teaching will be difficult for some headteachers. It may be that in the nineties we can no longer justify headteachers as surrogate teachers, for such an action may well be considered profligate in a system that construes headteachers as providers of strategic vision, as constructors of relevant networks, as entrepreneurs in a market economy . . . (p.209)

The emergence of the headteacher as entrepreneurial leader and chief executive in the 1980s and 1990s marks, insofar as these become dominant constructs, the final secularization and commodification of the educational process. The most important characteristics of effective school leaders are now less to be found in their moral, scholarly or professional qualities than in their 'streetwise' capacity to survive in and exploit market opportunities for education.[31] It is true that a shrewd awareness of market opportunities characterized many headteachers in earlier periods of English schooling, especially those in charge of private schools, but it is a major transformation of English state schooling culture for market relations to be dominant.

It is here that one of the sharpest contradictions of New Right ideological influence in schooling becomes apparent. One emphasis, which calls for a reinstatement of traditional moral values and spirituality at the heart of schooling, is negated by another emphasis, which celebrates the advance of market culture in education and which exalts entrepreneurial leadership and the competitive ethic. The strong cultural insulations between the schooling system and the market place in English society have been premised upon a deep, historical sense that market culture has the potential to corrupt and pollute the school's prime concern with moral, spiritual, cultural and human values. Much of English school culture, as Bernstein (1990) has argued, has been permeated by recontextualized elements of an earlier religious culture. This has included a strong, symbolic separation from the mundane world of parents, local community, politics, economic relations and the market place, and the development of knowledge and pedagogy within a relatively autonomous space.

The weakening of the cultural boundaries and the loss of the autonomous space in English schooling in the 1980s and 1990s has been a form of school reformation which has recontextualized the school firmly within secular and mundane culture. As Bernstein (1990) suggests:

> Market relevance is the key orientating criteria for selection of discourses, their research, their focus and their relation to each other. This movement has profound implications, from the primary school to the university. This can be seen in the stress on basic skills at the primary level, vocational courses and specialization at the secondary level, and new instruments of State control over higher education and research.
>
> There is a new concept both of knowledge and of its relation to those who create it, a truly secular concept. Knowledge should flow like money to wherever it can create advantage and profit. Indeed knowledge is not just like money, it *is* money. Knowledge is divorced from persons, their commitment, their personal dedications, for these become impediments, restrictions on flow and introduce deformations in the working of the market. Moving knowledge about, or even creating it, should not be more difficult than moving and regulating money. Knowledge, after nearly a thousand years, is divorced from inwardness and is literally dehumanized. (p.155)

Headteachers in England have historically been the guardians of the 'otherness' of the school, of its commitments to sets of values and ideals not much regarded in the wider world of the market place.[32] As Ball (1990) points out, 'the market is unprincipled, it allows no moral priorities in its patterns of distribution' (p.37). Its rise to power in education will have radical consequences for school culture. There will be major dilemmas for those headteachers whose conceptions of educational leadership have involved giving priority to moral and spiritual values or to professional, cultural and human values. Faced with the calculus of market imperatives in contemporary English schooling such values may easily be marginalized. On the other hand, some headteachers will see no necessary opposition between these values and the new trading conditions for schools. These will be the new market leaders in schooling who find no serious dilemmas in operating 'the Protestant ethic and the spirit of capitalism' in contemporary English education.

The discourse of the market place is in the process of reconstituting the nature of education and of knowledge, the nature of the school and its social relations, and the nature of the professionals working within it. For headteachers of secondary schools, in particular, what has been called the chief executive 'dimension' of the role in the past seems likely to become its defining characteristic in the 1990s and beyond. The position of headteacher is itself in radical transformation as executive, entrepreneurial and managerial functions become constructed as the prime responsibilities of the role. Such developments operate across the education system. Ian Craig (1989), in introducing a collection of essays concerned with the development of Primary Headship in the 1990s, has argued that 'The term headteacher in the 1990s will become a misnomer. The task of headship is management and much more than about being a good teacher . . .'.[33]

The title of headteacher has historically signalled the school leader's prime relation with knowledge, pupils, teachers and pedagogy. Its potential replacement with chief executive or senior manager indicates new priorities in the future operations of schools. Among these priorities a 'new managerialism'[34] which goes beyond the practice of the 1960s and 1970s is evident. Such new managerialism involves a much more sophisticated and specialized approach to the management of educational institutions as corporations or businesses. One of the effects of the introduction of local management of schools has been to constitute the school as a budget centre. This development has given heightened significance to financial and budget management in all schools. The new managerialism in the schools has involved more expert attention to budgeting control and forecasting; public relations and market research; performance indicators and quality control; and staffing and personnel relations. Headteachers have been encouraged to undertake courses provided by local education authorities, management consultants and finance specialists which have been designed to up-grade their management skills and, perhaps more fundamentally, to enhance their rapport with modern management culture. Substantial government investment has been made in a project to convert headteachers into modern managers. In 'Improving Education through Better Management: A view from the DES', Sir John Caines (1992) makes clear the official view that:

> If the Government's reforms were to be implemented effectively far more attention needed to be given to management issues. So in 1988 we saw the launch of the School Management Task Force to lever up the standards of management training and development. We have seen increases in the specific grant for school management training, including the grants for the implementation of the local management of schools . . . the total expenditure supported is over £80 million. (p.15)

As was noted in Chapter 1, a very considerable literature of Education Management Studies now exists whose purpose is to resource the new educational manager with the latest technical intelligence about every aspect of school operations.[35] The proponents of the managerial revolution in English schools claim that great benefits will result for pupils, teachers and parents arising from more responsive and efficient management of educational services which has been brought into close dialogue with other agencies in society. The critics of these developments believe that important educational values will be marginalized or corrupted by this process and that the key relationship for headteachers will become a relationship with a computer and a financial package rather than with other teachers and with the classroom life of the school.

An important emerging issue in the micro-politics of contemporary English schools relates to what effects the new managerialism is having upon the internal social relations of schooling. Are headteachers, as they become chief executives or senior managers, introducing line-management and hierarchical systems in the interests of rapid, executive action? Does the new management culture represent a serious weakening of the shared decision-making processes of the 1970s? What are the effects of the new managerialism upon headteacher–governor relations and upon headteacher–pupil relations? These questions constitute important issues for contemporary research inquiry into the changing nature of school management in England.

One of the most influential texts in the field is *The Self-Managing School* (1988). Its authors, Brian Caldwell and John Spinks, argue that the most effective schools, like the most successful business corporations, involve the use of collaborative styles of management. In an international programme of management seminars conducted in Australia, Britain, Canada and the United States, Caldwell and Spinks (1988) have advocated the superiority of:

> . . . the Collaborative School Management Cycle because it provides for the appropriate involvement of teachers, parents and students in an on-going management process of goal-setting, need identification, policy-making, planning, budgeting, implementing and evaluating. The focus is on programmes for students and the effective and efficient allocation of resources to support learning and teaching. (p.vii)

As the culture and practice of the new managerialism increases in both primary and secondary schools in England during the 1990s, the principles of management enacted by headteachers will be crucial for the shaping of the school's ethos and of its internal social relations. On the one hand, the hierarchical and authoritarian features of the English 'headmaster tradition' could be reconstituted in the position of the headteacher as expert chief executive. On the other hand, the shared decision-making practices of the 1960s and 1970s, i.e., the culture of professional collegiality, could continue in a new form, i.e., collaborative school management in the 1990s.

Written in this way, such management alternatives appear to have equal chances of realization within contemporary English schooling. In fact, the possibilities are not equal. In the 1980s and 1990s, despite a constant political rhetoric of democracy and freedom, the political practice of a strong Conservative state has demonstrated 'strong leadership', rapid executive action, low tolerance of opposition and little commitment to consultative procedures in policy formation. In other words, in a wider socio-political and ideological climate in which strong leadership is lauded, and in a new competitive culture in schooling in which rapid, entrepreneurial activity is believed to be essential for institutional survival, external factors work against the chances of collaborative school management and in favour of hierarchical chief executives. This situation is compounded when teachers have experienced considerable 'intensification'[36] of workloads and work pressures arising from curriculum and assessment reform in the same period. Teachers who are tired and stressed by deteriorating conditions of service are not in the best position to participate actively in collaborative school management even if they endorse its theoretical virtues.

Ball (1987) has argued that 'the political culture in schools, as in society generally, rests upon a limited conception of democracy and participation' (p.138). Such limited expression of democracy and participation as currently exists in English schooling is largely the outcome of the social democratic culture of the 1960s and 1970s. It is the outcome of a wider political culture which gave some credence to notions of consultation and shared decision making in policy formation and in management practice. It is the outcome of an educational system marked by more autonomy, less competition among schools and relatively stable operating conditions. External conditions supported internal, participative developments. If some headteachers are able to establish collaborative school management cycles in the schools of the 1990s against the grain of external conditions then this will be an eloquent testimony to the enduring power and influence of English headteachers as school leaders who can use leadership to facilitate and promote collaboration.

After a decade of strong political leadership in England, however, it would hardly be surprising if a construct of strong school leadership was given renewed emphasis. Taking a key policy issue, such as the decision to opt out of local education authority control and constitute the school as a grant-maintained school, it is instructive to note how Chubb and Moe (1992) report developments to their American readers:

> (Opting-out schools) must have strong leaders who want to take charge, who are unafraid of political conflict and who can convince their governing bodies and parents that opting out will succeed. While on paper the governing boards and the parents are supposed to be the prime movers in all this, the reality is that they lack expertise and experience and are often easily intimidated by the establishment. They need strong leadership . . . and it is the school head who must usually provide it . . . autonomy is quite manageable. Most school heads are eminently capable of running their schools all by themselves, without help from above. (pp.35–6)

A celebration of strong school leadership in the 1990s and of a capacity to manage 'without help from above' could, by extension, lead to a situation in which headteachers felt able to manage 'without help from below'.[37] Grant maintained schools may prove to be the new cultural relay for the amplification of notions of strong school leadership and for the reassertion of the headmaster tradition in modern executive forms. The discourse of strong school leadership is reasserting itself once more in English schooling in the 1990s.[38]

Notes and References

1   As Smyth (1989) notes, 'leadership covers a great deal of ground; as a consequence it is one of the most misunderstood concepts in our educational language. There is a sense in which leadership *is* understood in the conventional language of schooling as being a real phenomenon, one that does make a difference in schools.' (p.5)
2   It must be noted that a distinctive study of educational leadership is now re-emerging with publications such as Smyth (1989) and Hodgkinson (1991).
3   Foster (1989, p.48).
4   Bernstein (1990, p.168).
5   See Gordon (1974) for a detailed study of Victorian school managers.
6   Bernbaum (1976) notes that 'the reputation of great reforming mid nineteenth century heads, of whom Arnold was amongst the first, was not based upon great learning or scholarship, nor upon great administration prowess, rather upon their capacity to uplift their increasing number of pupils and assistant masters by a concern for their moral welfare and by the example of a Christian life fulfilled.' (pp.13–14)
7   Management as school dominance is encapsulated in Edward Thring's classic assertion of the authority of the headmaster: 'I am supreme here and will brook no interference'. (Quoted in Peters, 1976, p.2.)
8   See Bernbaum (1976) for evidence of this. Bernbaum notes in particular how a text written as late as 1968 on the 'Art of the Headmaster' could still assert:

> The responsibility of the head is to see that law and order prevail . . . Not only is the responsibility for overall discipline the most important of the head's charges, it is also one that he cannot avoid and one that he cannot delegate . . . A head will either rule his school, or there will be no rule; he will be the inspiration or there will be none . . . (p.25)

9   For an important analysis of the social democratic project in education, see Education Group (CCCS) (1981); see also Jones (1983, pp.51–67).
10   Musgrove (1971, p.61).
11   See Kogan *et al.* (1984, pp.58–62).
12   For an interesting account of the role of the headteacher in participatory school government, see Watts (1976).
13   The important role of the deputy headteacher in school organization and administration was recognized in research and analysis developed in the late 1960s; see, for instance, Burnham (1968).
14   In noting the undeveloped state of training for headteachers in English schools in the 1960s, Taylor (1968) commented:

> In educational circles it does not do to claim or to admit that one enjoys administration . . . To embrace the administrator's role with too much enthusiasm is to run the risk of separating oneself from the central objectives of the institution, to become embroiled in system maintenance . . .

> To express a fondness for administration attracts accusations of power seeking . . . None of this has helped to encourage the development of the study of administration in educational settings. (pp.141–2)

15 Part of the opposition to the growth of comprehensive schools in England in the 1960s and 1970s was based upon their size and the assertions that large schools would take on the characteristics of factories rather than communities.

16 Representative examples are Allen (1968), Barry and Tye (1972) and Poster (1976).

17 For a discussion of the symbolic value of managerial discourse, see Hoyle (1986, pp.156–68).

18 Taylor (1976) drew attention to such potential dangers in certain forms of managerialism in schools.

19 Musgrove (1971, p.88).

20 This also extended to relations with school governors. Kogan *et al.* (1984) concluded that 'the style of headship plays a large part in influencing the operation of the governing body' (p.62).

21 Difficulties in realizing full consultative management and shared decision making in schools are reviewed by Hoyle (1986, pp.86–100).

22 See Grace (1995) for a discussion of the social relations of respect and of rapport in English schooling.

23 See, for instance, Poster (1968).

24 In a widely read text of the 1980s, Hargreaves (1982) argued that 'comprehensive reorganization has distracted public attention in most areas of the country from what may, in the longer term, prove to be one of the most important innovations of the time: the emergence of the community school' (pp.113–14). Despite such advocacy, community schools did not become a widespread feature of English state schooling.

25 For various accounts of New Right ideological attacks upon English state schooling see Chitty (1989), Griggs (1989) and Jones (1989).

26 See Dale (1989, Chapter 6) for a discussion of 'Thatcherism and Education'.

27 For critical discussions of the commodification of education see Grace (1989) and Grace (1994).

28 Johnson (1991, p.81).

29 Chubb and Moe (1992, pp.45–6).

30 This classic assertion by Marx and Engels (quoted in Apple, 1989, p.1) as to the effects of capitalism upon production also encapsulates the experience of some educators when encountering market capitalism in the schools for the first time.

31 Ball (1990) notes the criticisms of the industrial lobby in English schooling that too many teachers and headteachers are out of touch with industrial and commercial realities. A new kind of headteacher is looked for by this lobby, one who can move 'forward to a vision of high-tech, state-of-the-art schooling, run like an efficient business, quick to respond to the changing requirements of the market' (p.129).

32 In some senses the insulated culture of English schools has allowed them to exist as sanctuaries for values and ideals which have weakening force in the external world. Schools have had an important values conservation function in English culture in the past. Waller (1965), in his classic text *The Sociology of Teaching*, believed this to be true also of American schools in the 1930s:

> Though most adults have left such ideals behind they are not willing to discard them finally. The school must keep them alive. The school must serve as a museum of virtue. (p.34)

33 Craig (1989, p.9).

34 For one account of the new managerialism in education see Ball (1990, Chapter 5).

35 Representative examples of this literature are Dean (1987), Bell (1989 and 1992), Cave and Wilkinson (1990), Briault and West (1990), Foskett (1992), Davies and Anderson (1992). The most recent texts show the salience of market culture in education in explicit form, as a sample of the titles show:

B. Hardie (1991) *Marketing the Primary School*
B. Davies and L. Ellison (1991) *Marketing the Secondary School*
L. Gray (1991) *Marketing Education*
R. Levacic (1991) *Financial Management in Education*
C. Barnes (1993) *Practical Marketing for Schools*

36 Apple's (1988) concept of the 'intensification' of teachers' work in contemporary schooling expresses well the sense of pressure and pace experienced by English teachers in the 1980s and 1990s.

37 It should be noted that Chubb and Moe (1992) qualify their earlier statement by adding, 'school heads cannot succeed alone. Above all else, they need to recruit able teachers who share the school's mission' (p.38).

38 For further evidence of this, see the emphasis on the importance of strong leadership in education which appears in the White Paper *Choice and Diversity: A new framework for schools* (1992, p.7).
See also the fundings of Halpin, Power and Fitz (1993) on headteacher leadership and Grant maintained status.

Chapter 3

Critical Perspectives on School Leadership

Historically, headteachers in English schools have been powerful definers of the culture, organization and ethos of schooling. It is no surprise therefore to find that interest groups who wish to change the culture and ethos of schooling in various ways realize the strategic importance of changing the consciousness, values and behaviour of headteachers and, more fundamentally, of changing the nature of the headship role itself. A significant contemporary struggle therefore exists in England to change the consciousness of headteachers and to change the historically constituted nature of what it is to be a headteacher.

The position of headteacher is at the focal point of attention from agencies with very different messages about the priority concerns of school leadership in contemporary conditions. A body of writings and discourse already referred to in earlier chapters as Education Management Studies (EMS) reconstitutes the position of headteacher as chief executive and market manager of 'Education plc'. A body of writings and discourse which has arisen in opposition to these tendencies and which may be called Critical Leadership Studies (CLS) calls upon headteachers to give a new kind of educative and democratic leadership for the future.

In 1988, the culture of EMS was given powerful impetus by the Department of Education and Science/Coopers and Lybrand Report, 'Local Management of Schools', and explicitly by its observation that:

> Delegation of management responsibility is one of the cornerstones of good management practice . . . At the school level, it marks a change from local administration to local management. The changes require a new culture and philosophy of the organization of education at the school level. They are more than purely financial; they need a general shift in management. We use the term 'Local Management of Schools' (LMS).[1]

In the dissemination of a new culture and philosophy for English schools, LMS has been the founding concept and EMS its cultural relay. The discourse and publications of EMS have been widely disseminated by many public and private agencies, and headteachers, faced with the immediate impact of financial budgeting of a new kind, have added EMS texts and primers to their professional development bookshelves.

The messages of Education Management Studies for the nature of school leadership in the 1990s and beyond have been the dominating messages. The reasons for this are quite clear: EMS has official and state legitimation as the cultural agency for the reconstitution of schooling and of leadership within schooling; EMS has professional legitimation as it meets, in a variety of practical ways, the new management demands upon headteachers in all types of school; and EMS provides the corpus of knowledge, skills and discourse which will need to be demonstrated for appointment to headships and progress within the headship category. It thus has career and demonstrable success legitimations.

There is, therefore, an unequal contest in the struggle to influence the consciousness of headteachers because the oppositional culture of Critical Leadership Studies (CLS) has none of these legitimations. Whereas EMS has been the focus of short training and development courses for headteachers under such headings as 'financial control and management information in schools', CLS will, in general, only have been encountered by those head-teachers undertaking advanced study of educational leadership in MA and EdD programmes.[2] However, as more headteachers and aspirant headteachers enrol in such programmes as part of a general enhancement of leadership qualifications in England, debates about the nature of school leadership can be expected to widen in scope.

Critical Leadership Studies consists of a corpus of writings generated, among others, by writers in the UK, the USA, Canada, Australia and New Zealand, who have reacted in various ways against what they have seen as an emergent hierarchical, 'strong leadership' and market-dominated culture of educational leadership in their respective countries. CLS does not represent a coordinated oppositional movement but rather a series of critical responses to developments in a number of countries. It can be claimed, however, that its intellectual coherence is to be found in a number of unifying themes which set out its alternative agenda for study. The first part of this chapter will examine some of the main themes in the literature of Critical Leadership Studies. The second part will contain reflections upon these themes with special reference to the changing conditions of English state schooling and of the position of the headteacher.

On the Need for a 'Humane Science' of Educational Leadership

An important impetus to CLS was given in 1986 with the publication of Thomas Greenfield's paper 'The Decline and Fall of Science in Educational Administration'. In a wide-ranging critique of the field of educational admin-istration, Greenfield argued that most existing studies were ahistorical, nar-rowly technical, mechanistic and unnecessarily boring. The study of educational administration and the study of educational leadership had become the pris-oners of a 'neutered science'.[3] Following Hodgkinson (1978a, p.272), Greenfield endorsed the view that 'the central questions of administration are not scientific at all. They are philosophical' and he pointed out that the devaluation of administrative studies had impoverished understanding: 'with the elimination of values, consideration of the conduct of organizations is reduced to technicalities'.[4] In setting out an agenda for future inquiry, Greenfield called for a humane science which would use interpretive and qualitative methods of inquiry; which would focus upon power, conflicts, values and moral dilemmas in educational leadership; and which would examine the changing role of language and discourse in constructing new administrative 'realities'. This need to develop a more humane study in the face of the existing limitations of the field has been powerfully elaborated in Greenfield's most recent writings (1993):

> The exclusion of values from administrative science, the exclusion of both the human and the humane, the exclusion of passion and conviction . . . does leave a residue for study—and one that is perhaps scientifically manageable. The most obvious consequence of this exclusion leaves a field that is regrettably and unnecessarily bland and boring. The difficult and divisive questions, the questions of purpose and morality, the questions arising from the necessary imposition of one person's will upon another, the questions that challenge the linking of ends and means—all these matters are set aside in a search for a pallid consensus and an illusory effectiveness. The great issues of the day in education are similarly set aside . . . (pp.164–5)

For Greenfield the critical study of educational leadership must engage with such issues and such questions.

This agenda for a new approach to the study of educational leadership has been endorsed and developed by Smyth (1989) and Bates (1992). In introducing the important CLS text, *Critical Perspectives in Educational Leadership*, Smyth (1989, p.4) argues, with others, against contemporary trends towards strong leadership and 'salvationist and hegemonic views of leadership' and for a study and understanding of leadership which is informed by critical theory.[5] Such critical theory will focus attention upon notions of the empowerment of all school participants; the educative potential of leadership; and the conditions necessary for the creation and sustaining of community in educational institutions. Whereas Greenfield argues that the study of educational leadership must become a form of 'humane science' and Smyth argues that it needs to be informed by critical theory, Bates (1992) has made a powerful case that educational leadership can only be understood in the context of its wider cultural setting. In other words, there is a crucial school leadership–culture relation which defines what it is to be a leader and which goes beyond the scope of Education Management Studies. The understanding of this leadership–culture relation requires insights from history, philosophy, religion, political economy and cultural analysis. Leadership, in this sense, is a more complex and comprehensive concept than that of management and its proper understanding requires a wider range of scholarship.

Bates points out that educational leadership often has to be exercised against a background of 'culture battles' in society. In contemporary conditions these battles involve:

> ... the battle between lifeworld and system[6], the dangers of a commodification of culture and the emergence of repressive regimes of power and truth. These are battles that affect both individual and collective futures. Schools are centrally concerned with such futures and those who would exercise leadership in such times need not only an understanding of such issues but also of ways in which they can be articulated through the message systems of the school.[7]

For Bates, therefore, the essential point about educational leadership is that it 'involves the making and articulating of choices, the location of oneself within the cultural struggles of the times as much in the cultural battles of the school as in the wider society'.[8]

In these ways, CLS has been constituted as a new framework for the understanding of educational leadership. It is a framework which not only attempts to move attention from educational management to educational leadership, but which also articulates new and emancipatory notions of what such leadership could be.

Leadership as Critical, Transformative, Educative and Ethical

In calling for new thinking about educational leadership and in resistance to its commodification in management culture, Foster (1989) has set out a radical agenda for educators. For Foster, 'leadership is at its heart a critical practice'[9] and this involves educational leaders in the necessary practice of reflective and critical thinking about the culture and organization of particular institutions and about the ways in which this culture may need to change.

There is at present a developing literature in education which has been stimulated by Schön's (1983) influential book, *The Reflective Practitioner: How Professionals Think in Action*. The concept of the reflective practitioner is thought to be particularly appropriate for professionals in education, since education as a process involves reflection as well as learning and activity. If, therefore, the reflective practitioner is becoming an influential model in teacher education and professional practice, Foster's argument that educational leadership should be a particular form of reflective and critical practice is a logical extension of this culture. There are, however, important differences between the celebration of a culture of critical reflectiveness in the literature and the practice of critical reflectiveness in contemporary conditions of schooling. Various impediments to leadership as critical practice exist. Indeed, a powerful argument can be made that the contemporary conditions of schooling in many societies involve an *intensification* of work for headteachers, teachers, pupils and governors, so that the spaces and opportunities for critical reflection upon practice have been seriously curtailed.

Closely related to Foster's concept of leadership as critical practice is his notion of leadership as transformative. From this perspective, the leader works with others to obtain transformations of undesirable features of schooling culture and practice. These features might be the existence of racism and sexism in educational practice; the existence of prejudice against particular religious or regional groups; or against those with a range of disabilities and disadvantages. The leadership intention is the intention to attempt a transformation of culture and social relations in a particular institution, not as an act of individual, charismatic leadership but as a shared enterprise of the teachers, the pupils and the community. Transformative leadership involves considerable social skills of advocacy, inter-group relations, team building and inspiration without domination. Foster (1989, p.52) prefers to talk of 'a community of leaders' rather than of *the* leader.

For the English schooling system, these ideas are radical and challenging. As earlier chapters have demonstrated, English schooling culture is familiar with the idea of transformative leadership but, in general, related to an individual and charismatic 'headmaster'. Transformation has been the outcome of individual, hierarchical and patriarchal forms of school leadership for the greater part of English educational history. The idea that transformative leadership could be exercised by a community of leaders rather than by a formal and hierarchical leader would itself require a significant transformation of existing consciousness among teachers, parents and pupils. This is not to say that such change could not occur but to observe that it would involve a profound reorientation of existing expectations and concepts and that it would directly challenge the emergent strong leadership culture of the 1980s and 1990s in English political life. If transformative leadership of this kind is to be a credible alternative to traditional concepts of transformative leadership then educational and professional development programmes would be necessary for its realization among headteachers and aspirant headteachers. In short, new forms of academic and professional education would have to resource new forms of transformative leadership in the schools.[10]

Foster recognizes this need in calling for leadership to be educative and not simply managerial. Drawing upon the work of Fay (1987), Foster argues that existing educational leaders have a responsibility to use education as a means of empowerment for all:

> This educative aspect of leadership is intended to have citizens and participants begin to question aspects of their previous narratives, to grow and develop because of this questioning, and to begin to

consider alternative ways of ordering their lives. The educative aspect, in other words, attempts to raise followers' consciousness about their own social conditions and in so doing to allow them, as well as the 'leader', to consider the possibility of other ways of ordering their social history.[11]

From this perspective, a responsibility of educational leadership is to ensure that all members of the institution have access to powerful information; have spaces and opportunities to debate policy and practice; and are freed as much as possible from the communication impediments of hierarchy, formality and status consciousness. The educative leader attempts to establish the conditions for dialogue, participation and respect for persons and their ideas. When written in this form and at this juncture in contemporary educational practice, such formulations appear impossibly idealistic and out of touch with schooling realities. If this is the case, then rather than dismissing such ideas as impractical in the present context we should perhaps look hard at what has shaped the present context and at what serious faults there may be in 'reality'. If present schooling arrangements limit, in various ways, dialogue, participation and respect for persons, then there are serious ethical issues to be addressed in a framework which goes beyond management culture. It does not seem inappropriate, in this context, that the leadership of an educational institution should be defined as primarily 'educative' in this whole institutional sense rather than primarily managerial or executive.

It also seems appropriate that ethical considerations should be a prime responsibility for educational leaders. Foster's view is that:

> Leadership in general must maintain an ethical focus which is oriented towards democratic values within a community. This has to do with the meaning of ethics historically—as a search for the good life of a community . . . Ethics here refers to a more comprehensive construct than just individual behaviour; rather it implicates us and how we as a moral community live our communal lives.[12]

This emphasis upon the ethical commitments and responsibilities of educational leadership is one that is familiar to English schooling culture. Notions of the good life and of education as one of the means for attaining this in an ethical sense are strong in the historical discourse of English schooling both in the state and private sectors. Notions of moral community and of the particular responsibilities of headteachers for generating such community in schooling similarly have a long history in English cultural life. What is much less established in the English tradition is that such ethical considerations should be shaped by democratic values. It is an important part of the agenda of Critical Leadership Studies that democratic values should not only permeate schooling but should transform the nature of leadership itself.

Beyond Domination: On Organizational Democracy

English schooling culture in the twentieth century has always had, at its heart, a major paradox and contradiction. Formally designated as the cultural agency for 'making democracy work' and involved, at specific periods, with explicit pedagogical projects to enhance education for citizenship, its own practice has remained largely undemocratic. Among a complex of reasons for this lack of democratic practice in school life, the influence of the hierarchical 'headmaster tradition' has been significant. While this tradition may have modified over time into more consultative forms, the fact remains that most headteachers are the operative school leaders and that few examples exist of serious organizational democracy involving major decision making by headteachers in association with teachers, pupils and other school staff.

This lack of democratic culture and practice in English school life, it can be claimed, is itself a mediated form of the historical hidden curriculum of English political and social culture. Despite an early achievement of formal political democracy in England, social and cultural forms have remained pervaded by aristocratic and hierarchical values; in particular, the notion that there is a leadership class. The hidden curriculum of English culture teaches its citizens that this leadership class *will* emerge as the natural leader of society by reasons of its confidence and its relevant cultural capital and that democratic processes will not seriously affect this outcome.[13] In a similar way, English headteachers have also historically constituted a leadership class in schooling and the idea that schools could be run 'properly' by forms of organizational democracy has always seemed far-fetched and improbable.

It was to challenge such aristocratic assumptions that Pat White of the London Institute of Education made two crucial contributions to the literature of Critical Leadership Studies. In her 1982 paper, 'Democratic Perspectives on the Training of Headteachers', White argued that headteachers should be given training opportunities to reflect upon their role in relation to the enhancement of democratic values and democratic practice in schools. For White, if the political ideal of participatory democracy in English society was ever to move beyond the level of rhetoric, then a prior educational practice must lay the foundations for its active realization. This would involve a new culture and ethos in English schools to be generated by a new form of democratic educational leadership:

> In an institution run on democratic principles there should be increased opportunities for individuals to exercise 'genuine leadership'. In saying that I am assuming that by such leaders people have in mind dynamic individuals who are able either to describe ends, or strategies for achieving ends, in such a way that other people are inspired to think that they might be possible to achieve. Clearly the organization of the school on democratic lines will present ample opportunities for

such 'inspirational' leadership without tying it to a person or an office . . .[14]

This notion of organizational democracy should, in White's view, extend beyond simply the involvement of teachers and other adults in educational decision making, to include the pupils:

The democratic head will also be keen that pupils should take a more active role within the school, both in the management of their own and others' learning and in the organization and running of the school itself . . . because for pupils such participation will be a part of their earliest formal political education.[15]

Reference was made in Chapter 2 to the pervasive influence of the 'cult of the amateur' in English cultural and political life. The cult of the amateur, in itself an aristocratic concept, assumes that no special 'training' is required to undertake particular social functions. It has already been demonstrated that the culture of the gifted amateur inhibited the development of training courses for headteachers on organizational planning in the 1960s and 1970s. In essence, White's argument is that the delayed recognition that headteachers do need forms of management training must be extended to include the recognition that headteachers need education programmes on how to operate with more organizational democracy. In other words, the crucial enterprise of educating for democracy and for participative citizenship cannot be left as an amateur enterprise. It requires systematic professional development with headteachers as the necessary preliminary for a systematic approach to education for citizenship in English schools.

These ideas were developed in greater detail by White's subsequent text *Beyond Domination* (1983) which elaborated arguments for participatory democracy in a range of social institutions. Making the interesting observation that among the few writers making serious cases for participatory democracy, women were prominent, White asked:

Is it that women are drawn to explore theories which plan for the control of power so that everyone can flourish and live autonomous, morally responsible lives, because, whatever their country or social class they are likely to have experienced domination in many forms? (p.5)

The question of gender relations and consequences for power relations and for *thinking* about power relations is an important constituent of Critical Leadership Studies and it will be examined in a later section of this chapter. For the present, it can be noted that Pat White's 'unashamedly radical' thesis of 1983 went beyond conceptions of the democratic headteacher to consider future scenarios where such a role would not exist:

> It might be expected that a good part of this chapter would be an elaboration of the role of the headteacher in such a (democratic) society, but this is not so. The reason is simple. There would not be headteachers, as we know them, and therefore special heads' training programmes would not be required. In a participatory democracy there would be training for the whole staff in school organization and the role of the 'head' would be radically different . . . for instance there may be administrative chairpersons with a limited term of office . . .[16]

The proposition that the role of the headteacher, as historically constituted in English schooling would, in the conditions of real participatory democracy, give way to elected, administrative chairpersons is as radical an antithesis to English headship traditions as can be imagined. Between Edward Thring's robust articulation of the headmaster tradition, *viz.* 'I am supreme here and will brook no opposition' and Pat White's advocacy for the elected chairperson of the future, an immense cultural divide exists. It is a divide between a schooling culture marked by hierarchy and patriarchy and one which aspires to be democratic and participative. The domination of English schools by their headteachers has a long history. The forms in which that domination is expressed may have changed over time and may appear now in modern management and chief executive modes. Despite surface change, however, power relations can be remarkably constant and, as White (1982) puts it, 'authoritarianism need not have an ugly face and yet it is authoritarianism for all that' (p.75).

Any project which attempts to transform the authoritarian legacy of English school headship has to recognize that it is dealing with a strong historical formation that will not easily yield to notions of real participatory democracy as opposed to its rhetorical endorsement. If such a project is to be successful it has, above all, to engage with pervasive ideas about the technical necessity of hierarchical leadership and about the impracticability of ideas of organizational democracy in schools.

It is precisely these objections to organizational democracy in schools which have been addressed by Rizvi (1989). Rizvi examines the arguments that hierarchical leadership is inevitable in complex organizations in the context of Michels' (1958) much quoted 'iron law of oligarchy'. He also critically analyzes the case that the existence of hierarchical leadership and control is necessary for the technical efficiency of an institution. Rizvi's counter-thesis, which constitutes his 'defence of organizational democracy' consists of two major arguments. The first is that:

> The iron law of oligarchy or indeed the 'inner logic' of bureaucratic organizations need not be regarded as inescapable. It is only under certain structural conditions that bureaucracy or oligarchy presents itself as natural and necessary—there is no reason to suppose that

under different conditions, human relationships might not be ordered differently.[17]

From the viewpoint of schooling, this is an argument which implies that schools would have potential to develop forms of organizational democracy in conditions where wider social and political change in a given society was itself moving towards greater participatory democracy. However, it would also be possible for schools to develop forms of organizational democracy where the schooling system itself possessed considerable relative autonomy from external agencies, as was the case in England in the 1960s.

Rizvi's second argument is that the idea that hierarchical decision making is more efficient is, in general, untrue:

> Many recent organizational thinkers, such as Fischer and Siriaani (1984) and Crouch and Heller (1983) have gathered a great deal of empirical evidence to suggest that participation is a necessary condition for bringing about greater 'efficiency' . . . Participation induces, they claim, enterprise, initiative, imagination and the confidence to experiment . . .[18]

For schooling, this argument implies that the realization of a school's mission statement is more likely to be achieved where a headteacher uses high levels of participation rather than hierarchical enactment.

Rizvi recognizes that the introduction of more developed forms of organizational democracy in schools will be a slow and locally variant process depending upon existing historical and cultural experience: 'each situation has to be examined in the context of its own unique historical and social features. Changes can only come about when the individuals who belong to a particular organization can see the point in changing.'[19] In coming to such a decision (or not) headteachers, teachers and community members will be influenced by local and national conditions and trends in the wider society. However, Rizvi makes the important point that much more use should be made of comparative studies in education which demonstrate the strengths and weaknesses of organizational democracy in schools in different national and cultural settings.[20]

The work of Rizvi is a significant contribution to Critical Leadership Studies, building upon and extending the arguments of Pat White and others that more participatory democracy in schools is a viable and necessary project for the future. However, his agenda is silent on gender issues and their relationship with forms of educational leadership. An important literature is emerging within CLS which suggests that many of the 'inevitabilities' of leadership theory and practice are an outcome of masculine and patriarchal assumptions rather than of some immutable features of these phenomena. In other words, a growing and significant feminist critique of educational leadership exists which challenges the conventional masculine wisdom about the nature of leadership.

Beyond Patriarchy: Women and Educational Leadership

The feminist critique of patriarchal education management studies and culture was given impetus by the work of Charol Shakeshaft, Chairperson of the Department of Administration and Policy Studies at Hofstra University, New York. In an influential text first published in 1987 and revised and updated in 1989, Shakeshaft argued that administrative and management studies in education had, in effect, been gender blind. What had claimed to be a comprehensive field of study was in fact only a study of male educational leadership. Shakeshaft offered her text, *Women in Educational Administration*, as a contribution to the critical extension of this limited field:

> This is not a book on how to make it in administration, nor is it a book instructing women to be more like men. If anything, it is a book that asks us to question the assumptions of the so-called 'self-help' tracts that have first analysed how men manage and then urged women to do the same. I am saying something quite different in this book. The effective woman does not copy the effective man, nor does she find that what works for him necessarily works for her.[21]

In calling for more research into the differences between the ways that women and men manage schools, an essential part of the thesis of *Women in Educational Administration* is that there are already indications that a 'female culture' of educational leadership and management exists with distinctive characteristics. These characteristics include: greater interpersonal and care sensitivities; a strong and central focus upon the quality of teaching and learning and of relationships with children and students; a more democratic and participatory style of decision making with different conceptions of relations with the wider community, of the use of power and of the nature of educational leadership.

While recognizing that notions of male culture and female culture applied to educational leadership do not refer to entirely distinct categories (i.e., cultural overlap does exist), Shakeshaft nevertheless contends that women approach the leadership and management task in education with different sets of priorities, values and modes of working. Her proposition is that 'this female world exists in schools and is reflected in the ways women work in school.'[22] If this is the case, then women headteachers in England might be expected to encounter sharper professional dilemmas than their male colleagues, as English school culture moves towards a line-management, business executive and market commodity style of operation. Women headteachers in primary schools might, in particular, feel a growing disjuncture between their interpersonal and pupil relationships and their increasing preoccupation with management and financial control issues more sharply than male headteachers.

While Charol Shakeshaft has characterized the distinctive aspects of a female culture of education management, Jill Blackmore (1989) has concentrated upon a feminist critique of educational leadership. Blackmore's critique of the field is more radical and more fundamental than that of Shakeshaft because she calls for a paradigm change in theory and in discourse and not simply for a change in the focus of research:

> Feminist theory does not ask merely to include women as objects in the patriarchal discourse, in which sameness is emphasised rather than difference. It rapidly becomes evident that it is impossible to incorporate or 'add on' a feminist perspective. Rather, a feminist critique ultimately leads to the need to reformulate the methodologies, criteria of validity and merit . . . Feminists demand not just equality, but that they become the subjects and objects of an alternative, autonomous discourse which chooses its own measures and criteria.[23]

For Blackmore, a feminist reconstruction of the concept of an educational leader is necessary. Such leadership would involve a move away from notions of power and control over others towards a leadership defined as the ability to act with others. Leadership would involve being at the centre of a group rather than at a hierarchical distance from it. A feminist discourse and practice in educational institutions would, from this viewpoint, encourage caring and reciprocal relations to be at the heart of organizational culture. In recognizing the qualities required for educational leadership, community activities and child-rearing experience should have equal status with male experience in the formal and public sphere of education. Educational leadership reconstituted in these ways would, Blackmore argues, hold out the possibility that schools might become, for the first time, fully human communities for the education of young people. However, it is recognized that the construction of this alternative culture for schooling and leadership faces major external cultural and political impediments as:

> This would require going against the renewed push towards more masculinist notions of leadership embedded in corporate managerialism, the impetus for current restructuring of secondary and tertiary education, which equates efficiency and effectiveness with organisational rationality and hierarchy.[24]

While Blackmore's specific references are to educational developments in Australia, they apply with equal force to changes in educational policy and practice in England. If there is a feminist project in English schooling to reconstitute the nature of educational leadership then it faces not only the accumulated weight of a historical, patriarchal tradition but also the potency of new forms of 'masculine' corporate management.

Two important sources for challenging patriarchal dominance in England appeared in 1993 with the publication of Jenny Ozga's edited text, *Women in Educational Management* and Sue Adler, Jenny Laney and Mary Packer's book, *Managing Women: Feminism and Power in Educational Management*. Ozga (1993) argues that:

> Education management, like management elsewhere, is largely done by men and is therefore defined by men. Such a definition may be very restricted: at best it may be inappropriate for women; at worst it is hostile to the fostering of management qualities which may represent more ethical and also more effective ways of managing people—and managing people is what educational management is primarily about. (p.2)

For Ozga a crucial part of the feminist project for reconstructing the nature of educational management and leadership involves the collection of accounts from women with such responsibilities who are able to demonstrate that different cultural styles exist which are based upon different sets of values.

Adler, Laney and Packer (1993) have pointed out that women in educational management are not an homogenous group and that analytical distinctions have to be made between 'women in management' and 'feminists in management'. From this perspective, a defining quality of feminism is a resistance to hierarchy and authoritarianism and a search for shared decision making. The possibility for realizing feminist principles in current educational arrangements is recognized as a difficult and contradictory project:

> We see a contradiction between being a feminist and being a manager in education today, although not between being a feminist and working with a feminist management style. There is an inherent contradiction between maintaining feminist principles and holding a powerful position in a linear hierarchy. A manager, by definition, is in a high position on the linear scale. Feminism is wary of pyramidal and linear models and looks to alternatives to hierarchies, to providing multi-dimensional ways of working.[25]

Nevertheless, for all the difficulties which beset the feminist project for the reconstitution of leadership and management in English education, Adler *et al.* argue that current trends in management outside of the schooling system are moving in the direction of principles of feminist management rather than of hierarchical and confrontational patriarchal styles.

It has been shown in earlier chapters in this book that English schooling has been marked by a strong hierarchical and patriarchal culture, established by the 'headmaster tradition' of the English public school and its cultural mediations in state schooling. As a feminist critique of this tradition is developed within Critical Leadership Studies it will be crucial to recover the marginalized history of women in leadership positions in the English educational system of the nineteenth and twentieth centuries. It will thus be possible to show that a feminist project for the transformation of schooling has always existed, even in the most hostile conditions. Feminism, in education, is not simply a trendy and short-lived phenomenon of the 1960s but a continuing oppositional culture for making schools more humane places.[26]

Educational Leadership: Philosophy and Morality

Within Critical Leadership Studies, the corpus of writings generated by Christopher Hodgkinson (1978a, 1978b, 1983 and 1991) provides a sustained critique of technical and reductionist views of educational administration and leadership. For Hodgkinson, 'administration is philosophy in action'[27] and its central preoccupations are with value judgments and the attempted resolution of value conflicts and dilemmas in organizational settings. Educational leadership is necessarily involved with moral questions and the generation of an appropriate moral climate in an educational institution is an important indicator of the quality of that leadership. From this view, therefore, it cannot be sufficient to provide courses for educational managers and leaders which have only a technical content. Educational administrators and managers require opportunities to reflect upon and gain greater insight into the value and moral dilemmas which constantly arise in organizational life. Hodgkinson quotes with approval the observation of Barnard (1972) that 'leadership is the conjunction of technical competence and moral complexity'.[28]

In *The Philosophy of Leadership* (1983), Hodgkinson raises the interesting suggestion that educational leaders have responsibilities which go beyond financial audit, teaching quality audit and learning outcomes audit, to include value audit:

> For the leader in the praxis situation there is an obligation, a philosophical obligation, to conduct where necessary a value audit. This is an analysis of the value aspects of the problem he [*sic*] is facing . . . It is the careful reflection upon such questions . . . prior to administrative action, which is the hallmark and warrant of leadership responsibility.[29]

It is necessary therefore for educational leaders to demonstrate some understanding of moral complexity and some capacity for making explicit the relations between values and proposed actions in educational institutions.

The model for educational leadership is that of practical idealism, i.e., a capacity to interrelate technical competence and moral complexity. Failure to achieve such a relationship leads, in Hodgkinson's view, to formal educational leaders becoming simply careerists, politicians or technicians. Hodgkinson is well aware that contemporary developments in education policy and practice in a number of societies give legitimation to leadership concepts other than that of practical idealism. The careerist leader can command much support in these circumstances:

> The careerist can easily endear himself to the non-administrative ranks of his organisation, he is easily perceived as a good leader. For the simple reason that when there is alignment between his own and the organisational interest, the conjoint dynamism often ensures

organisational growth and success. At the least, he will appear as a good fighter for the sectional interests who seek his leadership.[30]

The politician-leader attempts similar ends to those of the careerist but with greater use of diplomacy and apparent democratic endorsement, while the technician-leader finds legitimation in creating a sense of technical order and efficient operation within the organization.

Hodgkinson makes the point that the legitimation of various forms of educational leadership is related to the wider socio-political conditions in which an institution is operating and related also to the expectations and perceptions of the leader's colleagues or, in Hodgkinson's terms, to the leadership-followership relation.[31] Followers have expectations of leaders. As external socio-political conditions become adverse or as the internal politics of institutional survival become more problematic, followers tend to expect leaders to get them out of difficulty. Such times of institutional threat or crisis are particularly periods when careerist or politician leaders can appear as 'salvationist'. When institutional survival is in the balance, an awareness of moral complexity may not appear as the first requirement for leadership.

While recognizing the force of these contextual arguments, Hodgkinson (1991) nevertheless argues that, properly understood, educational leadership has to be seen as a moral art:

> The dialectic of history dictates three forms: active, passive and synthesizing . . . The educational leader as practical idealist learns to understand these rhythms and seeks, according to personal ideals, to prevent the bad from being born and the good from dying too soon . . . It is not too much to say that, properly conceived, education can be considered as the long sought after 'moral equivalent for war'. Certainly the conduct of its business and the leadership of its organization should be more than mere pragmatism, positivism, philistinism and careerism.[32]

Sergiovanni (1992) has also argued for the importance of moral leadership in education, making a case that the moral school will be also the effective school. For Sergiovanni the desired goal for publicly provided education in America is the creation of the 'virtuous school' characterized by 'a covenant of shared values' and by an ethos of caring and respect for persons. Leadership in such a school would be a demonstration of stewardship and of a manifest serving of the common good—'in the virtuous school, the leader would be seen as a servant'.[33] The religious discourse and imagery of Sergiovanni's thesis is very clear and in particular his construct of the leader as servant is one that is central to the culture of religious schooling, at least in its formal rhetoric. As part of the literature of Critical Leadership Studies, Hodgkinson challenges Education Management Studies to recognize the centrality of philosophical and moral issues in education. Sergiovanni challenges its rational and secular discourse with a discourse derived from a much longer religious tradition.

In a major research study in the USA, Anthony Bryk *et al.* (1993) have focused upon the continuing importance of this religious tradition within schooling. Focusing on Catholic education, Bryk *et al.* argue that Catholic high schools in America can be shown to have made significant contributions to the common good of society, i.e., in the effective development of the intellectual, moral, social and political dispositions of citizens. Indeed, Catholic high schools have, in particular, been historically a crucial sector of the schooling system in the USA, operating in inner city locations and providing a high quality education service for disadvantaged communities.

Both the academic and the social-personal achievements of the Catholic high schools studied are seen to be related to an effective communal school organization involving shared values, shared activities and an ethic of caring which permeated all social relations in the schools:

> Our notion of communal school organization involves a social context that significantly alters the nature of human interactions and the meanings conveyed through these interactions. The major effects of a communal school organization on teachers and students, we believe, are located most directly in the personal and social rather than in the academic domain. Nevertheless, we also maintain that the quality of the social engagement of adults with one another and with students is foundational to a school's academic mission . . . Active rituals, in turn, locate the current social group within a larger heritage, which can serve as a source of profound human meaning. Most important, the underlying values of the institution—shared by its members—provide the animating force for the entire enterprise.[34]

Also crucial to the success of the Catholic high schools studied by Bryk was the quality of commitment demonstrated by the teachers and the principals. This was a quality of professional commitment which still had resonances with ideas of a religious vocation in that extended service was given despite modest material rewards. Educational leadership was, in general, a form of dedicated service:

> The motivation for assuming the principalship more often focuses on the opportunities for institutional leadership than on individual career advancement. The economic rewards to the principalship are very modest and the individuals who take on the role are more likely to see it as a chance to help the school rather than as a means for personal gain . . . the Catholic school principalship is seldom viewed as a stepping stone to a 'plum job downtown'.[35]

Educational leadership as a 'vocation to serve' is not a concept or a discourse routinely found in text books of Education Management Studies. Neither is it found in the rational and secular discourse of Critical Leadership Studies.

However, it is alive in the discourse of many religious cultures, Christian, Jewish, Islamic and multi-faith. It constitutes a founding conception of educational leadership which pre-dates both EMS and CLS. Religious-educational cultures of many traditions carry messages about leadership which stand in a critical relation to those currently dominant or rising to dominance in secular culture. These traditions give pre-eminence to the spiritual and moral responsibilities of leadership, to notions of vocation in education and to ideas of commitment relatively independent of reward or status. The extent to which these ideas are realized in practice by the leaders of religious schools is an empirical question of great interest and relevance for the various faith communities and others. However, the very existence of a religious culture of leadership, when applied to education, provides a sharp antithesis to contemporary constructs of the principal or the headteacher as chief executive of a schooling corporation.

Critical Perspectives and Contemporary English Headship

Education Management Studies provides charts, check-lists and guidelines to assist contemporary English headteachers in a work setting characterized by rapid decision making, competitive market conditions in schooling and new managerial responsibilities. EMS is valued because it offers practical, concrete advice and guidance about what to do. Critical Leadership Studies, on the other hand, seem to inhabit another cultural world where there is time to ask questions about what is being done. CLS, in asking for various forms of reflection and analysis about 'the busyness of headship', seems to be asking for the impossible in contemporary schooling conditions. It is, in the derogatory sense, academic.[36] Contemporary developments in educational policy have accentuated the culture of busyness in schools (work intensification) at the expense of a culture of reflection (always a fragile and dangerous concept in state schooling). Despite a formal rhetoric that the critically reflective practitioner is the ideal of modern professional practice, there is little space in which to reflect and in any case the activity increasingly appears to be irrelevant. In Anne Jones' (1987) research, one of her headteacher respondents articulated the familiar idea that common sense rather than reflection was the contemporary requirement for educational leadership:

> Don't let the academics get hold of headteacher training and turn it into some rarified discipline of study. Needs to be up to date, relevant, practical, common sense and feet on the ground approach, preferably led by practitioners.[37]

One way of evaluating the claim that headteachers in England need only practicality and common sense to deal with their new challenges would be to obtain more information about headteachers' perceptions of these educational challenges and about their responses to them. This may demonstrate that while practicality and common sense are part of the profile of effective leadership, other qualities are required for its full realization. The following chapters will review fieldwork data obtained from samples of headteachers in England in an attempt to make explicit the changing nature of school leadership and its contemporary dynamics, opportunities and challenges.

Notes and References

1 Local Management of Schools (1988, p.5).
2 The recent development of MA courses in School Leadership and Management and of EdD courses in the same field marks an important recognition that simply 'training' for educational leadership is insufficient. The issues involved in leadership and management in education are of sufficient complexity to warrant advanced level study and research.
3 Greenfield, in Greenfield and Ribbins (Eds) (1993, p.141).
4 *Op. cit.*, p.146.
5 Brian Fay (1975) argues that in its educative role, critical social theory tries to enlighten social participants so that 'coming to see themselves and their social situation in a new way, they themselves can decide to alter the conditions which they find repressive' (p.103). One of the aspirations of critical theory is to raise the consciousness of social participants while respecting the intellectual autonomy of those participants, i.e., to avoid programmed 'solutions'.
6 Lifeworld refers to culture, values, interests and commitments; System 'to those activities within society that are organized through the medium of money and power (markets and bureaucracies)' p.9.
7 Bates (1992, p.19).
8 *Op. cit.*, p.20.
9 Foster (1989, p.52).
10 Similar points have been made by White (1982 and 1983) and by Al-Khalifa (1989)
11 *Op. cit.*, p.54.
12 *Op. cit.*, p.55.
13 Green (1991) argues that this aristocratic and leadership culture is sustained by a separate system of public (i.e., private) schooling in England:

> The public schools are the most notorious of Britain's old institutional anachronisms and the most out of place in a modern, supposedly democratic society. They are probably the feature of our education which most baffles foreign observers. Even the name is incomprehensible to most people, apparently saying the exact opposite of what it actually means . . . In England, a uniquely prestigious and influential private sector exists whose main purpose is to provide an intensive education for the children of the upper middle class which gives far better access to positions of influence, power and affluence than do other schools. (pp.14–15)

14 White (1982, p.75).
15 *Op. cit.*, p.77.
16 White (1983, p.118); see Chapter 4, 'Headteachers: a changing role' for further elaboration.
17 Rizvi (1989, p.222).
18 *Op. cit.*, p.216.
19 *Op. cit.*, p.227.

20 Comparative studies of organizational democracy in schooling are, as yet, a relatively undeveloped field of inquiry.
21 Shakeshaft (1989, p.12).
22 *Op. cit.*, p.196.
23 Blackmore (1989, p.120).
24 *Op. cit.*, p.124.
25 Adler *et al.* (1993, p.135).
26 See, London Feminist History Group (1987), *The Sexual Dynamics of History*.
27 Hodgkinson (1978b, p.3).
28 *Op. cit.*, p.219.
29 Hodgkinson (1983, p.207).
30 *Op. cit.*, p.150.
31 Hodgkinson's argument is that concepts of leadership cannot be discussed without a necessary relation to concepts of followership; see pp.141–94. However, the concept of 'follower' seems inappropriate when applied to the culture of professionalism with its traditional commitment to a 'primus inter pares' relation.
32 Hodgkinson (1991, pp.164–5).
33 Sergiovanni (1992, p.115).
34 Bryk *et al.* (1993, pp.276–9).
35 *Op. cit.*, p.300.
36 See Codd (1989) for an argument which is critical of these assumptions.
37 Jones (1987, p.114).

Chapter 4

Fieldwork and Analytical Approaches

Education policy scholarship implies that contemporary fieldwork data should be located in a developed historical and cultural framework rather than abstracted from it. Such scholarship attempts to make a conjunction of historical, cultural and socio-political analysis with the specifics of fieldwork, contemporary empirical data and personal accounts from participants in the research activity. The previous chapters have attempted to construct a theoretical, historical and cultural context in relation to which the fieldwork data can be located and interpreted. The following chapters (5–10) report the detail of a fieldwork inquiry undertaken with the cooperation of eighty-eight headteachers, mainly in schools in the north-east of England, between 1990 and 1994. The intention of the inquiry, which developed over time, was to obtain material which would be illuminative of the range and nature of contemporary headteachers' responses to a changing culture of school leadership. The collection of headteacher accounts as a basic data source was the prime purpose of the fieldwork. Such accounts were obtained from the participants by a cumulative and developing research strategy over a four year period. The accounts were generated either through the medium of semi-structured interviews with headteachers or through the use of survey methods of various types. The participative and collaborative nature of the research inquiry was stressed throughout and the headteachers were encouraged to suggest, define and elaborate the major issues in educational leadership as they saw and experienced them.

Michael Apple (1988) has argued that teachers in a number of societies have experienced a process of 'intensification' in their working conditions during the 1980s, i.e., 'a sense of work overload that has escalated over time' (p.106). This observation is widely endorsed by teachers in England and it was referred to explicitly by the headteachers as a permeating theme in this inquiry. In fact, the work intensification of headteachers in the 1990–1994 period proved to be a considerable impediment to the research process. Although the researcher was well received at headteacher professional conferences and committee meetings and although the objectives of the research were fully endorsed and indeed welcomed, the subsequent follow-through in interview and survey response was often modest. The irony of this situation was that many headteachers, on their own admission, were so preoccupied with day-to-day management 'busyness' that they did not have time to let a wider public know, via research activity, just how busy they were! It seems likely that the work intensification of all school personnel will provide increasingly serious obstacles to educational research in the future. As a result of these difficulties the active, participating sample of headteachers is small in relation to the total population of headteachers in the region and therefore the results reported later can only be regarded as illuminative of headteacher responses rather than definitive or generalizable. However, it can be argued that what the data lacks in numbers, it compensates for in the richness and range of the personal accounts from the workplace.

Fieldwork research activity proceeded in five phases across the period 1990–1994 as follows:

Phase 1: The Initial Interview Stage (1990)

A semi-structured interview schedule was designed to focus discussion of the changing nature of English school headship in both primary and secondary schools. Questions covered a range of issues including motivations for becoming a headteacher; reactions to changes in pedagogical leadership, especially in relation to the national curriculum; reactions to governor and parent empowerment; reactions to the introduction of local management of schools (LMS) and reactions to a more salient market culture in education. The schedule concluded with reflections about school headship in the 1990s and invited headteachers to develop their ideas on this theme.

The cooperation of the two major headteacher professional associations, i.e., the National Association of Headteachers (NAHT) and the Secondary Heads Association (SHA), was obtained for the north-east region. Letters inviting participation in 1 hour interviews focused on these themes were sent to local headteachers.[1] Twenty-one headteachers (eleven Primary and ten Secondary) agreed to be interviewed and 1 hour tape-recorded interviews subsequently took place. The tapes were transcribed and returned to the participants for further reflection before being subject to content analysis. The twenty-one transcripts of Phase 1 were analyzed for their central meanings and categories (see later). From this analysis an interim report was written in 1991–92 with the title 'School leadership in England: Moral values, professionalism and market relations'. This account indicated the range of headteacher responses to changes in these three sectors.

Phase 2: The Focused Survey Stage (1993)

In 1993 an edited version of this interim report was circulated to local headteachers in the target population, inviting them to respond to this first analysis in the following terms:

It is for every headteacher to decide what are the key issues which deserve comment. However, two major points of interest for the research are:

(i)   How are headteacher–governor relations changing or expected to change?

(ii)   Do headteachers experience conflict and contradictions in trying to meet three sets of demands:
  * moral and spiritual responsibilities?
  * professional leadership responsibilities?
  * market executive responsibilities?

The research intention at this stage of the fieldwork was to submit 'key issues' of leadership, as defined by the initial interview sample, to the evaluative judgment of other headteachers in the region. This gave an opportunity for new participants in the inquiry to make critical responses to key issues already defined or to suggest further items as key issues in school leadership.

Twenty-two headteachers (eight Primary and fourteen Secondary) returned written responses to the edited account and to the questions arising from it.[2] These responses were analyzed according to the central meanings and categories approach adopted in Phase 1.

Phase 3: The Moral and Professional Dilemmas Survey (1994)

Headteacher discourse in the first two phases of the inquiry was largely taken up with changing professional and power relations and with changes in school management and the market culture of education. Moral and professional dilemmas in relation to the latter were commented upon by some headteachers but in general their responses were brief and undeveloped.

In order to encourage more reflection upon these issues an open-ended survey document on possible dilemmas in contemporary school headship was designed. This document suggested three areas in which dilemmas for headteachers might arise:

* from pupil and parent behaviour and attitudes;
* from changing professional relations with pupils, teachers and governors;
* from issues generated by a more market related culture in schooling.

In this context, moral and professional dilemmas in schooling were defined as 'situations where two more sets of value judgments conflict and where a resolution of the conflict must be made in the interests of the pupils, the teachers and the school'. However, the document invited headteachers to 'make your own judgment about what constitutes a moral dilemma in schooling'.

The survey document was sent to local headteachers[3] in January 1994. Nineteen headteachers (fifteen Primary and four Secondary) returned written responses. These responses were analyzed for central meanings and categories.

Phase 4: The Catholic Headteachers Survey (1994)

There is a strong Roman Catholic voluntary school sector in the north-east of England and preliminary research activity in phases 1–3 had resulted in twelve headteacher responses (out of sixty-two) from Catholic schools. The opportunity to address a national conference of Catholic headteachers in 1994 provided the basis for widening the sample beyond the north-east region. An open-ended survey relating to possible moral, ethical and professional dilemmas facing Catholic school headteachers was circulated at the conference and the participation of a further twenty-two headteachers was obtained.[4]

The intention of this aspect of the fieldwork was to investigate any qualitative differences which might exist between conceptions of educational leadership in Catholic schools when compared with such conceptions in state schools. To the extent that the 'special mission of the Catholic school' is a distinctive social and cultural phenomenon, the research interest here was, did it generate distinctively different moral and professional dilemmas for the headteachers?

Phase 5: Women Headteachers (1994)

School headship in the north-east of England still shows a strong pattern of male dominance even in primary education.[5] The four phases of research activity already described had resulted in a data source consisting of sixty-four accounts from men and twenty accounts from women. Attempts were made by a further targetted survey to increase the representation of women school leaders and to sharpen the focus upon gender issues in school leadership. An edited extract of material based upon the writings of women academics concerned with school leadership was circulated to a small sample of women headteachers.[6] Four further accounts were generated by this process.

Analyzing Headteacher Accounts

Each phase of the fieldwork activity had been designed to generate a headteacher account based upon an interview situation, a focused survey or a relatively open-ended survey. The formation of the participating sample of headteachers was slow and time-taking and it was entirely dependent on the exigencies of the researcher's other work commitments and upon those of the headteachers. It can only be described, from the perspective of both the researcher and the participants, as a limited opportunity sample.[7]

However, eighty-eight headteacher accounts, by this cumulative field-work process, were available for analysis. These accounts represented the participation of headteachers differentiated in the following ways:

- Sixty-four men headteachers: twenty-four women headteachers
- Forty-seven secondary school headteachers: forty-one primary school headteachers
- Fifty-four state school headteachers: thirty-four Catholic school headteachers
- Sixty-nine north-east region: nineteen other regions

The accounts were subjected to content analysis. Content analysis was based upon a process of initial discourse 'saturation', followed by the identification of the central meanings and categories used by the participants in their responses. Close and repeated readings of the accounts was undertaken in order to achieve in-depth understanding of the content and texture of headteacher discourse.

On the basis of this close knowledge of the accounts, central meanings and categories for each participant were identified. These were defined as those aspects of headteachers' discourse to which they devoted most time and to which they returned as a point of reference and/or in relation to which they exhibited particular engagement in interview or in written response.[8] In the elucidation of central meanings and categories every attempt was made by the researcher to preserve the integrity of the account, i.e., that the edited versions to be used in direct quotation should be faithful to the overall stance of the participant on a particular issue.[9]

The headteacher responses were analyzed first for patterns of reactions in four sectors of leadership relations in English headship, i.e.,

(a) changing power relations with governing bodies
(b) changing curriculum and pedagogical leadership
(c) professional relations and market–management relations
(d) the moral and professional dilemmas of school leadership.

Preliminary analysis suggested the existence of three broad ideal-type headteacher responses to the changed culture of leadership in English schools. The *headteacher–managers* as a group, in all categories of school, celebrated their perceived empowerment in the local management of schools initiative and were confident about their new working relations with governors and the likely success of their schools in a new and competitive market culture in education. They saw the role of the headteacher as becoming primarily managerial but believed that greater management effectiveness would generate an improved professional performance from the school and its teachers. This group was predominantly male in composition. In general, they believed that the autonomy of headteachers had been enhanced and they did not experience either empowered governing bodies or a prescribed national curriculum as a serious constraint upon their school leadership.

The *headteacher–professionals*, on the other hand, had various concerns about loss of important professional relationships and values in a management and market culture in schooling. In particular, this group was concerned that the managerial preoccupations of headteachers would distance them from the pupils, the experience of direct classroom teaching, collegial relations with their own staff and with other headteachers in the locality. This was a concern expressed particularly by women headteachers. In general, while they did not oppose the concept of a national curriculum they were critical of the lack of professional consultation in its formulation and implementation, especially with regard to assessment and testing. Despite this, they were attempting to find a professional response to what they perceived as an unworkable assessment regime. Members of this group believed that a significant cultural change was taking place in schools, with market values strengthening and their particular professional values weakening. However, some headteachers believed that it might be possible to evolve a workable compromise between the two cultures over time, i.e., to 'make the best of things' in the interests of the children.

Given their responsibilities for professional leadership and for institutional (and personal) survival, it is not surprising that relatively few headteachers articulated what might be called a cultural resistance or subversion response. However, a small group, *the headteacher–resistors*, did so with some vigour, especially in relation to what they had experienced as curriculum and assessment impositions by central government and a lack of appropriate consultation. They looked to their professional associations to make a stand on these issues.

Others indicated resistance to the growth of market culture and market values and to the fragmentation of local education services implied in the opting-out initiative for grant maintained status. However, this group faced the dilemma that policies to which they objected on philosophical and professional grounds were policies which, if adopted, could bring to their schools and their pupils considerable material and resource benefits. For some Catholic headteachers in particular, these moral and ethical dilemmas of contemporary school leadership were particularly sharp.

More detailed analysis of the accounts indicated much more complexity in headteacher responses, and the fact that such broad characterizations had internal contradictions and were mediated by phase-level of the school, by state or voluntary status and by gender sensitivities.[10] The following chapters report and comment upon that greater complexity in the responses to a changing culture of school leadership in England.[11]

Note In the following chapters, numbers in brackets used after quotations refer to the code numbers of the headteachers' accounts.

Notes and References

1 Ninety headteachers working in partnership schools with Durham University, School of Education, in the field of initial teacher education were approached for participation in March 1990.
2 The focused survey stage took place in July 1993 and approaches were made to the ninety headteachers in the original target population. Twenty responses received were from headteachers who were not involved in phase one of the inquiry. Two responses were from participants in the initial interview stage.
3 The moral and professional dilemmas survey was sent to a sub-set of sixty headteachers from the original sample. Of the nineteen written responses received, eighteen were from headteachers who had not responded to earlier phases of the inquiry.
4 The Catholic survey took place in March 1994 and focused upon potential moral and professional dilemmas for Catholic school leaders. An open-ended survey designed on these lines was circulated to fifty-four headteachers representing a national distribution of Catholic schools in England, Wales and Scotland.
5 Analysis of the gender composition of school headship in two of the major Local Education Authorities (LEAs) involved in this inquiry revealed the following patterns:

LEA (1)	Secondary headteachers	42 men	1 woman
	Primary headteachers	168 men	73 women
LEA (2)	Secondary headteachers	39 men	5 women
	Primary headteachers	119 men	59 women

6 The edited extract was sent in May 1994 to a targetted sample of fifteen women headteachers, mainly in the north-east region. The names were suggested by one of the women participants in the inquiry. In addition to the extract itself, a covering letter invited these women headteachers to reflect upon questions such as:

(a) Is there a female style of management?
(b) Do women have significantly different ideas about educational leadership to those held by men?

7 'Limited opportunity' refers both to the limited size of the sample and to the limited possibilities which both the researcher and the participants had to generate a more extensive inquiry. The research was accomplished against the grain of work intensification among headteachers.
8 For an earlier use of this method, see Grace (1978, pp.112–14).
9 Bernstein (1977, pp.147–8) has pointed to certain dangers in qualitative research in education, particularly a tendency to use 'invisible control' in the editing and interpretation of data, and has argued that 'the methods of this transformation must be made public so that its assumptions may be criticized'. Young (1976), in commenting upon collaborative research with teachers, warns against a tendency to 'appropriate' fieldwork data into the theoretical framework of the researcher.
10 As the analysis reported in the following chapters demonstrates, there were important differences between primary and secondary headteachers, between state and Catholic school heads, and between men and women.
11 Headteacher-managers, as defined here, numbered 25 (28%); headteacher-professionals, 45 (51%) and headteacher-resistors, 18 (21%).

Chapter 5

The Power Relations of School Leadership: Change or Continuity?

As part of a complex strategy of empowering educational 'consumers', controlling professional autonomy and making schools more responsive to market considerations in education, Conservative governments in England have re-empowered school governing bodies *vis-à-vis* headteachers during the 1980s. Arising from the changes in school governance introduced by the 1986 and 1988 Education Acts, an apparent transformation in the power relations of school leadership has taken place and as Deem (1990) observes, 'Governors now have the power, in theory, to run the schools' (p.169). School governing bodies possess a significant jurisdiction over issues of curriculum and pedagogic effectiveness, the internal organization of schools, financial and resource decisions, staffing priorities, business and community relations and the appointment and remuneration of headteachers and teachers.

From a policy scholarship perspective, the historical and cultural transformations involved in this attempted change in the nature of school leadership are profound. As previous chapters in this book have demonstrated, English headteachers in state schools had emerged from an earlier period of class-cultural surveillance to enjoy an exceptionally strong form of autonomous school leadership dating from the early twentieth century. Both the power relations and the cultural symbolism[1] of this form of manifest school leadership were legitimated and sanctified by the legacy of the public school 'headmaster traditions' and by later social democratic notions of professional expertise and authority.

While contemporary English headteachers in a more professional and consultative culture have moved away from the robust autocracy of headmaster Edward Thring ('I am supreme here and will brook no opposition'), they remain the inheritors of a school leadership position with particularly strong claims to professional and moral authority. Historically, the position of headteacher has commanded a measure of deference (mediated by school level) and its association with hierarchical leadership has been an obstacle to the development of more democratic and participative forms of school governance.

The culture and ritual of English school headship may have moved away from the autocracy of 'I will brook no opposition', but during the social democratic era of the 1960s and 1970s it achieved no significant or large scale transformation towards power-sharing with parents, governors or the

76

community. Autocratic headship may have given ground to professional headship but the professional culture of the 1960s and 1970s still retained a strong sense that 'interference' in the life of the school was not welcomed from parents, governors or other external agencies. The intention of the educational legislation of the 1980s which re-empowered the governing bodies of English state schools was that a concept of lay 'interference' should be replaced by a legitimate involvement of parental, business and community interests in the operation of schools. There is considerable research interest in charting the dynamics of this attempted transformation of school leadership in England. Writing in 1990, Deem concluded:

> It is unclear at present whether headteachers will continue to dominate governing bodies in the way they did prior to the new legislation.[2]

and in a later paper, Deem and Brehony (1992) warned that 'we must be careful not to attribute too much influence to educational legislation' (p.4).

The focal point of research interest is the extent to which a new culture of governor power and leadership can in fact be realized in the face of an existing and powerful culture of headteacher leadership. No simple answer to this will be forthcoming because examples of accommodation or conflict between these two cultures will be mediated by the histories, cultures and socio-political contexts of different educational institutions. At this early stage of research inquiry, case studies of the changing culture of leadership in English schools will at least give some pointers for future investigation. The following fieldwork data gives some indication of these dynamics as reported by headteachers in the north-east of England.

The Continuity of Headteacher Leadership

The headteachers participating in this inquiry had been asked to describe their working relations with their governing bodies following the empowering legislation of the 1980s. Close examination of the headteachers' accounts and of headteacher discourse revealed that the majority of them had not experienced, at that time, any sense of a changed power relation with governors. The reaction of these headteachers may be summed up as saying in effect despite the government's intention to empower the governors, headteacher leadership remains in practice. In short, these headteachers were confident that they were 'still in charge'.

The sense of continuity of headteacher manifest leadership was constituted in a variety of ways. In many cases, headteachers reported that working relationships had not changed qualitatively although much more preparation for governors' meetings was now required. Headteachers attributed this cultural continuity to their fortunate possession of 'good' governors. Others felt that the sheer volume and complexity of education reforms taken together with the increased responsibilities for finance and staffing arising from local management of schools meant that in practice the governors could be 'led' or 'managed' by a well-informed and organized headteacher.

When Nell Keddie (1971) elucidated the concept of the 'good pupil' in her classroom ethnography research, she pointed out that good pupils were socially and morally acceptable to their teachers and caused no trouble, either behaviourally or intellectually. When headteachers in this inquiry used the concept of the 'good governor' they implied that good governors similarly gave no trouble. Such governors were prepared to continue in a pre-reform culture of governance and were not inclined to challenge the manifest school leadership of the headteacher. This view was expressed with varying degrees of nuance depending upon the age-phase of the school or its social and cultural setting:

- This is a head's comment but I have got a good group of governors. In other words, they follow my lead.
  *(Male Primary School Head) (1)**

- The governing body are very good; they have never disagreed with me up to this point in time.
  (Female Infant School Head) (15)

- They are not giving me any trouble. They are giving me support where I need it. They are not interfering in those areas where I feel that they needn't get involved, and they are happy to continue with that kind of set-up at the moment.
  (Male Secondary Head) (11)

- I am very fortunate with my governing body. I have always managed . . . to maintain a good relationship . . . Since the changes after the 1986 Act and the 1988 Act that has carried on . . . I wouldn't say that I've lost independence *vis-à-vis* the governing body . . .
  (Male Primary School Head) (16)

- We have never had any major confrontations . . . They leave the business of running the school to me entirely. When I want their help, it is there, but they don't interfere. I have probably got more power than I really need or want.
  (Male Secondary Head) (6)

The majority of headteachers participating in this inquiry responded in these terms. However, it was recognized that work intensification for headteachers

---

* *Note* Numbers in brackets used after quotations refer to the code numbers of the headteachers' accounts.

had occurred in relation to school governance. There were more meetings of the governing body and of its various sub-committees. Meetings were much longer and the documentation required for them had also increased in volume and complexity. For some headteachers the continuity of headteacher leadership was reinforced by the governors' 'needs' for information and guidance:

- It is really another management task, i.e., managing the governors and keeping them informed of things you want them to know about.
  (Male Primary School Head) (14)

- You give it to them but you also lead them through it . . . several of the governors have welcomed the leading through things that you cannot expect them to understand in so much detail.
  (Male Secondary Head) (21)

Headteachers who took this view were confident that professional leadership manifesting detailed knowledge of legislation, documentation and policy implications for a particular school would be able to maintain dominance by 'leading' and 'managing' a formally empowered lay leadership. However, it was recognized that a headteacher's capacity to sustain manifest professional leadership would depend crucially upon the particular constitution of a school governing body. Power relations could be affected by the social, political and cultural composition of the school governors and by the relative activism and attitudes of the Chair of the governing body in particular.

Given the conservative cultural traditions of the region and its social class profile it is not surprising that many headteachers emphasized the continuity of power relations between heads and governors or the ability of professional leadership to maintain its existing historical advantages in an apparently re-formed model of governance. What was surprising and interesting were the accounts of those headteachers who believed that government reform of English education had actually resulted in an unintended enhancement of the power position of headteachers.

The Empowerment of Headteacher Leadership

Historically, the north-east region of England has been characterized by a local state organization and culture which, in its Labour politics, has celebrated the importance of publicly provided education and of the proper role of local education authority members and officials in the provision and oversight of schooling. Richard Johnson (1991) gives an evocative description of this local political and professional educational establishment:

In January 1988 I attended the North of England Education Conference which is held in a different northern city each January. I was struck by the occupations on the attendance list: county education officers and directors of education, chairpersons and members of local education committees, inspectors and advisers at local and national levels . . . It was an overwhelmingly masculine gathering, though Labour and northern. (p.42)

In his 'critical history of the 1988 Act', Johnson's argument is that such local educational state power was vulnerable to charges of organizational conservatism, undue bureaucracy and County Hall dominance over local community participation and the direct involvement of the parent/consumer. The weakening of the powers of the local educational state by the Conservative reforms of the 1980s was premised upon an apparent transfer of such powers to school governing bodies and to parent/consumers in each local area. As Kenneth Baker, Secretary of State for Education in 1988, expressed it:

So far as financial delegation is concerned, the purpose of the legislation is to ensure that responsibility is shifted—not from local education authorities to the centre—but from local education authorities to the individual schools and colleges. It is thus a devolutionary not a centralizing measure.[3]

Many critics of this political rhetoric have pointed out that the devolution of education management responsibility to each school site level does in practice empower the centre as no unitary body will exist (if the local state is emasculated) to act as a 'check and balance' against the power of the centre. In other words, under the appearances of surface devolution of educational responsibilities to governors and parents, the deep structure of central educational control is actually strengthened.[4]

Other examples of disjunctures between the apparent empowering of school governors in educational leadership in the 1990s and the actual reality of power relations at individual school sites were given by a small group of headteachers in this inquiry. These participants argued that there had been unintended consequences of government education reform which had actually enhanced the power position of headteachers rather than having limited or constrained their power. Their argument was that government action to weaken the control of the local state in education (local education authorities) taken together with the relative inexperience of the newly constituted governing bodies had generated a local power vacuum which headteachers could exploit in various ways. Thus, contrary to government policy and intentions to limit professional leadership power *vis-à-vis* lay leadership, headteachers, in some cases, had the potential for greater autonomy in the reformed system:

- LEA power has been reduced. At present, many governing bodies are unable or unwilling to exercise new powers through lack of understanding. The vacuum created allows more scope for headteacher autonomy.
(Male Primary School Head) (29)

- Headteachers have had the opportunity to 'dominate' the new governor selection in 1992 and 'steer' the new committees as the lead professional, without LEA control either politically or through the advisory services and/or administrative officers.
  (Female Secondary Head) (28)

- The relationships between a Head and his/her Governors will largely determine the effects of empowerment legislation. A Headteacher who provides strong leadership for Governors and whose informal relationships with Governors are very cordial, may be in an even stronger position than previously.
  (Male Secondary Head) (22)

The thesis of greater headteacher empowerment in school leadership in the 1990s depends crucially upon the existence of a 'power vacuum' in particular local settings. This feature may only be a phenomenon of transitional cultural change in English school leadership. It may refer to a delimited period marked out by the initial weakening of local state educational control of schooling before a new culture of confident and informed school governor leadership becomes established in many schools. Deem (1993) has argued, on the basis of her intensive studies of school governing bodies in England, that some governing bodies are 'beginning to display a distinct organizational culture of their own'.[5] Where that culture involves the confident assertion of new forms of governor leadership in education, then headteachers will encounter the beginnings of a changed power relation and the beginnings of various challenges to their historically dominant position in English schooling. There was evidence from this inquiry that such changes were beginning to emerge.

School Governors: A New Culture of Leadership?

In accounts covering the period 1990–1994, ten of the participating headteachers made explicit reference to what they interpreted as emergent or potential difficulties in the new forms of headteacher–governor relations. In general, such headteachers' concern focused upon examples of a changed organizational culture among the governors involving more assertion or activism with a potential for 'interference'. Others predicted difficulties for the future when empowered but inexpert governing bodies began to exercise the full extent of their powers. The most explicit form in which the new power relation in English schools was expressed, occurred in a large secondary school in a locality with a significant representation of middle-class and professional parents. Given the status and manifest success of the school, the headteacher was clearly surprised by an experience of a new assertive culture among the governors:

- One of the problems that we faced was an initial, acute enthusiasm for power. . . . [In reporting to the Governing Body], I used the expression that 'senior management think', i.e., the Head and the Deputies, and he [the Chair of the governors] stopped me immediately and said, '*We* are the senior management now'.
  (Male Secondary Head) (9)

No other account provided such a dramatic example of a new culture of leadership among school governors but other accounts indicated in various ways that change was emergent or expected:

- Dealing with the governing body was something that took an hour or two a month. Suddenly, overnight, the Education Reform Act has made it a major part of my job, more than anything. It's not just altered my job, it's altered my life . . . there are very few days, certainly no weeks, when I do not either have to be in contact with the Chairman of Governors, having meetings with the Chairman, or having meetings with other governors. Having much longer meetings and preparing papers . . . falls at my door.
  (Male Secondary Head) (7)

For this headteacher, the increase in workload associated with a new pattern of shared leadership with governors was 'massive'. It was also qualitatively different from the relationship before 1988:

- There is a significant attempt, by some of them, to take a higher profile and there is a bit of a battle going on at the moment, and that's probably the case in other schools, between those who are happy to be there and monitor what is going on and those who actually want to interfere.
  (ibid.)

The distinction between 'monitoring' governors and 'interfering' governors was to be found in the discourse of other headteachers. One headteacher represented the changes in power relations and the culture of leadership in terms of a growing conflict situation within the school:

- From 1984 to 1988 the Governors were very much *laissez-faire* and virtually left me to get on with the job. However, more recently, many more decisions are being questioned and a firmer line demarcated as to who makes decisions. . . . Where one has done what has always been done, now it is questioned . . . The Governors fall into two camps, the activists and the 'press-ganged'. Activists have ready-made agendas and build up their power bases so that they can force their viewpoint through. They are generally articulate, knowledgable and have done their homework. The 'press-ganged' are well-meaning people but have a narrow personal view of education that hardly fits in with the demands of educational needs and changes. Often these people struggle to comprehend the issues and tend to be persuaded not by argument but by force of personality.

(Male Primary School Head) (25)

From the perspective of this headteacher, a process of attrition was occurring in school governing bodies with the gradual loss of the services of 'well-meaning' governors and a drift towards the 'activist' model of school governorship.[6] The change in school governors' leadership in this account was from a *laissez-faire* culture to an 'adversarial' culture.

The ten headteachers whose accounts expressed various degrees of concern about a new culture of governor leadership made distinctions between supportive action by governors and 'interference'. The concept of 'interference' in headteacher discourse may be unique to English school culture. In its strongest historical form it is a linguistic manifestation of an insulated and powerful pedagogic authority. It is a classic response of the culture of the 'headmaster tradition' to any change in power relations. In a more contemporary setting it is also the response of a relatively autonomous professional culture when faced with reforms involving greater parental and community involvement in the governance of schools.

'Interference' is a way of signalling an illegitimate intrusion of lay power into a specialized professional culture. Although most headteachers in this inquiry had not experienced 'interference', being fortunate in their possession of 'good' governors, a minority of their colleagues had not only experienced the beginnings of such interference but believed that government reform was encouraging such interference in the name of greater accountability. For some headteachers, the whole philosophical and theoretical basis for empowering inexpert governors in English schooling was seriously flawed:

- He who controls the strings of appointments and dismissals, finance and teacher discipline, when put to the test, is in a position to control the Headteacher. Where once it was an LEA, advised by educational experts . . . now power resides in the hands of the non-expert governors and cannot be justified in many instances of schooling . . . While the LEA loses its powers to the governors and the headteacher does not have the power of County Hall to support and strengthen his role, the governors will take control of the head and the school. This is a crisis in authority and leadership writ large. It is an unjustified attack upon the moral claim of knowledge and expertise as instruments of decision making. Where rationality, moral exhortation and judgments of expertise were once recognized as the rightful tools of leadership in schools, now

> there is a void where anybody on the governing body can take part in a power struggle to control the school . . . As the LEA loses its powers to the governors, who do not have the same expertise to justify their control, such control is not leadership but power unjustifiably exercised.
> *(Male Secondary Head) (37)*

This was the most eloquent and detailed defence of the moral superiority of headteacher professional leadership in English schooling when faced with a new and active form of leadership from 'inexpert' governors. There was some evidence that the vigour of this professional case was related to conflict between the headteacher and a group of active governors over teacher appointments in the school.

What one group of headteachers may characterize as 'interference' by school governors in a specialized, professional world, could on the other hand be represented as an appropriate and long overdue move towards a more democratic and consultative culture of school leadership. Given the historical tradition of insulations between school and community in England, it is not surprising that few headteachers positively celebrated the empowerment of governors. However, there were some examples where greater governor involvement was welcomed.

Power to the People?

In contrast to those headteachers whose discourse about school governors centred upon notions of 'interference', a small group of participants saw the empowerment of governing bodies as a necessary and welcome reform. For these headteachers, the Education Reform Act opened up possibilities for a more democratic, shared and community-related form of school governance and leadership. From this perspective the social and community exclusions involved in both the 'headmaster tradition' of school leadership and the 'expert professional' form of leadership could be overcome in ways more appropriate to a democratic culture. Some of these headteacher-democrats were strongly critical of the residues of the 'headmaster tradition' still operating in English schools:

- Even after ten years' headship in English schools, I have never quite got to grips with the concept of 'my' school and the inherent autocracy encapsulated in it . . . Too many English schools were 'ruled' by none-too-benevolent despots! Many working-class governors have real power in school now. I applaud this.
  (Male Secondary Head–Australian in origin) (38)

- I believe that any Head who sets out to 'manage' Governors is sadly mistaken. In this generation of Headship, many will 'get

away with it' but their schools will not benefit from the vitality
that an empowered Governing Body can give a school. In the long
run, Heads will have to learn . . . There are potential conflicts, but
only those irked by the diminution of the illegitimate power that
Headteachers may have wielded in the past find these threatening.
(Male Secondary Head) (43)

- There may have been a golden age of English headship—but only
  because heads were able to lead, govern and rule without any real
  challenge to their authority and without needing to be accountable
  . . . It shouldn't surprise anyone that those Governing bodies which
  have been patronised by a termly tea and biscuits cosy chat . . .
  suddenly begin to exercise their new powers . . . This is the excit-
  ing potential of ERA. It would be great to see real community
  power taking over.
  (Male Secondary Head) (26)

Such criticism of the autocracy and unaccountability of the headmaster tradition of school leadership was not generated by young radical headteachers or
by politically correct new headteachers of the 1980s but by experienced
headteachers who had worked under such regimes in the early phases of their
careers and whose conceptions of headship had been forged in opposition to
this historical and cultural tradition. While they were critical of other aspects
of government reform in education, the empowerment of governors as a means
of empowering community influence in schooling received their positive
endorsement.

Other headteachers welcomed the changes in school governance because
in their view greater accountability in English schooling was required:

- The enhanced role of the governing body is something I welcome.
  In my experience it has increased local accountability immeasur-
  ably. The headteacher very properly has to win the hearts and
  minds of governors, many of whom are parents themselves. This
  has, in my experience, made the role more fulfilling, challenging
  and rewarding. I have found the governing body giving priority
  to the best interests of all children. It is the proper task of the
  headteacher to explain, share and, if appropriate, modify his vision.
  There are tensions and conflicts in the process. This is the price of
  leadership in a democratic society.
  (Male Secondary Head) (36)

- I think many of the radical views of educationalists in the 50s and
  60s did great harm to the education service and that a return to
  accountability to a balanced [in terms of race, gender, etc.] group
  of people is a step in the right direction. School governing bodies

have been extended to enable a wider range of people to be involved in the education of the next generation (and in some cases
are being educated themselves!)
(Female Infant School Head) (23)

As Deem (1994) has argued, 'school governance has the potentiality to be
a key form of democratic participation' (p.24). The majority of headteachers
in this inquiry either asserted or implied that the governing bodies of the
schools had been changed from control by a dominant political bloc to a more
distributed pluralistic control from parents, community members and business interests. For some, this was an obvious manifestation that governance
and leadership in schools was becoming more democratic and community
focused. Others were sceptical about such claims:

- School governors are not, by any stretch of the imagination, a
  democratic body representing parents.
  (Male Secondary Head) (34)

For the headteacher–democrats, the potentiality for greater community involvement in school leadership from reformed governing bodies was something to be celebrated. Whether in practice the reformed governing bodies
would be more representative of local communities in class, race and gender
terms remained an open question. It is noteworthy that headteacher discourse
on this issue made little reference to the class, race or gender composition of
school governing bodies. For most headteachers, the key issue was not the
representativeness of school governing bodies but whether or not such bodies
were 'good' or 'interfering', 'activist' or 'cooperative' and, in particular, whether
or not harmonious working relations could be established with the Chair of
the Governing Body, seen as a strategic power holder.

Democracy, Governors and Headteachers

Among the various intentions the Conservative governments in the 1980s had
for the re-empowerment of school governing bodies, the establishment of a
stronger agency for accountability to parent/consumers and to business interests was prominent. In other words, a long established professional autonomy
for headteachers to be manifest school leaders was to be constrained in the
name of greater efficiency, effectiveness and responsiveness. Accompanying
such changes in the nature of school leadership in England was a discourse
which celebrated parent power, reconstituted as 'consumer power' and the
school reconstituted in enterprise culture as an emergent business, with a
Board of Directors (The governors) and a Chief Executive (The headteacher).
The most politically effective strand in this discourse of legitimation for radical
school change was that the reassertion of governor power was in fact an

assertion of democratic and community control of state schooling over and against the insulated control of education professionals.

Given the political and ideological context of the reforms in school governance duing the 1980s and given the historical and cultural traditions of strong, autonomous leadership from headteachers in English schooling, it is hardly surprising that the initial reactions of the majority of participants in this study were largely defensive rather than celebratory. The strong insulations (or 'classifications' in Bernstein's, 1977, terms) between school culture and community or mundane culture in England have deep historical roots. The origins of such insulations and separateness are to be found in a religious culture of scholarship and learning which sought to keep the secular world at arm's length as potentially a corrupting and polluting agency. In more contemporary educational settings this culture of 'necessary insulation' has been reconstituted and reformulated in the claims of modern professionalism for autonomy in which to exercise its specialized knowledge and understanding. Headteachers, in English schools, have exercised a form of educational leadership with this historical and cultural pedigree and this accounts, to an important extent, for their defensive reactions to the possibility of 'interference' from empowered school governors rather than their celebration of the possibilities for greater democratic and community involvement in the life of schools.

The defensive response of headteachers in this study to greater governor power is not simply, however, the response of an entrenched cultural interest group when faced with demands for greater openness and accountability in matters of schooling. Throughout the accounts of the majority of headteacher participants in this study was a sense that the education profession (including headteachers) was under ideological and political attack from governments hostile to the interests of public service professionals. This hostility and perceived contempt had been shown in the dictatorial manner in which a whole range of education 'reforms' had been 'imposed' on English schools, with scant regard for the views of education professionals and with little serious attempt to consult them in the process of change. Many headteachers were therefore sceptical of the good faith and intentions of government reform. What could be represented as a legitimate extension of accountability mechanisms within the school, could also be represented as an illegitimate constraint upon headteacher and teacher professional autonomy. What could be legitimated as an extension of democratic control within schooling, could also be interpreted as an extension of control by small groups of 'activist' parents or by business interests.

Nevertheless, even in these socio-political circumstances, a minority of headteacher-democrats appreciated the potential of the reforms in school governance for the beginnings of a real change towards greater democracy in schools and stronger forms of community involvement. These headteachers were aware, from their own experience, of the limitations of headteacher autocracy and accepted that a modern form of headteacher professional leadership had to be constructed in partnership with school governing bodies. As one headteacher put it:

- Some headteachers, and I am one, view the traditional hierarchical aspects of leadership differently . . . The school's ethos can be different and can produce a less possessive type of Headteacher . . . If leadership is promoted at all levels in the teaching staff so that ownership of problems is disseminated much more widely, and if Governors themselves support this concept, the ethos of the school can develop contrary to the intent of Government legislation.
  (Male Secondary Head) (22)

Rizvi (1989, p.227), in making the case for more organizational democracy in schools, has accepted that such democracy will be a slow and locally variant process depending upon existing historical and cultural features and that 'changes can only come about when the individuals who belong to a particular organization can see the point in changing'.[7] This judgment is endorsed by the findings of this study. One headteacher represented the changes in the culture of school governance in the region in these terms:

- The role of the Governors has certainly changed and with it the relationship with the Headteacher. Some Governors see the ERA as their way of exerting power but some are frightened by the power they corporately hold. Relationships with Governing Bodies vary from school to school. Some colleagues have very little say in what happens; they have to have Governor permission for almost everything. Others manage to 'manipulate' their Governing Bodies and thereby retain some leadership of their school. One has to very carefully learn what games must be played and with whom. Much depends on the social and political constitution of Governing Bodies.
  (Female Infant School Head) (30)

The reformed culture of English school governance has various potentialities for future development. There is a potentiality for continued manifest leadership from headteachers using strategies of governor management (at its best, 'professional guidance', at its worst 'manipulation'). There is a potentiality for governor dominance of headteacher leadership ('We are the senior management now'). There is a potentiality for the strengthening of sectional or particular interest groups in the running of schools but there is also a potentiality for more representative and democratic control of English schooling. Such potentialities are currently being realized in different school settings and in different socio-cultural contexts. Current and future research on school governance will be crucial to the elucidation of these various patterns and forms.

Headteachers will not simply be the passive recipients of these changed forms of educational leadership but, on the contrary, active agents in their constitution and realization. At this historical junction in the development of English schooling, headteachers have a critical role to play and this role will depend upon their own philosophical and ideological reflections upon the proper nature of school leadership and governance in a democratic society. They may choose to continue historical traditions of manifest headteacher leadership on the grounds that they have the professional and moral authority to give such leadership with the 'support' of the governors. On the other hand, they may take the view that school leadership must become less hierarchical and leader centred and more a shared and participative responsibility of education professionals and community members. To realize the former model, headteachers simply have to build upon their existing historical advantages, consolidating this by expert knowledge of legislation and documentation and by the appropriate deployment of micro-political strategies. To realize the latter model, requires a more radical and fundamental reappraisal of the conditions for democratic school leadership. Just as action by the 'strong state' has been the necessary preliminary to the advance of market forces in social and educational life, it may be, ironically, that action by 'strong headteachers' will be the necessary condition for the emergence of greater democratic and community involvement in the governance of English schools. Here, the key questions are: Will headteachers be prepared to share their historical powers of leadership with members of local communities? What advantages could possibly accrue to headteachers in moves towards partnership in leadership as opposed to relative autonomy in leadership? Does the rhetoric of greater democratic involvement mean 'interference' in practice?

The minority of headteacher–democrats in this study were prepared to share their powers of leadership with newly constituted governing bodies and welcomed this possibility as a necessary development in the culture of English schooling. For such headteachers, the more active involvement of school governors in leadership and management enriched and strengthened the cultural, personal and material resources available for educational developments within the school. In these contexts, empowered school governors were looked upon as educational allies and not as potential sources of 'interference' in professional matters. It seems clear that the headteacher–democrats adopted this positive stance for a variety of reasons. In some cases, there was a principled commitment to the serious realization of community education in practice; in other cases, a shrewd awareness that, in difficult times, schools needed support networks and that active and involved governing bodies could provide such networks for the future. The potential for 'interference' was reconstituted by such headteachers as a potential for supportive partnership. They were confident of their ability to make the new constitution work for the good of the school and the community and confident that they, as headteachers, could make the transition to a shared concept of educational leadership. Such headteachers were prepared to give a form of strong leadership, not directed towards the historical models of powerful, individual headteachers but towards greater community involvement in the governance of schools.

Their responses were, however, exceptional and not typical of the overall stance of headteachers in this study. For the majority, inheritors of a tradition of strong, patriarchal authority and of strong professional autonomy, such transitions were radical in their redistribution of power in leadership; dubious in their political origins; and uncertain in their practical outcomes. A form of compliance with the new arrangements had (in most cases) to be given but to celebrate them was regarded as premature. The historical forms of strong headteacher leadership were not to be so easily transformed.

The Local Educational State and Headteachers

While Conservative government reform of education in England has sought to empower school governing bodies, it has, as a concomitant strategy, sought to de-power the local education state in its control of school governance and management. Chitty (1992) has pointed out that 'the 1988 Act has also been seen as an attempt to undermine, and even destroy, Local Education Authorities' (p.39), and Simon (1993), in a powerful critique of 'The Destruction of Local Democracy', has argued:

> The current attack on local authorities is being carried through because these provide the indispensable infrastructure and support for systems of comprehensive education. To transform such systems into something quite other (which is the objective) it is necessary first to destabilize, then to disrupt and finally to abolish local education authorities.[8]

The reaction of the headteachers participating in this study to the weakening of local education authorities will be dealt with in detail in a later chapter, because such reactions were integral to headteacher reactions to the introduction of local management of schools (LMS) and to the development of market values and market forces in schooling.

In general, headteacher responses to central state initiatives which weakened the powers of local education authorities were mediated by their prior experiences of the local state and its bureaucracy. Where those experiences had been positive and the LEA had been a valued resource and support network for the headteacher and the school, the diminution of their powers was regretted. However, those headteachers for whom the LEA had been a source of unwelcome political and bureaucratic constraint in their own exercise of school leadership and management regarded their weakened position as a source of 'liberation' for headteachers.

The particular style and nature of local education authority jurisdiction in the region and the particular culture of local politics and bureaucracy is central to any understanding of headteacher responses to a weakened LEA. Those headteachers who saw themselves as modern, progressive, dynamic and enterprising in educational leadership and management tended to be critical of a local culture of politics and bureaucracy in schooling which they had experienced as conservative and constraining. Those headteachers who regretted the weakening of the LEA did so on the basis of a past loyalty rather than a principled defence of the necessary role of local education authorities. In the ideological struggle between notions of individual, school-site leadership and management, and notions of local authority leadership and management, the former appeared to be in the ascendant. After a decade of sustained central state ideological and material support for 'liberated, school-site management' this finding is not perhaps surprising.

The State and Educational Leadership

Throughout the 1980s a strong, interventionist central state in education had demonstrated a radical form of educational leadership of a type not experienced in English culture since the nineteenth century. The consequences of such state action had impacted upon the working world of the headteachers in this study in various ways and it had decisively altered the conditions in which their own concepts of school leadership could be realized. Just as the power relations with the local state had changed, so too had the power relations with the central state in education. It was important to know how the headteachers had responded to this.

In an attempt to preserve the authenticity of headteacher discourse on power relations, it was decided not to raise central state action as a major focus for the interviews or for responses to the open-ended surveys but rather to allow references to the central state to emerge in any discourse relating to changes in school governance, curriculum, local management of schools, and the growth of market culture in schooling. Throughout the inquiry, the headteacher participants were encouraged to introduce the issues which they defined as central to educational change and it was open to them to comment upon the strong leadership which they had experienced from the central state if they wished to do so.

It is characteristic of the deep professional inhibitions in English schooling culture about references to explicitly political issues, that out of the total sample of headteachers' accounts only fourteen made any developed references to the political action which had transformed the conditions of education. I have traced elsewhere the socio-historical origins of this particular form of English teacher and headteacher professionalism which eschews wider political or economic discourse as inappropriate for professional discourse. Such inhibition has been a central feature in the creation of legitimated professionalism for teachers in England (Grace, 1987).

Arising out of socio-political factors in teacher-state relations, what began as an occupational distancing of party or class politics extended over time to a culture and a discourse which attempted to distance political issues *per se*. Far from being a radically politicized profession, teachers and headteachers in England have been, in general, much less political in consciousness and action than their colleagues in the USA and in other societies.[9] Headteachers, in particular, in enacting a model of responsible professional leadership, have been restrained, at an individual level, in commenting upon the nature of state policy in education, although their professional associations have made more explicit statements with political connotations.

Most of the headteachers in this study did not comment upon their experience of central state power in education despite early warnings to the profession that the politicization of education was taking place in the 1980s. Walter Roy, a headteacher and leading member of the National Union of Teachers, had warned his colleagues in 1983 that:

> The attack on teaching . . . has its roots in a philosophy resting on the belief that it is central government, its ministers and its civil servants, that must determine not only the shape of the school system but of the curriculum and methodology of the teaching process. Teachers must therefore be subordinated to a political will based on the notion that only an all powerful state knows what is best for its citizens . . .[10]

Ten years later, it was as if the majority of headteachers in this inquiry had become resigned to the power of the central state in education and that they took it to be an immutable fact of the political and professional world in which they had to survive. What was to be gained by the generation of either protest or critical comment in the face of a strong and active ideological state?

A minority, however, broke through the culture of resignation and inhibition to offer their views on the nature and effect of central government policy upon schooling and upon the role and working conditions of headteachers. Most of these 'political' accounts made reference to the dictatorial style of educational reform or to its various negative consequences:

- Our targets are now being set externally. We are not being involved in the debate. The so-called consultation over the Education Reform Act, the national curriculum and everything that has followed through, is laughable . . . I see no possible reason why a Minister with very limited experience in education, who doesn't seem to listen to advice at all, should be in a position to decide what is best for all children.
  (Male Secondary Head) (2)

- Paperwork responses to idiotic government legislation and the like are threatening to engulf me . . . part of Mr Patten's bureaucratic framework for schools . . . I am buried in the new Attendance Regulations . . . amendment of all staff job descriptions . . . an Annual Review and a statement of salary position for every teacher . . . a whole range of instant requirements for the School Prospectus, listed in DFE Circular 4/93.
  (Male Secondary Head) (22)

- I am disillusioned about what has been done to schools. I have said that I have a very loyal, hardworking staff, but most of them would like a job somewhere else and that upsets me terribly. The net results of the Education Reform Act . . . is that it has demoralized teachers and it is making a lot of them want to leave. I have also heard that it is difficult to find certain candidates for headships. *(Infant School Head) (17)*

Other critical comments referred to 'the adversarial methods for bringing about reform' and to inability of government ministers (and many civil servants) to understand the culture of English state schooling, especially in primary education, given their own private school backgrounds.

For some critics of the central state, serious constitutional issues had been left unresolved in the reform of school governance, with great potential for conflict in the future:

- There is no clear demarcation between governor and headteacher responsibilities. By not drawing a line here, after the Stratford School conflict,[11] the government has enabled a power struggle to ensue, that the professional is likely to lose.
  (Male Secondary Head) (37)

Very few headteachers made explicit reference to the ideological context of educational reform and in particular to the influence of the New Right on the formulation of policy. The following account was exceptional in the detail of its analysis and in its critical stance:

- It is difficult to divorce the changing patterns of leadership from the ideology currently propounded by the 'New Right'. Indeed there is a growing consensus of opinion amongst my colleagues that the sheer amount of change being heaped upon schools is a deliberate attempt to destabilize the system, by wrenching power away from LEAs, thereby *apparently* increasing the autonomy of schools and consequently requiring new patterns of leadership to emerge. Much of this has more to do with economics than curriculum, of course—and far from the 'classless society' envisaged by John Major, is actually designed to perpetuate the class system. Headteachers are therefore being required to lead something (ironically under the guise of improved standards and quality) over which they have little real control—and even less faith!
  (Male Secondary Head) (27)

Although this headteacher represented his account as part of a growing consensus among his colleagues, it was a consensus which did not make itself explicit and visible in the great majority of responses.[12]

Dale (1992) has argued that 'A focus on the State is not only necessary, but the most important component of any adequate understanding of education policy' (p.388). From a policy scholarship perspective this is a powerful argument, because it insists that the state and the agencies of the state, structure the new working conditions and social relations experienced by educators. However, because of the pressure and intensity of the reform process the attention of participants tends in practice to be focused upon changed local circumstances rather than upon their structural origin. For most headteachers in this study, their focus in terms of the changing power relations of school leadership was firmly upon the reconstituted governing bodies rather than upon the central state as such. In other words, at the level of professional practice, the policy of the central state as mediated by new relations with governors and with communities was for these headteachers the important component in schooling in the 1990s.

Notes and References

1   Peter McLaren (1993) has argued that much more attention needs to be given to the analysis of cultural (and religious) symbolism in processes of schooling. Many of the concepts used by McLaren in his original and scholarly study of a Catholic school in Toronto have relevance for the study of educational leadership and these concepts should be more widely used. From the perspectives of a policy scholarship, understanding of educational leadership 'culture' and 'ritual' have high theoretical and analytical potential. As Colin Lankshear (1993) expresses it in his Foreword to the second edition of *Schooling as a Ritual Performance*:

> Culture refers to a system of symbols . . . an historically transmitted pattern of meaning embodied in symbols . . . Rituals are forms of enacted meanings . . . (and) . . . are components of ideology, helping shape our perceptions of daily life and how we live it. (p.xiii)

The argument of this present study is that school leadership in England, especially as manifested in the position of the headteacher, cannot possibly be appreciated without an adequate understanding of the cultural symbols and the ritual forms associated with headship in English schooling. English school headship has been powerfully and richly endowed with cultural (and religious) symbolism and its historical, hierarchical traditions have generated an associated set of rituals. These may now be in transition but they remain active in contemporary settings.

2   Deem (1990, p.168).

3   Quoted in Johnson (1991, p.67).

4   As Johnson (1991) observes:

> An individual school can hardly be said to counterbalance a national state. It cannot even claim to speak for a whole locality or arbitrate competing local needs. So the effect of the erosion of LEA competence is to reduce local power overall as a counterbalance to the centre. (p.68)

5   Deem (1993, p.214).

6   Many headteacher accounts contained references to the workload expected of school governors and the level of responsibility which they were expected to assume. Such accounts also predicted difficulties in retaining the services of 'well-meaning' governors as pressures increased.

7   Rizvi (1989, p.227).
8   Simon and Chitty (1993, p.23).
9   One of the greatest ideological successes of New Right lobbying, campaigning and media activity has been the construction of a highly political image of the teaching profession in England. This image has resulted from the skilful amplification of a minority of explicit left wing and radical political activits within the profession. In fact, the great majority of teachers and headteachers in England are characterized by 'moderate' professionalism and 'moderate' politics. The profession as a whole has a much less developed political culture than right wing publications have claimed.
10   Roy (1983, p.1).
11   For a discussion of the issues at stake in the Stratford School conflict, see Cumper (1994, pp.174–6).
12   A small number of headteachers argued that New Right attacks upon state education had resulted from the activity of a minority of left wing teachers and the policies of a minority of LEAs:

- This government thinks that so many of our profession are left wingers.
  (Male Primary School Head) (19)

- The Education Reform Act could be described as a sledgehammer to crack a few nuts, in that certain LEAs and certain schools were underachieving. They received an incredible amount of adverse publicity, particularly politically.
  (Male Primary School Head) (17)

Chapter 6

Headteachers: Curriculum and Educational Leadership

In the changing culture of English school headship one of the major trans-formations historically has been from a general conception of the headteacher as moral leader to a general conception of the headteacher as curriculum and educational leader. The relatively strong autonomy for schooling in the 1960s and 1970s, when combined with an amplification of progressive notions of curriculum and teaching reform, empowered headteachers to be radical agents of educational change if they chose to be so. While there were always constraints upon headteachers' cultural power, Pollard (1985) has argued that headteachers, especially in primary schools, enjoyed, 'very great autonomy over many aspects of teaching processes and curriculum decisions' (pp.103–4). Once the majority of primary schools in England were freed from the pedagogic constraints of preparing pupils for the 11 plus selective secondary examination by the late 1960s, innovative headteachers had the potential for radical change.

Some headteachers, despite the new freedom, pursued a policy of cultural continuity and a traditional reputation for 'high standards' and 'disciplined' teaching in primary education (i.e., the continued production of 11 plus school-ing culture despite changing circumstances). Others used their new freedoms to introduce more child-centred approaches to teaching and learning, mixed ability grouping, integrated curricula with emphasis upon topics and themes rather than discrete academic subjects, and flexible and varied approaches to assessment and recording (i.e., progressive forms of primary education—the Plowden culture[1]). To an important extent, the educational cultures of pri-mary schools and of secondary schools in this period were constructed as 'traditional' or 'progressive' largely as a result of the pedagogical leadership of headteachers. Headteachers were able to exploit their institutional power, their status as professional leaders and their influence over staffing and promotions to either maintain or change the educational ethos of a school. Opposition to such cultural power was possible and in certain circumstances successful but powerful headteachers, either as staunch traditionalists or committed progress-ives, were a force to be reckoned with in English schooling culture.

The configurations of this professional world were, however, dramatic-ally changed by the educational legislation of the 1980s. Pollard (1994) gives a succinct account of these changes:

> The National Curriculum and its associated assessment procedures
> were introduced in England by the passage of the Education Reform
> Act 1988 . . . Among many significant features of these reforms was
> the specification of nine subjects, which with Religious Education
> were to structure the basic content of the curriculum at primary school
> level, and the introduction of a ten level scale of attainment through
> which pupil achievements could be assessed and recorded throughout
> their school careers. (p.2)

Pollard observes that this major reform of the curriculum and educational
culture of both primary and secondary schools was introduced rapidly and
with minimal consultation involving headteachers and teachers. The mode of
its introduction made it clear that a strong state was imposing a particular
curriculum and pedagogic regime upon maintained schooling in England and
was making a decisive break with an earlier culture of curriculum autonomy
for schools. In Bernstein's (1977) terms, 'how a society selects, classifies,
distributes, transmits and evaluates the educational knowledge it considers to
be public, reflects both the distribution of power and the principles of social
control' (p.85). The educational legislation of the 1980s in England was a most
explicit manifestation of the new distribution of power and of the new principles of social control which were intended to shape schooling in the 1990s.

The principles of social and educational control were most sharply realized
in the area of educational assessments. Broadfoot *et al.* (1994 p.1) provide this
account:

> Assessments were to be made and recorded against each of the different
> Attainment Targets into which the curriculum for each subject was
> divided . . . Following the Act, schools were required to report an-
> nually to parents in written form. The reports were to give a detailed
> commentary on progress in each subject and, at the end of the Key
> Stage, to report the levels achieved by the student in each subject. In
> addition to the communication of information concerning the achieve-
> ment of individual students to their parents, schools were required to
> provide aggregated data concerning their overall profile of results.
> These data were collected by Local Education Authorities and pub-
> lished as 'league tables' of their relative achievements. . . . In requir-
> ing teachers to implement externally derived tests and in imposing on
> them externally determined requirements for recording and reporting
> children's progress and achievement, standardized National Assess-
> ment represented what was arguably the most novel, the most coercive
> and the most difficult part of the 1988 Act's provisions to implement.

The requirements to test school pupils at ages 7, 11, 14 and 16 by standardized
National Assessment had strong resonances with a nineteenth-century schooling culture in England in which headteachers and teachers were the monitors

of a prescribed cultural code and paid according to the results achieved in the tests of that code. The long struggle by the teaching profession in England to establish a legitimate sphere for professional autonomy in curriculum and assessment matters appeared to have been nullified to an important extent by the reassertion of central state power over both curriculum and assessment. Headteachers in both primary and secondary schools who defined their role strongly in terms of its potential for curriculum and educational leadership found themselves in a cultural world 'turned upside down'. From conditions of relative cultural autonomy, especially in primary education, they now faced, in Tomlinson's (1993) terms, 'a return to central control in a form more detailed, assertive and comprehensive than ever before' (p.94).

The question of how headteachers had responded to such a transformation of their leadership potential in curriculum and assessment issues was a key focus for empirical inquiry in this study. While all headteachers had been affected by the cultural revolution[2] of the 1980s, it seemed plausible to expect a sense of sharper disjuncture between the professional commitments of primary school headteachers and the values embodied in the new curriculum and assessment regime. Attention focused first therefore upon the responses of primary school headteachers participating in this inquiry.

Primary School Headteachers and the Culture of the National Curriculum

Croll *et al.* (1994), in reporting upon a research inquiry into primary school headteachers' reactions to 'imposed change', have suggested that a useful analytical framework could be 'compliance–mediation–resistance, denoting a range of school responses to externally imposed change'[3]. Using such a framework, the Primary Assessment, Curriculum and Experience (PACE) project concluded that the forty-eight primary school headteachers participating in the inquiry adopted either compliance or mediation responses to imposed curriculum and assessment change. In particular it was noteworthy, and surprising in terms of earlier primary school cultural autonomy, that 'none of the heads interviewed could be classified as resisting or contesting change'.[4]

The fieldwork accounts of the present study, derived from forty-one primary school headteachers, largely confirm these findings but add some regional variation to them. In referring to the introduction or 'imposition' of the national curriculum, the reactions of the primary school headteachers in this study may be described as *celebration, compliance, mediation* and *resistance*. In contrast to the PACE continuum, the responses of these headteachers were more extensive. On the one hand, a group of headteachers went beyond compliance and celebrated positively the arrival of the national curriculum. It will be seen later that such celebration was closely connected with changing the power differential between classroom teachers and headteachers. On the other hand, a small group did articulate a discourse of criticism of, and resistance to, the national curriculum. Their stance was that as educational leaders in primary schooling they could not remain silent in the face of curriculum changes of which they disapproved but they recognized, as did all their colleagues, that they could not in practice resist the full power of the central educational state in curriculum reform.

Celebrating the National Curriculum

From an historical perspective, the fact that any primary school headteacher should celebrate the arrival of a government imposed national curriculum seems remarkable. Why should relatively autonomous curriculum leaders in primary education welcome a prescribed curriculum code? Analysis of the fieldwork accounts revealed that a positive response to the national curriculum was either autonomy-related or power-related. For some headteachers, the conditions of relative curriculum autonomy predating the 1988 Education Act had resulted in distortions or defects in curriculum and in learning which were professionally indefensible. The requirements of the national curriculum were therefore welcomed as a framework for the enhancement of the primary school curriculum:

- The idea that it should be a broad and balanced curriculum is correct. I know from experience in this school that without this being dictated, the previous head was allowed to run this school, missing out great chunks. There were no environmental visits, no physical education and no collective worship . . . I think telling us that we must provide a broad and balanced curriculum is a good thing.
  (Female Junior School Head) (3)*

- I always saw the need for national curriculum guidelines. I have admitted children to this school and I have often wondered 'what on earth have they been doing?' They knew nothing . . . There was too much freedom for schools and heads. They could follow their own whims and fancies. I think a lot of the ills in education are down to the HMI . . . their suggestions are so ridiculous but we are afraid to disagree with them. We implemented what they said. So we have gone through a period of crazes if you like . . . I am all for child-centred learning, but it has been ridiculous.
  (Male Junior School Head) (19)

What is of interest in these two accounts is what they reveal about the manifest practice of some primary school headteachers. No simplistic judgment

---

* *Note* Numbers in brackets used after quotations refer to the code numbers of the headteachers' accounts.

can in fact be made about the nature of headteachers' curriculum and educational leadership even before the Education Reform Act. The situation as described in these fieldwork accounts is complex and contradictory. In Account 3, the 'previous headteacher' (a long-serving man) *decided* the curriculum and was proof against all external influences. In Account 19, another long-serving (and confident) headteacher suggests that for all the apparent autonomy of headteachers in primary schooling they were 'afraid to disagree' with the educational suggestions of Her Majesty's Inspectorate of Schools. In Account 3, the national curriculum is celebrated by a new headteacher for its specification of a broad and balanced educational experience. In Account 19, it is welcomed by an experienced headteacher as a protection against educational 'crazes'.

Other headteacher accounts celebrated the arrival of the national curriculum in primary education in terms of its effects upon the micro-politics of the school and in particular upon the power differential between headteachers and classroom teachers. In Chapter 5 of this book, it was noted that some headteachers, contrary to expectation, saw in the 'reform' of local education authorities and of school governors, opportunities for the greater empowerment of headteachers. In a similar way, some headteachers saw empowerment possibilities in the greater specification requirements of the national curriculum i.e., some change in micro-political power differentials in favour of headteachers:

- In general, I welcome it . . . I think schools were drifting . . . The national curriculum has put us back on the rails if you like. We have goals which are quite clear cut and I think the structure is good. I am very supportive of the national curriculum . . . another reason I am happy with it, is that it requires a type of working within the classroom to be able to get everything done, which I am sympathetic to and which I have been trying to get in this school ever since I came. Suddenly, the national curriculum has brought about the realization by the staff that this is the only way to go . . . the national curriculum is great for the headteacher.[5]
  (Male Junior School Head) (14)

- The imposition (of the national curriculum) makes it a little bit easier in that those staff who wouldn't take part in ownership of the school curriculum, now have it imposed, so it has got to be done.
  (Male Junior School Head) (1)

- The national curriculum has enabled headteachers and teaching staff to focus their teaching far more . . . I certainly don't envisage a constrained future and less job satisfaction—in fact, the opposite!
  (Female Infant School Head) (23)

Pollard (1985) has argued that while the curriculum power of primary school headteachers was considerable in pre-1980 schooling culture, it was in practice constrained by classroom teachers' sense of their own professional autonomy. Classroom teachers:

> teach and have contact with children far more than any headteacher can manage . . . Headteachers are thus in a position of being largely dependent on their class teachers for the quality of the education provided in the school and this can give class teachers a significant degree of power . . .[5]

In other words, the cultural autonomy which primary headteachers possessed *vis-à-vis* the central and local state could be limited, in the micro-politics of particular schools, where classroom teachers had a strong sense of their own classroom autonomy. For some headteachers, therefore, the political effect of the national curriculum in sharply reducing classroom autonomy had the useful effect of strengthening their own position as curriculum managers i.e., 'it has got to be done'. A similar reaction was in fact noted in the PACE project (1994): 'Some heads saw the National Curriculum as a lever which they could use to make changes which they judged needed making and where they had encountered resistance in the past.'[7]

It is salutary to reflect upon these findings. In a stereotyped and ahistorical view of English primary education, the headteacher can easily be projected as the guardian of child-centred education and of a progressive and relatively autonomous learning culture within the school. In practice, the educational philosophies and ideologies of primary school headteachers in England are as complex and various as those of their secondary school colleagues. The supposed hegemony of progressive Plowden culture in primary schooling has in fact been largely the creation of media agencies and of right-wing ideology.[8]

For some primary headteachers the power relations of the curriculum are just as salient as they are in secondary schooling. While it may be the case that the culture of secondary schooling is more visibly political in both macro and micro relations, there is also a politics of the primary school. Part of that politics is the nature of the power differential between headteachers and classroom teachers relating to the curriculum and assessment. The culture of the national curriculum provided, for some headteachers, new conditions for changing the balance of that relationship and for introducing a more directive style of curriculum.

Compliance and Mediation

The majority of the primary school headteachers in this study reacted to the imposition of the national curriculum by adopting a compliance–mediation response. There were important qualititative differences between compliance and mediation and yet there was also a sense in which they were linked in the discourse of some of the headteachers' accounts. The most obvious cases of compliance involved statements which were critical of curriculum imposition by the government, while at the same time recognizing that it had legislative force which could not be resisted:

- The national curriculum has presented a number of dilemmas. Whilst I feel that there is an overload, I have a duty to implement it. Thus, while my sympathies are with the staff, I do my best to ensure that it is covered, even though I realize the problems faced by the staff.
  (Male Primary School Head) (52)

- I felt that we had a good structure developing and we now have got to . . . try and tie it up with at least 5000 statements of attainment across the curriculum . . . we now have to say, is what we have already done, right by the national curriculum?
  (Male Junior School Head) (16)

Both of these accounts of headteacher compliance with curriculum 'reform' articulate with the compliance findings of Croll *et al.* (1994) that 'implementation was very much a response to external requirements rather than as a development of internal practice' (p.7). Other headteachers, however, emphasized a continuity between their internal curriculum practice and the requirements of the national curriculum. Their stance was that, in terms of curriculum structure at least, the new arrangements presented no major problems for the school and that a process of mediated change was proceeding.

In the analysis of headteacher discourse on reactions to imposed curriculum change, 'mediation' responses were more complex and sometimes contradictory than other responses. Accounts involving 'celebration' of the national curriculum, 'compliance' with it or 'resistance' to it were in general characterized by an internal consistency. 'Mediation' accounts were more complex and sometimes contradictory and linkages between compliance and mediation were often apparent. It could be argued here that some primary headteachers were attempting to minimize the sense of radical curriculum change, perhaps because there was actual cultural continuity with their own curriculum practice or because, in an attempt to preserve staff morale, they intended to claim such continuity. A classic example of a compliance–mediation response of this type was given by the headteacher of an infant school:

- As a headteacher, I need to be positive. I need to help my staff through changes by pointing out the benefits wherever there are any. . . . I have tried with my staff to investigate the positive parts of them rather than the negative. We haven't always agreed with them. We haven't always been happy about them but if they are

> going to come in by statute, then we are stuck with them and we
> try always to make the best of them. That's been our policy . . . try
> as far as possible not to get too worried about the pieces that don't
> suit or are counter-productive to what our pupils do, and to use
> the best of it for our pupils. As far as the national curriculum is
> concerned, we have been doing it for years. *(17)*

For this headteacher, educational leadership consisted, in the curriculum and
assessment sector, of mediating, as positively as possible, the imposed changes.
In other words, the imperative for headteacher leadership in a situation of
unwelcome educational changes was 'we try always to make the best of them'.
For the interests of staff morale and for the interests of the pupils, many
headteachers in this inquiry adopted a policy of 'mediation/being positive'.
This was central to their understanding of what being a headteacher in difficult times required. However, it was apparent from the accounts that mediation strategies were more convincing in the curriculum contents and structure
area—'we have been doing it for years'—than in the assessment area. The new
regime of assessment made it particularly difficult for headteachers to claim
continuity with previous practice or to find a convincing discourse of mediation.

For the present it can be said that primary school headteachers, in adopting a strategy of compliance–mediation, of 'making the best of it', were enacting
a professional response with deep historical and cultural antecedents. Viewed
historically, compliance and mediation was required of the teaching profession
for many decades before the development of modern professional autonomy.
As a necessary response to state power in education it has a long historical
pedigree. Even in more autonomous conditions, certain versions of English
teacher professionalism have stressed that 'making the best of it' is an occupational imperative for placing the interests of the pupils before the interests
of teachers themselves where conflict of interests has been generated by state
action.[9] These historical and professional features have combined together to
produce a strong culture of mediation among headteachers and teachers in
England. It is not surprising, therefore, to find that many primary school
headteachers felt that it was their duty to give 'mediation/being positive'
leadership whatever their own personal and professional views might be about
curriculum and assessment change. As one infant school headteacher put it,
'we have got to meet the challenges because of our children'.

Resistance

Faced with legislative change in the form of a national curriculum imposed by
a strong educational state, there could be no serious and major resistance in
practice by individual headteachers. This was *'force majeure'* and the participants
in this study recognized it to be so. However, for some their own sense
of professional integrity as primary school educators and leaders made it

necessary to articulate at least a discourse of criticism and of 'resistance where possible':

- One has to fight harder and harder to maintain one's profession-alism as more and more is imposed from above. As a staff we resist 'jumping through hoops' and fix our own priorities within the parameters of the national curriculum.
  (Female Infant School Head) (60)

- We are not about trying to turn out standard children like standard meals on standard trays in *Macdonalds*. We are about celebrating the individuals in our care while educating them to the best of our, and their, ability.
  (Female Junior School Head) (57)

In general, however, there were few examples of the discourse of criticism and resistance arising from the imposition of the national curriculum in primary schooling. The great majority of headteachers either welcomed its arrival or adopted the compliance–mediation strategy.[10]

This was much less true of responses to the new regime of testing and assessment. Broadfoot's (1994) argument that 'reforms' in primary school assessment were likely to be the 'most coercive and difficult part' of the 1988 Act to be implemented was borne out by an extensive and vigorous discourse of criticism from the participants. Here, there was a much stronger sense that inappropriate and unworkable models of assessment had been imposed upon primary education and that there would have to be resistance both at individual school-site levels where possible and certainly at a collective level by head-teachers associations and by teacher unions:

- We've been put into a strait jacket . . . assessment and recording are barmy . . . We have already said to our members (National Association of Headteachers), if you are involved in this and you think it is not viable, refuse to do it, and we will back you all the way.
  (Male Junior School Head) (19)

- I feel very angry at the amount I am obliged to demand of my teachers in terms of useless paperwork over and above the large amount I expect of them in the course of their work.
  (Female Infant School Head) (57)

- What we are being expected to do is to get pupils to jump through hoops by hitting attainment targets . . . I did work out that if each teacher in my school took an equal share of the assessments in a year they would have to do about 1400 assessments, which is absolutely ridiculous.
  (Infant School Head) (17)

- To give us these restrictive and extremely detailed forms of assessment and recording will, I think, cause a good deal of rebellion. *(Female Junior School Head) (3)*

The anger and strong sense of need for professional resistance articulated by the majority of primary school headteachers in relation to the new regime of assessment had various but interrelated causes. Such headteachers resented the lack of adequate consultation in the formulation of the new procedures. It was quite apparent to many of them that their professional status as educational leaders in primary education had been given very little recognition. Assessment changes, in their view derived either from the practices of secondary schooling or from the preparatory school experiences of government ministers and civil servants, were being imposed upon the culture of primary education. A form of assessment imperialism from other educational cultures was, from the perspectives of these headteachers, being attempted under the guise of greater accountability to parents.

Campbell and Emery (1994) have pointed to 'a reinforcing contradiction between the broad and balanced curriculum espoused in the ERA (Education Reform Act) and DFE (Department for Education) regulations for assessment, recording and reporting' (p.19). Such contradictions and their consequences for teacher stress and bureaucratic workload would, in the view of most of the headteachers, provoke resistance and even rebellion. This resistance and rebellion might even extend to headteachers themselves as Account 19 indicated.[11]

The possibility that headteachers, as educational leaders, might refuse to implement the assessment requirements of the 1988 Education Act was an historical juncture in teacher–state relations of great socio-political significance. The position of headteacher in English schooling culture has always symbolized relations of moral correctness, discipline, social order and control and task achievement. Headteachers were and are the cultural antithesis of tendencies to resistance or rebellion again lawful authority. As the lawful authority within their own schools, there are strong inhibitions against resisting lawful authority in the wider social context. However, insofar as headteachers are educational leaders and not simply educational managers, can they implement assessment arrangements which they believe to be detrimental to the interests of children, to the educational values and effectiveness of primary schooling and to the interests of their own classroom teachers? This was the great dilemma which faced English headteachers in the early 1990s.

The visible and explicit resistance of classroom teachers to the new assessment regime in primary education occurred in 1993 during the fieldwork stages of this study. Broadfoot *et al.* (1994) have argued that:

The formal assessment and reporting requirements of the Education Reform Act which culminated in the publication of league tables of relative school performance, represented the biggest single challenge to the understanding, the values and the professional power of English primary school teachers. Their boycott of the reporting of the 1993 Key Stage One SATs (Standard Assessment Tasks) was a rare example of collective and sustained teacher resistance to the Act's provisions. (p.2)

In 1993, primary school headteachers were under a legal obligation to implement Key Stage One testing and to report and publish the results of such testing. In their roles as educational managers, their obligations were clear. In their roles as professional leaders, in a collegial relation with their classroom teachers, their position was, as one headteacher put it, 'at the focal point of contradications—we are pulled in all directions'. How they responded to such contradictions and to other professional and moral dilemmas of school leadership will be examined in Chapter 9.

Primary School Headteachers and Strategies of Educational Leadership

The fieldwork accounts of this study have demonstrated that the majority of primary headteachers saw educational leadership as working to safeguard the interests of children and of teachers in a situation which they judged to be largely inimical to both. This was a leadership of mediation which at the individual school-site level was designed to sustain morale by emphasizing the positive aspects of curriculum reform wherever possible. Such leadership was not dramatic or charismatic but it was judged to be necessary for institutional and professional survival in the changed schooling conditions of the 1990s. It was a contemporary form of a long professional and cultural response of 'making the best of it'. Such leadership could be interpreted, at a superficial level, as lacking in principle and as conformist and weak, but this would not be a fair evaluation. The leadership of mediation can of course have such characteristics but in this study the overwhelming sense of the quality of the leadership was that it had a commitment to the protection of children and teachers from stress and disruption so far as this was possible. Mediation was seen to be the professionally responsible form of leadership for the individual school situation.

Resistance was a leadership strategy which was very problematic for headteachers, given the historical and cultural symbolism of their position and the legal obligations laid upon it. However, such a strategy could be realized in collective form through the agency of their professional associations and unions, especially in the face of an assessment regime which they knew to be professionally unworkable. It is a measure of the extent to which state educational agencies in England had alienated responsible school leaders, that strategies of resistance and even rebellion were being considered by headteachers in the early 1990s.

For a small group of primary headteachers in this study, changes in curriculum and assessment practices changed the power differential between classroom teachers and headteachers. The reduction of autonomy for class-room teachers empowered those headteachers who wished to enact a more directive and controlling style of educational leadership in the future. In these cases, leadership concepts of a more hierarchical and monitoring nature appeared to be emerging.

Secondary School Headteachers and Changing Cultural Leadership

It was expected that there would be some qualitative differences in the responses of primary and secondary school headteachers to curriculum and assessment changes. As some of the primary school headteachers had observed, these changes were in a closer cultural relation with the practices of secondary schooling than of primary education. In other words, secondary school headteachers appeared to face less dramatic transformations of any curriculum leadership role that they had been pursuing before the Education Reform Act than their primary colleagues. Nevertheless, it was important to analyze the responses of secondary school headteachers to such changes. Insofar as they regarded themselves as curriculum leaders in secondary education, how did they respond to an imposed national curriculum? How did they respond to a schooling situation which now demanded more of their time to be given to institutional management and marketing rather than to curriculum leadership *per se*? What was their response to a system of national assessment which curtailed the relative autonomy which they had possessed before?

In investigating some of these questions with a small sample of secondary headteachers, Mortimore *et al.* (1991b) concluded, 'these heads appear to have responded remarkably positively to the National Curriculum—accommodating it . . .' (p.165). The fact that these researchers found such accommodation 'remarkable' indicates an expectation that secondary school headteachers might have resented and resisted such curriculum imposition from the central state in England. In the present study, only two participants argued that the general characteristics of curriculum leadership for secondary headteachers had been constrained, and this was more by the growing culture of management and marketing than by the national curriculum itself:

- I detect that colleagues are less than happy with what they perceive to be a diminution of their role in providing curriculum leadership (in the face of other demands) which they regard as vitally important . . .
  (Male Secondary Head) (27)

Analysis of the accounts provided by the forty-seven secondary school head-teachers participating in this study revealed that, in general, such headteachers adopted either a compliance–mediation response or a celebration response to the national curriculum. Only a minority argued that they had lost a 'vitally important' curriculum leadership function. There was, however, as with their primary school colleagues, a much stronger negative reaction to the new regime for assessment.

For some secondary headteachers there was no sense of loss of curriculum leadership because this concept had never been a significant part of their understanding of secondary school headship:

- I have never felt 'in control' of the secondary curriculum. It is/was controlled by Heads of Department. Headteachers have only been able to influence the fringes of the curriculum since the advent of the comprehensive school. The national curriculum actually restricts Heads of Department, not Headteachers.
  (Male Secondary Head) (43)

This account indicates, in a very explicit way, the more distanced relationship of secondary school headteachers, especially in large comprehensive schools, to specific curricular and pedagogical issues. These matters are regarded as within the professional jurisdiction of heads of department and their teaching colleagues and it is here that stronger reaction to curriculum change can be expected.

Many of the secondary headteachers in this study were able to be relatively 'accommodating' to the national curriculum because its concrete pedagogical implications and its associated workload could be delegated to a 'middle management' level within the school. In a study of the changing role of the secondary school headteacher, Earley *et al.* (1990) have noted the critical importance in secondary school organization of middle management and of departmental and faculty heads in particular. For secondary schools the hard reality of curriculum and assessment 'reform' crystallized at this level. As one of the headteacher respondents in Earley *et al.* (1990) noted, 'the pressures that come to heads can be transmitted to middle management' (p.32). It is not surprising, therefore, that the majority of the secondary headteachers were either accommodating to the national curriculum or positively welcomed it. As with their primary colleagues, compliance responses emphasized *force majeure* by the state:

- I am in a fortunate position in some respects in saying that the teachers take the assumption that it is outside my role, it's the law, it's the Act.
  (Male Secondary Head) (8)

and mediation responses argued that much of the national curriculum was already in place in the school:

- It's as though the HMI and the DES actually selected national curriculum from this school. I'm not taking all the credit for this.

> My colleagues and I put together a package in 1984 . . . We
> anticipted the national curriculum.
> *(Male Secondary Head) (6)*

Those headteachers who celebrated the arrival of the national curriculum
did so for a variety of reasons which included their belief that it would improve standards in primary education and therefore levels of achievement at
entry to secondary schooling, as well as having a beneficial effect upon standards and coverage in secondary education.[12] The specification of a national
curriculum was thought by many to be in the interests of young people in a
more mobile society so that problems in school transfers were reduced.

As with the responses of some of the primary headteachers, a number of
the secondary participants had an awareness that changes in curriculum and
assessment arrangements had the potential to empower headteachers in their
relations with departmental and faculty heads. With more of the academic
subject content specified in the national curriculum and with more standardized assessment procedures, some headteachers believed that a new form of
curriculum and educational leadership might emerge with an emphasis upon
effective teaching and learning:

- Given that little energy has to be expended in deciding 'what to
  teach', nowadays our creative energy can go into 'how to teach'.
  Here there is more possibility of a Headteacher influencing his
  colleagues because there is much more in common between different departments in matters of methodology.
  (Male Secondary Head) (43)

- As far as secondary schools are concerned, we were always limited
  on curriculum matters by the need to fulfil examination requirements. I have not found the national curriculum a problem but
  would argue that less choice at 14 has actually made life easier and
  there is still a need to innovate to develop the most effective framework for delivering the national curriculum.
  (Male Secondary Head) (35)

These accounts suggest the possibility that the curriculum and educational
leadership roles of headteachers during the 1990s will be shaped by an effective delivery of the national curriculum imperative rather than by broader
cultural or educational innovation. From the perspective of a secondary
headteacher in the 1990s, arguments about the cultural content of English,
mathematics, science, history, etc., raised by departmental heads and subject
teachers may appear to be a distraction from the prime institutional purpose
of delivering the national curriculum.[13] It could be argued that insofar as
secondary headteachers define their curriculum leadership responsibilities as
the efficient *delivery*[14] of the national curriculum and of the pedagogy to meet

its assessment requirements they will have become more explicitly managers of cultural transmission rather than facilitators of cultural development. In other words, the culture and discourse of management in schools, already apparent in the salience of financial and marketing considerations, will extend its hegemony to curriculum and educational decisions.

For some headteachers in this study, the suggestion that the 'delivery' of national curriculum and national assessment requirements had seriously constrained their roles as educational leaders was vigorously denied:

- I believe that the proper prescription of the national curriculum and national assessment does not make innovation or development impossible. The autonomous cultural leadership (of headteachers) has been, in my view, rightly restrained . . . I believe that one of the tasks of education is cultural transmission and we cannot avoid the traditions of which we are the inheritors. Cultural and pedagogic innovation remain possibilities but they should be restrained. In no sense, in my experience, does this mean a serious loss of job satisfaction.
  (Male Secondary Head) (36)

The oppositional minority of headteachers disagreed with this stance and took the view that the nature of curriculum and educational leadership in secondary schools had been seriously constrained, with consequent loss of job satisfaction. For one headteacher, in particular, these changes were so unacceptable that they had resulted in his decision to take (an unwanted) early retirement. Constraints upon educational leadership from this perspective resulted not only from the specifications of the national curriculum but because of the imposition of externally determined targets:

- I think that in the 1970s when I commenced being a headteacher you had a leadership role in the sense of being a person who decided the agenda or at least put things on the agenda for development . . . We were accountable continually through this process but it meant that the targets were our targets and so the staff team, the parents' involvement etc., were all geared towards achieving targets and ambitions which we set for ourselves, which were ours . . . Now, targets are being set externally . . . so this is where I feel this is one of my motivations for getting out of the job. I am no longer even a navigator of the ship, let alone captain.
  (Male Secondary Head) (2)

This response was exceptional in that the headteacher in question defined his role very strongly in terms of its potential for curriculum development and took pride in his association with curriculum development in a number of schools. From his perspective these possibilities were now curtailed:

- One of the things that really does concern me is that if the head of an institution is concerned with input and output only—input in terms of financial and staffing resources and output in terms of national curriculum targets, how on earth can he or she not be concerned with the process by which the input is translated into the output?

Despite this headteacher's personal decision to leave because of the radical changes in headteachers' responsibilities, he nevertheless believed that the resistance to curriculum and assessment imposition (which had just started) would achieve success over time:

- I know that we [the teaching profession] will subvert all that is bad in the national curriculum and the Education Act. Whatever projects take place, we have always managed to subvert and make it good . . . We will always overcome problems that are set for us by our masters.

This theme of professional resistance to government policy in education was taken up by other headteachers who pointed to the beginnings of successful resistance in the schools:

- The assessment/recording/reporting element of the national curriculum did threaten to choke the life out of schools but they (the government) have adapted it very quickly. Growing resistance to the restrictive assessment procedures of the government is strengthening.
  (Male Secondary Head) (22)

On the basis of the accounts of the forty-seven participating secondary headteachers in this study, it can be concluded that there was no overall sense of loss of important curriculum leadership functions arising from the education reforms of the 1980s and early 1990s. What is apparent from an analysis of their discourse is that the great majority of secondary headteachers did not define their roles strongly in curriculum leadership terms, regarding this as the proper province of their heads of department or faculty heads. Problems of curriculum content, assessment specification and pedagogical change could therefore be delegated to 'middle management'. For most headteachers, the efficient delivery of the national curriculum was their prime institutional responsibility, although most of them also believed that its assessment requirements would have to be modified in the future.

The Politics of Cultural Management and Cultural Leadership

Bernstein (1990) notes that:

> School systems and university systems are now more and more engaged in a struggle over what should be transmitted, over the autonomy of transmission, over the conditions of service of those who transmit and over the procedures for evaluation of acquirers. (p.86)

While Bernstein is right to draw attention to this contemporary struggle, headteachers, both primary and secondary, have always been caught up in the politics of cultural struggle. In historical periods, in which the state has prescribed a curriculum and assessment regime, headteachers in state maintained school systems have had an obligation to be managers of that regime. Where the macro-politics of cultural transmission has, in Bernstein's (1977) terms, 'strong framing', then headteachers in state schools are expected to be cultural managers rather than cultural leaders. When the macro-politics of cultural transmission is more weakly framed then there is scope for headteachers to be relatively autonomous curriculum and educational leaders and even innovators.

The politics of school curriculum and assessment in the 1980s and 1990s is one of strong state control and within this political context, headteachers have to define or re-define their own role. For those headteachers, both primary and secondary, who, in more autonomous conditions preceding the 1980s have seen themselves as curriculum leaders, significant professional dilemmas can arise. As one of the primary school headteachers reported earlier commented, 'We are at the focal point of contradictions—we are pulled in all directions'. The central dilemma for such headteachers is the simultaneous recognition that the state requires them to be cultural managers of prescribed curriculum and assessment changes which in their professional judgment, as educational leaders, are inappropriate and unworkable. In these circumstances their options, as has been shown, are compliance–mediation, some form of professional resistance, or early retirement from headship.[15] In this study, the experience of serious dilemmas in relation to curriculum and assessment change was, however, a minority phenomenon. The great majority of primary and secondary school headteachers adopted a response of compliance–mediation, and were apparently prepared to take on the role of cultural managers of the new arrangements.

It is clear that in the political circumstances in which they found themselves, most headteachers accepted that becoming effective managers of the national curriculum was the key to institutional survival[16] whatever their own professional reservations might be. This realization was obviously easier for secondary school headteachers who in the context of large comprehensive schools had already moved further in the direction of cultural management and away from conceptions of innovative professional curriculum leadership.

Cultural management can be interpreted in various ways. At its best, it can imply the organization of resources to facilitate the most stimulating learning experiences for the pupils. At its worst, it can imply an enactment of government requirements for curriculum and assessment against professional judgment. Headship in English schooling culture appears to be moving towards a concept of cultural manager as a result of imposed, external requirements. The crucial question for the future of maintained schooling in England is what sort of cultural management will be developed by headteachers. In some formulations, the headteacher as cultural manager might involve a significant transformation of professional values and of collegial relations with other teachers resulting in a more distanced, utilitarian and directive relationship. In other words, if headteachers become increasingly preoccupied with the technical mechanics for efficient delivery of the required cultural output, professional debate in the school about the legitimacy of the process may seem an irrelevance. From this perspective, the management of culture and of pedagogy will have taken its place alongside the management of staff, resources and buildings, as part of the responsibilities of the school's chief executive (formerly the headteacher). In other formulations, headteachers as cultural managers may adopt a strategy of compliance–mediation for the necessity of institutional survival but continue to work with their teachers in a professional and collegial way to modify what they see to be educationally undesirable features of the new pedagogic regime.

What seems to be at stake here is the relation of the headteacher to the central cultural and educational purposes of the school. In schooling cultures which pre-dated the Education Reform Act, the relation of headteachers to the cultural messages of the school was mediated by their status as leading professionals. Their direct and personal involvement in classroom teaching, limited in secondary schools but more extensive in primary schools, was a powerful symbol of that relationship and of its significance. To the extent that new managerial demands in schooling have distanced both secondary and primary headteachers from direct cultural experience in classrooms, an impetus may be given to more distanced forms of cultural management in schools. It is therefore important to consider in more detail headteachers' responses to the growth of management and market culture in English schools and the effects which this may have upon the nature of headship and upon the working relations of headship. These issues will be examined in the following chapter.

Notes and References

1   As Pollard (1985) notes, 'In the late 1960s, particularly after the publication of the Plowden Report *(Children and their Primary Schools*, 1967), primary schools developed a reputation for so-called "progressive" and "child-centred" teaching methods. The Plowden Report advocated a new type of education for young children with special stress on first-hand experience and individualised learning. (p.16)'
2   Some headteachers used this language explicitly e.g., 'it is a sort of revolution and revolutions tend to move fast'.
3   Croll *et al.* (1994, p.6).
4   *Ibid.*

5   It is important to note, however, that this headteacher welcomed the national curriculum because he believed that it would help child-centred education. At the same time he recognized that the national curriculum put 'tremendous pressure' on his staff.

6   Pollard (1985, p.133).

7   Croll *et al.* (1994, p.7).

8   Galton, Simon and Croll (1980) reported in their study of fifty-eight junior school classrooms that 'progressive' teaching hardly existed in practice and that 'the weight of evidence shows very clearly that the general pattern of the traditional curriculum still prevails' (p.155). See also Carrington and Tymms (1994) for examples of media and ideological misrepresentation of primary education schooling culture.

9   This characterizes the position for instance of The Professional Association of Teachers.

10 A compliance–mediation strategy can also involve some element of resistance or 'situational adjustment'. For an interesting account of such a case, see Riseborough (1993).

11 At the 1993 Conference of the National Association of Headteachers, the Secretary of State for Education received a hostile reception from the delegates which was unprecedented as a public display of headteacher alienation.

12 The celebration of the national curriculum was often accompanied, however, by strong criticism of the mode of its introduction e.g.:

> • I think the national curriculum is a good thing. What I don't like is the political element and I think that some kind of a Schools Council type of body (but not run by the wretched NUT) should have been formed to develop it . . . and not have it subsequently changed by ministerial diktat.
> *(Male, Secondary Head) (7)*

13 This could be a source of conflict in the micro-politics of schools, especially secondary schools. The resistance of subject teachers to specific curriculum contents may conflict with the headteachers's desire as curriculum manager to 'deliver' the national curriculum smoothly and efficiently.

14 The language of curriculum 'delivery' is an ideological form of the 1980s and early 1990s. It implies that the curriculum is a commodity or a package which can be delivered. As such it is part of a wider process of commodification of education taking place in the 1980s and 1990s.

15 A number of the respondents in this inquiry claimed that the rate of early retirement from headship had increased considerably in the region.

16 As one headteacher put it:

> • Survival has always been the bottom line—it's just more acute now.
> *(Female, Secondary Head) (28)*

Chapter 7

Management, Markets and School Headship

John Chubb and Terry Moe (1990) in their major research into the deficiencies of the American school system concluded that a radical reform of institutional and organizational arrangements was required if American schools were to become more effective. The programme of radical reform advocated in their book, *Politics, Markets and American Schools*, called for decentralization of control and management (i.e., school-based management), and for conditions of greater competition and choice among schools (i.e., the application of a market system in schooling). In the analysis of the available data on school effectiveness in the USA, Chubb and Moe argued that the greater success of private schools when compared with public schools suggested the key elements necessary for a reform programme. Private school success did not, in their view, arise from the privileged conditions of such schooling (e.g., better resources, smaller classes, selected students) but from the institutional and contextual conditions in which they operated. If the system of public schooling in America could be reshaped to approximate to those conditions, great improvements would result for the education of all citizens:

> People who make decisions about education would behave differently if their institutions were different. The most relevant and telling comparison is to markets, since it is through democratic control and markets that American society makes most of its choices on matters of public importance, including education. Public schools are subject to direct control through politics, private schools are subject to indirect control through markets. What difference does it make?[1]

From Chubb and Moe's perspective, the operational conditions for schools are the key variables in explaining variation in effectiveness. In answering their own question they conclude:

> Our analysis suggests that the difference is considerable and that it arises from the most fundamental properties that distinguish the two systems. A market system is not built to enable the imposition of higher-order values on the schools, nor is it driven by a democratic struggle to exercise public authority. Instead, the authority to make

educational choices is radically decentralized to those most immediately involved. Schools compete for the support of parents and students, and parents and students are free to choose among schools. The system is built around decentralization, competition and choice.[2]

During the course of a public debate in America which these assertions have generated, Chubb and Moe (1992) have subsequently argued that school reform in England has pointed the way for school reform in America:

The landmark was the Education Reform Act of 1988 which in one stroke imposed a radically new institutional framework on British education—a framework built around the same three types of reforms that American activists were pushing for at the time, and still are. Under the Act, power would be decentralized through 'local management of schools', another name for what Americans call school-based management. Choice would be enhanced in important ways: by spelling out the rights of parents and students to choose their own school, by giving schools the right to 'opt out' of their local education authorities and by creating new kinds of schools—city technology colleges—for people to choose from. Finally, this population of more autonomous schools would be held accountable through a new national curriculum and a comprehensive battery of tests.[3]

Much of the public debate in England about the advantages and disadvantages of the new operational conditions for schools has been informed by writers and agencies external to the direct experience of implementation. It is important in this debate that the voice of headteachers should be heard. Headteachers are at the focal point of the translation of policy into practice and they are in a strategic position to evaluate ideological and political claims and counter-claims about the consequences of change for schooling culture and for its outcomes.

English headteachers in the 1970s were, in general, regarded as leading educational professionals, charged with the administration of personnel and resources provided by the Local Education Authority (LEA). They were regarded as the responsible agents, with the LEA, for the efficient and effective provision of education as a public service in a given locality. They were, in short, public service professionals. This culture of English school leadership began a process of radical change in the 1980s and 1990s with the introduction of Local Management of Schools (LMS), with a de-regulated policy on school admissions ('open enrolments') and a new market relation arising from the publication of school results in a hierarchical League Table[4] (without reference to the social setting of the school). The intention of government education reform encoded as the 'Five Great Themes' of quality, diversity, parental choice, greater school autonomy and greater accountability[5] was to transform what was seen to be an unresponsive public bureaucracy into a competitive and market-orientated series of individual educational enterprises or corpora-tions. In this regime, educational institutions would live or die according to their measurable success in market conditions. A new management and market culture in English state schooling has necessarily involved every headteacher in the process of becoming a site manager (rather than administrator) and a market analyst (with school survival issues high on the agenda).

The fieldwork inquiries with the headteachers participating in the study detailed in this book were designed to elucidate headteachers' responses to these changed conditions of leadership and management. How had they re-sponded to local management of schools? What effects were greater competitive and choice conditions in schooling having upon their schools and upon their own experience of school headship?

Local Management of Schools

Reviewing early experience of financial delegation to schools in what was originally known as Local Financial Management (LFM) developed in a number of LEAs,[6] Thomas (1988) concluded that 'LFM enhances the capacity of the Head as an educationist because it increases the degree of control over the resources available for achieving educational objectives' (p.182). In the wider dissemination of LMS in England following the Education Reform Act, such arguments featured strongly. The decentralization of management and finan-cial decisions to most schools appeared to empower headteachers and teachers *vis-à-vis* local education bureaucracy. LMS held out the promise of greater educational effectiveness arising from that autonomy. In the early years of the development of LMS culture in English schooling there was considerable emphasis upon its potential benefits.[7] However, the actual process of imple-mentation of local management was itself bound to show a balance sheet of advantages and disadvantages. The impact of the new system, it was recog-nized, would be felt by headteachers in the first instance, who would be expected to mediate it to the school governors, their senior management team, the teachers and the parents. As Thomas (1990) observed:

> Local Management presents a major challenge to the education service. At the heart of the response will be the requirement upon headteachers to acquire new and unfamiliar skills, related to finance, staff and com-petition. While this is happening, there is little doubt that they will also play the crucial role in assisting most governing bodies to come to terms with their new reponsibilities. (p.84)

How had the headteachers in this study responded to this 'major chal-lenge'? Analysis of the accounts of the eighty-eight participants revealed the celebration–resistance continuum which had already emerged in relation to other educational changes. Within that continuum, however, marked differ-ences were apparent between secondary and primary school headteachers.

Secondary School Headteachers and the 'New Freedom'

The majority of secondary school headteachers in this study welcomed what they saw to be the empowering effects of local management of schools. This sense of relative empowerment related both to their own role (as senior managers and as educational leaders) and to the institutional context of the school:

- I am partly prepared to work as hard as I do because of the new freedom that LMS gives us . . . I am now in a position where I can do some of the things which I have been so frustrated at not being able to do through the 1980s. I can now virtually decide on my staff.
  *(Male Secondary Head) (7)**

- The impact of the 1988 Act has given the Head Teacher more power, particularly in the area of finance.
  (Male Secondary Head) (35)

- LMS has considerably enhanced school autonomy.
  (Male Secondary Head) (32)

- LMS has given Headteachers much freedom.
  (Male Secondary Head) (43)

It should be noted that while these headteachers gave strong endorsements to the empowered management capacity for heads under the LMS system, many of them claimed that this managerialism was not in conflict with professional values or professional relations. They believed that their greater managerial autonomy could be used for the benefit of the professional and educational goals of the school.

There were, however, interesting differences between those headteachers who were 'winners' and 'losers' in the actual budget allocations to the schools in the region. While support for the principle of LMS was strong among almost all the heads, it was constantly mentioned that there was a winner–loser syndrome in the actual practice of financial delegation.[8] Some headteachers were in the fortunate position of being budget 'winners' i.e., their new financial allocations were greater than the historical budget for the school. Other headteachers were 'losers' i.e., their new budgets were less than the historical budget for the school and this placed them in a deficit position at the commencement of local management responsibilities. Headteacher–'winners' were, not surprisingly, the most robust in their celebration of financial delegation

---

* *Note* Numbers in brackets used after quotations refer to the code numbers of the headteachers' accounts.

and some of them had already adopted a hard-headed managerial stance about its consequences:

- I see it all as a process of accountability. If one doesn't know what something costs, you don't appreciate the problems or the financial implications of the decisions you are trying to take. As far as I can see there are quite a number of advantages in having LMS. However I can understand those who are the losers as opposed to the winners.
- Q   You are a winner?
- Yes, I am a winner, so we're coming out of it reasonably well because we are oversubscribed . . . we did quite nicely . . .
- Q   So you don't start with a deficit as some schools have done?
- No . . . but I can give advice to those who have a deficit and tell them exactly what to do.
- Q   What would that advice be?
- Go to the biggest budget and prune that, and that is the teachers.
  (Male Secondary Head) (8)

This account brought into sharp focus those aspects of LMS in schools which had not been featured in its initial celebratory rhetoric. The balance sheet of LMS in practice included 'losers' as well as 'winners' and for those headteachers who found themselves in a deficit situation the new freedom included also a new management experience, that of making teachers redundant.[9] Indeed, those headteachers in a deficit situation maintained that while the principle of LMS was progressive, its actual application was retrogressive. In their view, an inappropriate funding formula largely based upon pupil numbers irrespective of social context and the special needs of pupils had not led to a 'new freedom' but to new constraints upon less favoured schools. These critics of LMS-in-practice argued that decentralization of inadequate finance would increase managerial stress for heads in 'losing' schools:

- At worst, the mechanism for directing resources actually works against schools with great social need and in favour of schools with lower social need, but greater numbers.
  (Male Secondary Head) (53)

- (Headteachers') new roles which include managing less palatable aspects such as redeployment/redundancy of staff in a declining economic situation—something which hitherto could always be left to/blamed on the LEA—are more stressful than they could possibly have imagined. Thus we witness a vast increase in early retirement/health breakdowns etc. among headteachers.
  (Male Secondary Head) (27)

The consequences of local management of schools and of the decentralization of decision making had generated new forms of managerialism in the secondary schools of the region. Headteachers were preoccupied as never before with the close detail of school finance and its associated key variables, pupil enrolments and staffing levels. The majority believed that the new managerialism would enhance school effectiveness and they were prepared to acquire new skills to facilitate this. A minority believed that the new managerialism was an ideological cover for policies leading to greater social differentiation among schools and policies leading to public expenditure cuts and teacher redundancies. In all cases, it was accepted that the new managerialism was taking up a large proportion of the time of headteachers as school leaders. Most participants appeared to accept this as an inevitable consequence of secondary school headship in a decentralized system. A minority however were concerned that managerial preoccupations had now become so dominant that their professional relationships with classroom teachers and with the pupils in the school had become seriously distanced. Their status as professional leaders and as head*teachers* was in a process of fundamental change. In general, this seemed to be accepted, with regret, as the inevitable price of being an empowered school manager in the LMS system and as the next historical stage in the development of managerial culture within secondary schooling:

- I think that the task of managing a school is now so much more complex than it ever was before and I think that heads do have to accept that they can't continue to do all the things that they previously have done, and manage the school successfully. I think I have accepted as inevitable, I suppose, the increased remoteness of me from the pupils. But at the same time, I do feel that I ought to be out and about in the school and be seen to be interested in what is actually going on.
  (Male Secondary Head) (11)

For a minority of secondary school headteachers there was a dilemma in the conflicting demands of the new managerialism and historical expectations for professional leadership and involvement in the actual teaching culture of the school, but it was a dilemma that they believed would have to be resolved in favour of managerialism.[10] In other words, there was a general acceptance that the size, complexity and managerial responsibilities of secondary schooling in the 1990s had resulted in a cultural transformation of school headship. Headteachers could no longer think of themselves primarily as head*teachers* with priority relationships with classroom teachers and with pupils. The priority relationships, in new organizational conditions, were managerial.

In one sense, the hegemony of managerial culture over professional culture in English seondary schooling can be seen as the culmination of a process which began in the 1960s with the formation of large comprehensive schools.

Local management of schools, in the view of the participants, had accelerated that process sharply and changed its nature i.e., there *was* a new managerialism, requiring new skills, new ways of thinking and changed relationships. What was still emerging was the organizational forms of the new managerialism. Would it result in a line-management culture i.e., the reconstitution of old hierarchies in new forms? Would it result in enhanced power for the Senior Management Team (SMT) in the micro-politics of the school? Would it build upon a consultative professional culture (where that existed) to produce a consultative management culture? Some consideration of these questions will be undertaken in a later section of this chapter.

What was, for many secondary school headteachers, the final stage of the transformation of school headship, was for the primary school headteachers the beginning of a managerial revolution in primary school culture and it is not surprising that their responses were significantly different.

Primary School Headteachers and the New Managerialism

In research studies undertaken before the impact of local management of schools in primary education, both Davies (1987) and Southworth (1988) concluded that primary school headship had distinctive characteristics that differentiated it from secondary school headship. Davies (1987) found that:

> The traditional headteacher function of pedagogical leader and disciplinarian played an important part in the heads' role. The primary heads studied paid much attention to being in classrooms, either visiting or actually teaching. A quarter of contacts were made in visits to classrooms and nearly half their time was spent there. (p.45)

Southworth (1988), in reporting the findings of the Primary School Staff Relationship Project carried out at the Cambridge Institute of Education, produced a profile of primary school headship in these terms:

> Heads expected to set the school's guiding beliefs and saw it as their job to provide a sense of mission . . . Heads taughts classes and groups of pupils and used their school assemblies as opportunities to demonstrate their skill as teachers . . . The heads spent a lot of time involving themselves with the staff. They saw staff individually and collectively. They were frequently in the staffroom and touring the school . . . These aspects appear to combine to create the conditions for a particular kind of leadership. These heads were educative leaders. (pp.54–6)

As educative leaders, the primary school headteachers in this study were faced by new management demands which, in the view of many of them, threatened that educative leadership:

- Headteachers are now school managers and are increasingly told to 'manage' whatever situations arise. We are expected to have financial, administrative and business expertise—without the training. In my own case, I trained as a Nursery/Infant teacher, not as an accountant. My love is for children—not business and high finance.
  (Female Infant School Head) (30)

- My response, I think, is that you can't successfully and efficiently manage a school unless in your heart or soul (to be more profound) you have got some desire to be with children . . . I would not want to be primarily a manager. I would prefer to be a manager along with the desire to work with children. I have been advised at various meetings that I must consider myself a manager and I won't bend to that. I didn't come into teaching to be told that.
  (Male Primary School Head) (14)

- When I first started, I possibly spent 30 per cent of my time on administration during the actual hours that children were in school and 70 per cent of my time in the classroom or related activity. Now I spend maybe 75 per cent of my time on administration and 25 per cent of my time on the children, so I resent it . . . especially because I don't think the changes are doing our children a lot of good.
  (Infant School Head) (17)

- We have been told, and this comes from a senior adviser in this Authority, that 'the term headteacher is an anachronism and you are manager' . . . I respond to that with despondency . . . I enjoy kids. I like them . . . but the general, in-school relationship, knowing the kids . . . is slipping away and that I think is a backward step for any headteacher.
  (Male Junior School Head) (16)

- Always promised myself that decisions would be educationally led, not financially led. But increasingly I long for the day when my one small class is through the school—I can't afford them! This is against all I've ever believed and yet I am driven into this corner.
  (Female Primary School Head) (57)

Of the forty-one primary school headteachers involved in the fieldwork for this study, twenty-two of them adopted a stance that educative leadership was under threat from the new managerialism in LMS culture. For these headteachers, educative leadership was the priority. Educative leadership was the defining quality of primary headship. It involved direct participation in the teaching culture of the school; direct working relations with children and with classroom teachers and decision making based upon educational principles and values i.e., the realization of an educational culture. The new managerialism into which they were being socialized by management courses provided by the local education authority or by the stark budgetary categories of the LMS formula was experienced as a form of alienation from the primary commitments of primary headteachers. Primary school headship was being socially and culturally reconstructed on the model of secondary school headship and this was resented.

In contrast to this view, ten of the primary participants took an explicit stance that the new managerialism could be made to work in the interests of primary education if a balance of management and professional commitments was achieved:

- I am quite happy to become a school manager but I also feel that there has got to be a place within that management where you have contact with the children, where staff can still feel that you are contributing to part of the curriculum in some way, partly to keep your contact and relationship with the pupils, because you do need it, and also so that you never lose the practical experience of the problems which the teachers experience.
  (Female Junior School Head) (3)

The responses here were, once again, those of compliance–mediation rather than of criticism–resistance. The mediators believed that a balance between the new managerialism and traditional forms of primary educative leadership was possible. Underlying such responses was the view that particular pressures and stresses were occurring in the transition stages of local management of schools. With greater experience of the LMS system, primary headteachers need not lose the essential commitments of educative leadership.[11] In only two of the primary school accounts was there a discourse which unequivocally celebrated the realization that primary school headteachers were in fact managers and should operate upon that basis:

- I want to manage the school. There are some of my colleagues in the primary school who are still very naive, they still say they are a 'headteacher'. They like to teach. I gave up teaching as such, except in emergencies, a long time ago . . . I don't think that the teaching of children is now part of a headteacher's role. I think that if we do, we are looking for a luxury. We are indulging ourselves.
  (Male Primary School Head) (19)

> • I am better suited to being a manager than I am to being a teacher.
> I enjoy teaching but to be absolutely frank I am not interested in
> teaching now. I am interested in managing the school. In fact, any
> time that I spend not managing the school I tend to get a bit
> irritated because I feel now that whenever I go into a classroom I
> am not doing the real job.
> *(Male Junior School Head) (12)*

The attempt to transform English school headship from a prime identification with professional and educational leadership to prime identification with school management is still in progress. Strong government initiatives to strengthen the latter concept are clearly making progress in the secondary sector of schooling where they have a form of institutional and organizational credibility. However, there is significant criticism of, and resistance to, this transformation in the primary school sector. Linking both sectors are key questions about what forms of new managerialism will emerge and about the consequences of these forms for school leadership and for school effectiveness.

The Discourse and Practice of 'Senior Management'

As the culture of management has become more salient in English schooling culture in the 1980s and the 1990s, an enhanced discourse of management has been generated. Central to this discourse, especially in secondary schools, are various conceptions of 'senior management', which are distinguished from 'middle management' and even 'junior management'. The positioning of the School Governing Body in this discourse is a matter of some interest. In some cases (as demonstrated in Chapter 5) governors may assert 'we are the senior management now'. More generally, as analysis in this study indicated, governors may be compared to a Board of Directors to which the senior management team of the school makes its report.

The rise of the senior management team (SMT) in English schooling culture and practice has accompanied the education reforms of the 1980s and 1990s. Gillborn (1989), in investigating the reactions of a small sample of secondary school headteachers to rapid educational change, found that:

> Two main sources of support emerged as critical in helping head-
> teachers cope with the current situation: the first was an informal
> network of peer contacts between secondary school heads in the LEA;
> the second was an increased reliance upon senior management col-
> leagues within their own schools . . . an increasing interdependence
> between headteachers and their senior staff which reflected a micro-
> political, practical, (and possibly psychological) need to share prob-
> lems and responsibilities among a larger team.[12]

The growing importance of senior management teams in the organization of secondary schooling has been confirmed by the work of Earley *et al.* (1990), Bell (1992) and Wallace and Hall (1994). Senior management teams may be constituted in various ways, sometimes consisting only of the headteacher and the deputy headteachers, and in other cases including a larger range of senior staff.

As Gillborn and others have suggested, the rise of the senior management team to prominence in English schooling, and indeed the greater visibility of 'team' culture, has been an organizational response to rapid and complex educational change. Even by considerable extensions of work time and work load, many headteachers have found it impossible to keep up with the pace and range of educational and organizational change without the support of their senior colleagues. The reform process, intentionally or unintentionally, has given senior management teams a new significance in school organizations.

What are the implications of this development for the exercise of school leadership and management in English secondary schooling? Senior management teams might be interpreted as a significant move away from conceptions of the headteacher as hierarchical leader and manager. From this perspective, they could be seen as a progressive and functional development. On the other hand, they could be experienced as nothing more than the replacement of hierarchy by oligarchy or, at the worst, nothing more than an 'SMT front' for the strong, directive management of the headteacher.

In a small scale study of team approaches to leadership in secondary schools, Wallace and Hall (1994) pointed to 'a core contradiction' between the relatively egalitarian culture of teamwork and 'the ability of heads to create the conditions under which other SMT members could participate in fulfilling a shared leadership role.'[13] In other words, in any assessment of the growth of senior management teams in English schooling culture, important distinctions have to be made between its discourse, which may celebrate 'team work', 'participation', 'flexibility', and its practice, which may involve none of these things.

The investigation of the practice of senior management in the participating schools was beyond the scope of the study detailed in this book. However, analysis of the discourse of the secondary headteachers' accounts made clear that many of them had constituted a senior management team and regarded it as an important development in the changing management of schools. In some cases, this was part of a conscious attempt to change the historical culture of leadership and management which they had inherited from their predecessors:

- My predecessor was very much the old school headmaster . . . authoritarian, dictatorial to a large extent, although in many ways very caring and very innovative in a number of areas . . . but nevertheless he was still 'the headmaster' and even though there was a senior management team in name, it wasn't really a team in the

way in which it operated. We are now certainly closer to being a team and working as a team.
(Male Secondary Head) (11)

- I don't like the 'spider culture' management style which I have seen headteachers operate where all knowledge and authority was at his desk. The only access was through him/her and I don't think that this is the way schools should operate. You need a much wider delegation of power and authority to let people get on with the job. In my experience, the 70s were all of that type, authoritarian, hierarchical, 'spider cultures'. I think that in the 1980s this is gradually changing in the new generation of heads.
(Male Secondary Head) (6)

There was a qualitative distinction in the accounts between those head-teachers who were enthusiasts for management by team work and critical of 'spider culture' and those whose references to SMTs were more technical and instrumental i.e., recognizing that SMTs were necessary to get the work done. Whether these qualitative differences in discourse are related to differences in the practice of senior management is an intriguing question for further research.

Wallace and Hall (1994) have argued that:

Team approaches to school leadership offer great potential for making a coherent and sophisticated response to national reforms and other changes but, our research indicates . . . they are difficult to bring off. (p.8)

Part of this difficulty resides in the historical traditions of strong headteacher leadership in English schools. Even when a headteacher wishes to change that tradition and to inaugurate a senior management team approach there are impediments to that process. The legal and constitutional obligations of headteachers can be a constraint but more pervasively and perhaps more importantly, are the social and cultural expectations for the role of the headteacher. A number of headteachers participating in this inquiry drew attention to the conservative nature of these expectations i.e., that many pupils, parents, teachers and governors still have expectations for 'strong' leadership and management from the headteacher.[14] If a headteacher yields to the force of these traditional expectations then the resulting management style threatens the integrity of the senior management team culture. The transition from the 'headmaster tradition' to team approaches to school leadership and manage-ment is a cultural change and not simply an organizational change. As such, it will take time and quick transformations are unlikely.

Local Management of Schools and the Local Education State

The introduction of local management of schools has had obvious implications for the power relations between schools and their local education authority and for the status and jurisdiction of the local state in education in the national provision of educational services. Monck and Kelly (1992) have noted that:

> LEAs have traditionally had an important role in holding together a planned and integrated system of education, balancing the tendency for each school to regard its own needs as paramount. This role is seriously threatened by LMS . . . The Education Reform Act 1988 . . . appears to move away from the former consensus that schools existed within the local context of a wide range of education services provided by a democratically elected local education authority (LEA). Much of the ERA seemed to be based on the notion of schools as free-standing institutions owing little to anyone except their 'customers'.[15]

In the ideological, political and educational debate which has taken place in England as a result of the introduction of local management of schools, supporters of LMS have stressed the good management sense of delegating decision making to each school-site level; the empowering effect which delegated decision making can have for governors, headteachers and teachers and, in some cases, the sense of liberation from local bureaucracy which has ensued. Critics have argued that while the principle of delegation may be sound, the particular forms of local management of schools which are being implemented have serious deficiencies and that, in any case, LMS is not so much a device for empowering schools as a device for depowering and weakening the role of the local state in education. In short, the supporters of LMS have tended to concentrate upon its managerial utility, while the critics have focused upon its political intentions.

The headteachers participating in this study were affected less by the arguments of the national debate than by their own professional experiences of the local education authorities in the region. Crucial to the response of each headteacher to the changing management of education was the perception of the LEA as either a source of support for headteachers' work or as a bureaucratic impediment to that work. Those who felt 'liberated' by local management of schools had experienced the local education authority as a constraint upon fast-moving and effective management. In this study, such comments came almost exclusively from secondary school headteachers:

- Well, I very much welcome the principle of LMS because I feel that given the way things have been handled by the local authority, headteachers have felt that they could do a far better job keeping the cash themselves because they know their own particular

priorities within their own schools. There are some ridiculous practices going on at local authority level which, in my view, are totally out of date.
(Male Secondary Head) (4)

- I found no golden age in the 60s and 70s. Working in LEA schools at that time, one found the deadening hand of the bureaucrat all about one.
(Male Secondary Head) (43)

- In previous decades, the headteacher's autonomy was dependent on the style of the LEA, and in many cases, I suggest that the LEA may have disempowered heads to a greater extent than many Governing Bodies do.
(Male Secondary Head) (32)

- I welcome the opportunities which LMS gives to Governing Body and the management of the school to make decisions at a local level based on local priorities and I think, working in a very bureaucratic county, there is an awful lot to be gained from being freed from the shackles of the County mechanisms.
(Male Secondary Head) (11)

Within the total sample of participating headteachers, however, the celebration of LMS as a form of liberation from constraining local bureaucracy was a minority response. The majority, especially of primary school headteachers, emphasized the important role of the LEA in providing advisory and special needs services to the schools. While its defects, especially in terms of slowness of response, were recognized, it was perceived to be a valuable agency for supporting headteachers rather than constraining them. The weakening of LEAs and perhaps their ultimate abolition would, from this perspective, increase managerial pressures and stress upon headteachers:

- I would be very, very sad to lose the support of the local education authority, and losing its support would not necessarily enhance a headteacher and give them more freedom. As a matter of fact, I would see the disappearance of the local education authority as causing more problems.
(Male Primary School Head) (31)

This view of the local education authority as an essential support agency for the work of primary schools was also endorsed by a group of secondary headteachers who were not prepared to celebrate the arrival of LMS if it involved the effective abolition of the role of the LEA:

• I have been in headship long enough to know which sections of the LEA I need support from and their expertise in a number of areas cannot be replaced, especially in the special education needs area . . . I think it's wrong to depower the LEA. I think they should have been made more responsive to the needs of the school instead of the needs of their elected members. That's always been the problem in this authority . . . but I certainly don't subscribe to the view that the LEA should be decimated or removed entirely because that would be stupid. They do perform a very important role.
(Male Secondary Head) (6)

While recognizing the potential benefits of local management of schools for the exercise of their own autonomy as school leaders and managers, the headteachers in this study, in the main, wanted to work with reformed LEAs rather than as free-standing institutions. Their accounts stressed a requirement for local authorities which were more responsive to school needs, which were quicker to respond to such needs, and which were less bureaucratic in operation.[16] Support for the continued existence of the local state in education was therefore based upon technical and utilitarian considerations i.e., its value as a support services agency. Without such an intermediary agency between the individual school and the central state there was an apprehension that too many pressures would focus upon school governors and headteachers. In their examination of various models of educational governance under current discussion in England, Cordingley and Kogan (1993) concluded that:

Control of education is being shifted to centrally appointed bodies and largely autonomous schools. Many believe that education can not be governed by the centre . . . Education requires a public service to respond to the geographical, ecological, demographic characteristics and political cultures of diverse areas . . . (p.110)

This was the dominant view of the headteachers in this inquiry. However, it was also their view that this local public service, as expressed in the local education state, could be greatly improved.

Headteachers, Market Culture and Competition

The headteachers in this study were involved not only in adjusting to the implications of local management of schools but also in negotiating strategies to respond to a more salient market culture in schooling. In other words, they were caught up in a process of school reform which had two institutional and cultural stages. The first stage involved more managerial autonomy (in theory) through the local management of schools initiative. The second stage, encoded officially in a discourse of 'choice', 'diversity', and 'responsiveness to consumers', involved pressures for a much more radical change i.e., a change to entrepreneurial and market values in education.[17]

The headteachers operated as school leaders and managers in a political and ideological context strongly influenced by New Right arguments for free markets in education or at least for the concept of an internal market in education. In English political culture in the early 1990s writers such as Flew (1991) argued for a free market in education:

> . . . if . . . all existing maintained schools were to be deprived of their present monopoly privileges and thus become completely individual firms subject to the incentives and disciplines of the market . . . reliable measures of the teaching effectiveness at all levels of those schools would . . . be rapidly evolved and publicized. For everybody knows that firms competing to sell their products strive to demonstrate the quality of those products to possible purchasers. (pp.43–4)

In ideological positions of this type, headteachers of English schools at all levels faced an attempted cultural transformation of the school into a 'firm' and the commodification of its educational services into 'products' in the market place. The Health and Welfare Unit of the Institute of Economic Affairs in London was particularly active in the early 1990s in the publication of texts in support of market forces in public services (e.g., *Empowering the Parents: how to break the schools' monopoly*, 1991) while at the same time constructing a moral and ethical defence of market institutions as essential elements of 'free' societies (e.g., *The Moral Foundations of Market Institutions*, 1992: *God and the Marketplace*, 1993).[18]

As another strand within this attempted cultural transformation of educational culture and institutions, writers such as Chubb and Moe (1992) argued for at least the establishment of internal markets[15]:

> As we see it, choice is by no means a free market approach to education. It is a governmental system, just as the current one is. It is simply built to provide education in a different, more productive way, through a new governmental structure that does most of its work through markets rather than politics and bureaucracy. The government's job is not to abandon the schools but to use markets to see that schools flourish and prosper as effective organizations . . . educational markets operate within an institutional framework and the government's job is to design the framework[20] . . . If this framework is designed with care and concern, markets can be allowed to work their wonders within it—for everyone's benefit. (pp.10–11)

The argument that internal markets in education have great potential to improve the quality and effectiveness of publicly provided education 'for everyone' has provoked considerable debate. In England, Tooley (1992 and 1993) in a series of papers has argued for the benefits of market forces in education, while Ranson (1993) has warned that market forces in education will result in the commodification of education and a reinforcement of existing social divisions and disadvantages.

The headteachers in this study were fully aware of the general political and ideological delineation of market thinking in education but, in some senses, this was a large debate being carried on around the schools in a national context. What brought this debate directly into their professional experience was the new emphasis on management and marketing which had resulted from local management of schools. They all recognized new imperatives in the areas of financial management, personnel management and marketing relations. To facilitate these new imperatives a literature of Education Management Studies (see Chapter 1) had developed and it was these texts which brought market messages directly into the schools, generally through the agency of management courses.

Writing of the dissemination of progressive primary school teaching culture in an earlier period, Bernstein (1977, p.142) used the evocative concept of 'innovating message'. In the 1970s, the innovating message was transmitted in the new pedagogic experience of the child, i.e., 'the child becomes an innovating message to the home'. In the dissemination of market culture in English schooling the innovating messages have become management courses and the management texts which have multiplied everywhere.[21]

Of all the innovatory messages that headteachers in English schools have received in the 1980s and 1990s, perhaps the most radical have been the messages of marketing. Headteachers, as public service professionals, have not, historically, given much attention to market culture or market strategies. This situation has changed with local management of schools and with an open enrolment competitive regime. Now headteachers are advised that:

> The Education Reform Act 1988 promotes a market driven education system in which individual schools will need to sell their product in a competitive environment . . . The Education (Schools) Act 1992 will further intensify competition. This requires all schools to publish their public examination results including the SAT results for key stages 1, 2 and 3.[22]

How did the headteachers in this study respond to such innovating messages? Analysis of their accounts revealed two dominant responses which may be called market insulation and market regulation.

Market Insulations and Local Circumstances

The development of internal markets in education will be affected by a considerable number of variables. Among these will be the historical and cultural features of an area, its social and political traditions and the pattern of its rural and urban demography. In particular localities a primary school or secondary school may have no serious competitors in terms of easy access to alternative schools. This will be a characteristic of many rural and small town settings, i.e., the school is *the* school of the community. This situation applied to a number of the headteachers in this study who felt that market culture in education would not seriously impinge upon their school or upon their style of school leadership:

- We are not in a competitive situation here at all.
  (Male Secondary Head) (5)

- The market is too imperfect to be of the influence that the New Right would like.
  (Male Secondary Head) (43)

- It worries me and it's a whole idea that we have never considered before . . . I am lucky in that I don't really think it will happen in this immediate area.
  (Male Junior School Head) (14)

- Some headteachers are being forced pragmatically down the market line and others are embracing it almost excitedly. On the other hand, in geographical areas like my own, where this school is the only one in the catchment area and where a bus journey to another town is the only alternative, the market is less dominant.
  (Male Secondary Head) (22)

Whereas local management of schools was an 'innovating message' for all headteachers regardless of location, the impact of market forces in education was seen to be crucially mediated by location. However, location was not the only factor which could create feelings of relative insulation from market forces in education. In urban contexts with a higher 'choice and diversity' potential, some headteachers felt insulated from new challenges by their existing 'oversubscribed' status:

- The school is sited in an almost exclusively middle-class area. The school has always been over-subscribed so marketing has never been an issue.
  (Male Secondary Head) (35)

The generation of a competitive culture as between different schools was not therefore a 'real' issue for headteachers as school leaders in these two categories. Market insulation arising from either community setting or from the cultural capital of established success kept these issues at a distance and constituted no pressure upon the headteachers to change their leadership styles. However, where these conditions did not obtain, headteachers were being faced by an emergent market culture and, as school leaders, had to find some strategy for dealing with it. The most characteristic response was that of market regulation.

On the Professional Regulation of Education Markets

In a memorandum on 'The Marketing of Schools' issued by the National Association of Headteachers to its members in September 1990, headteachers in England were reminded of the conflicts between professional and collegial values in education and those of the market:

> [for] every school which 'wins' in a competitive market others lose and as a result the chances of their pupils will be damaged.[23]

For those headteachers in this study who found themselves in a potentially competitive situation for pupil enrolments, this expressed the professional and leadership dilemma to which they had to respond. While a muted expression of school marketing had existed in earlier decades, the cultural and ideological changes of the 1980s and 1990s constituted both a celebration and a legitimization of market values in education. The previous hegemony of collegial professional relations among headteachers of state schools in England which had largely eschewed explicit marketing of the school was now under sustained attack. The marketing of schooling was officially approved by the state, propagated and empowered, and a new hegemony of values and practices was in the process of formation. The innovating messages to headteachers were clear and unambiguous:

> Notwithstanding ethical objections to marketing education, circumstances dictate its inevitable use by schools if they are to survive.[24]

Many of the headteachers in this study attempted to operate, once again, a strategy of mediation when faced with such a cultural and operational transformation of the conditions of schooling. This strategy of mediation was widely expressed in various forms of, or aspirations to, professional regulation of the worst excesses of market forces:

- I have great difficulty in coming to terms with spending money on marketing the school which should, I believe, be spent for the direct benefit of the pupils . . . the secondary heads in this area meet regularly to devise strategies for persuading parents to keep their children in this area (in whichever school they wish to choose) instead of sending them to a school in another LEA.
  (Male Secondary Head) (44)

- We have seen people trying to operate competitively yet ethically. We have an agreement about ethical advertising, for instance, where we are trying to advertise ourselves, but not at the expense of others. We obviously respond to people who come to us but we don't go and parade our talents, as it were, in neighbouring areas and so far this is holding up very well . . . it is my intention that we should behave in a professional fashion . . .
  (Male Secondary Head) (9)

- It is probably because so many demands are being put upon us . . . that we have started to pull together more. Local heads have tended to start grouping . . . they have been morally supportive . . . we are fighting against it (the market).
  (Male Primary Head) (1)

From the perspectives of the New Right, such professional groupings and agreements among headteachers would be seen to be professional cartels seeking to impede the free operation of market forces in education and actually to reduce choice possibilities for parents. From the perspectives of these headteachers as school leaders, such action was represented as professionally responsible and in the best interests of pupils and the community.

Viewed historically, the growth of 'support groups' among headteachers in England has been given an added impetus by the sheer intensification of the work pressures upon such school leaders. There is thus an interesting paradox and contradiction emerging in English schooling culture. On the one hand, local management of schools is clearly premised upon a construct of the individual, empowered school manager. On the other hand, the intensification of work pressures and the propagation of market forces in education is causing headteachers to combine together in local and regional groupings more intensively than before. While those groupings exist to fulfil a range of professional, managerial and personal needs of headteachers, it is also clear that they provide possibilities for professional regulation of the full impact of market forces. There is thus both an individualizing and a collectivizing tendency in the complex of contemporary educational change in England. Both of these tendencies have important consequences for the nature of school leadership in the future. While attempted professional regulation of market forces was at its more explicit and visible in the headteacher 'support groups', other headteachers expressed their faith in the ability of professional and moral values to regulate the cruder aspects of marketing. In short, they believed that the professionalism of most headteachers would not be 'corrupted' by market forces and that some mediated compromise would emerge:

- Marketing the school isn't necessarily following the market place mentality or the market place ideas of 'whizz kid' business men.

Marketing the school can be making the community aware of the positives that the school has to offer for the children of the area.
(Male Primary School Head) (31)

• Headteachers should be moral, rational professionals. Implicitly such a headteacher may view the market place for education . . . as amoral but in need of moral guidance to control personal and managerial machinations.
(Male Secondary Head) (37)

• I have not developed a marketing policy as I am concerned that it could be perceived . . . as an attempt to 'poach' pupils from an adjacent County School.
(Female RC Primary School Head) (49)

Such headteachers were reluctant to abandon a professional culture which they regarded as morally and ethically superior to that of the market place. To do so would in their view radically change the nature of schooling itself and the nature of school leadership. They believed that professional and moral regulation of markets in education was possible and desirable.[25] Nevertheless there was also a recognition that the schools of the region were in the early stages of their encounter with market forces. Some of the participants recognized that both the headteacher support groups and faith in professional values and integrity might prove to be fragile defences against the powerful forces of institutional survival which were now at work. If the 'professional line' was broken by just a few institutions then the maintenance of market regulation would become even more problematic:

• I am realistic enough to know that this spirit of cooperation is fragile and is likely to disappear if one of the schools in the area begins to fear closure because of the effects of falling rolls.
(Male Secondary Head) (44)

Of all the issues which were seen to threaten local professional solidarity most fundamentally, the decision of any local school to seek grant-maintained status and to opt-out of LEA control was critical. At the time of the research inquiry, no school in the region had 'opted out' of LEA control but the material advantages of grant-maintained status were becoming more visible to both parents and headteachers. Whether headteachers should give leadership on this critical issue and what sort of leadership it should be was an emergent dilemma for some of the participants (the detail of this dilemma will be examined in the following chapter).

The majority of the headteachers in this study were seeking to maintain in various ways a professional and collegial culture. In general, they had no wish to be drawn into competitive marketing for pupil enrolments, nor did they wish to become entrepreneurial school leaders. They could accept a professionally regulated form of educational marketing which consisted of ethical and responsible promotion of the achievements of the school and of the resources and opportunities which it offered to local communities. As one of the participants put it:

- I'm not against marketing if you market the good things that the school does. I'm against marketing if you are advertising the school like people advertise soap powder . . . If marketing means promoting the image of the school then I'm not against that. What I am against is people who market things that aren't actually true. *(Male Secondary Head) (5)*

Resisting Markets: Visibly and Invisibly

The majority of the research participants did not generate a discourse of developed criticism about market forces in education. Their stance, characteristic of the occupational group, involved concentrating upon strategies of professional regulation and survival rather than upon principled or ideological criticism. However, for a minority of the headteachers in this study strategic response was not sufficient. Such headteachers discerned, in the advance of market culture, an attempted transformation of the nature of education and of the constitution of the school and its pupils. For these participants this process amounted to an attempted commodification of education so that in 'product' form it would be harmonized into market discourse and market practice. For these headteachers, being a school leader involved the articulation of a principled criticism of, and, if possible, resistance to, these reductionist tendencies of the market. They decisively rejected conceptions of the school as a firm or business and conceptions of school leaders as market executives or entrepreneurs:

- I don't see that to be my role—a business manager I am not. If I was I'd be working for *Marks and Spencers* . . . School is *not* a business with simple input and output measurement . . . Education is not about getting money for us. It's about helping people worse off than us.
(Male Secondary Head) (2)

- Much of what we are being asked to do in terms of marketing and competition is against my basic principles and I find this intolerable that a government should inflict a particular philosophy onto a profession and take no account of their opinions and expertise. The process of education is not the same as producing a tin of beans. Business practices are often inappropriate for what we do.
(Male Primary School Head) (50)

- I resent being placed in the position of 'marketing' at all. I feel we should serve the needs of our pupils to the best of our ability and not be placed in direct competition like some 'best brands' in a supermarket.
  (Female Primary School Head) (49)

- Today you are made to feel as though you are producing a product . . . I don't see children in those terms. I see children as people and I am not happy with an industrial model being placed on children.
  (Male Primary School Head) (14)

It could be argued, following Bernstein (1977), that headteachers' responses to market culture were mediated in visible and invisible forms. The visible form was an explicit discourse of criticism which focused upon the fundamental incompatibility between educational culture and market culture. Despite government sponsorship of market values in schooling, some headteachers believed that their integrity as school leaders required them to make a visible and explicit critique of such developments. The majority, however, engaged in invisible critique through the various strategies for professional regulation of education markets. In other words, strategies for professional regulation were *in fact* critiques of market forces but realized in different forms.

Explicit critique of market values constituted, for some headteachers, a necessary defence of fundamental principles in schooling. Invisible critique, on the other hand, constituted leadership for institutional survival in schooling. Most headteachers recognized that invisible critique had a dual advantage. It preserved some elements of professional integrity while at the same time not impeding institutional survival. It was therefore a leadership response which seemed particularly appropriate for the changed power relations and operational autonomy of contemporary English schooling.

'Winning' in the Market Place

Ranson (1993) has argued that:

> Action in the market is driven by a single, common currency: the pursuit of material interests. The only effective means upon which to base action is the calculation of personal advantage: clout in the market derives from the power of superior resources to subordinate others in competitive exchange. (p.336)

Thus expressed, market values in education are clearly at odds with many religious, humanistic and personal values which have been historically dominant in English schooling culture. While muted forms of competition have existed in English state schooling, the single-minded pursuit of 'winning' at the expense of other schools and of professional colleagues has been exceptional. However, in contemporary ideological conditions involving the publication of league tables of school results, 'winning' in the market place has been given a new salience.

At the time of this research inquiry the culture of competitive institutional 'winning' received virtually no public legitimation from the headteachers of the region.[26] Only one participant, in a situation of high competitive potential, was explicit on this issue:

- If you have a village school where there is no competition, you have no problems. The situation here is that there are four schools within half a mile of each other and there is going to be terrible competition and as far as I am concerned, we are in the business of winning.
  (Male Junior School Head) (12)

From this study it became apparent that there are local conditions which constitute various forms of market insulation and there are local conditions which result in market intensification. It is in these latter conditions that headteachers as school leaders may feel that they are inevitably driven into the role of being market winners. In this way, the education market establishes a winner–loser syndrome with profound consequences for schools and communities.

Management, Markets and Morality

Headteachers in England are the inheritors of a school leadership culture which for over a hundred years gave priority to moral leadership and subsequently, in recontextualized form, to various expressions of professional and educative leadership. This leadership culture has been subjected in the 1980s and 1990s to a sustained attempt to transform it as part of a larger political and ideological reconstruction of the education system and of schooling culture, driven by New Right doctrines.

Headteachers in this study had encountered a new managerialism, arising out of local management of schools, which all of them recognized to have significant implications for school leadership roles in all types of school. Managerialism, with its practices, values and perspectives, was in the process of establishing its hegemony in the whole schooling system. At the same time, market culture was beginning to impinge upon some headteachers as the new conditions for competitive enrolment and competitive visible success were socially constituted in their localities. For some headteachers, these transformations in schooling culture and the transformations in school leadership which they required generated no major problems. New constructs of school leaders as empowered local managers and as successful market entrepreneurs were experienced as modern, progressive, dynamic and stimulating developments. Such responses, not unexpectedly, came from those headteachers whose schools were already strong in the market place, in terms of established reputation, existing cultural capital, high pupil enrolments and non-deficit financial budgets. Such headteachers were poised for further success in a schooling culture shaped by the new managerialism and by market forces. In general, they experienced few dilemmas in negotiating the changed culture of school leadership.

For many of their colleagues, however, the transformation was more problematic because the changed culture of school leadership generated for them moral, ethical and professional dilemmas. Such headteachers had difficulty in reconciling the principles and values which they had upheld in the past, as part of their understanding of the culture of professional schooling, with the new principles and values now in power. Many of them found themselves in difficult and contradictory situations. At a national level they were being informed by a Secretary of State for Education that the traditional spiritual and moral values transmitted in English schooling must be maintained for the good of moral cohesion in society as well as for the good of individual pupils. At a local level they were encountering new conditions for schooling which seemed to negate those messages with an emphasis upon individual competitive survival, visible and measurable success, and a market culture in which 'winning' was the ultimate value. The contradictions between national, political rhetoric and local professional experience had the effect of producing a range of leadership dilemmas for these headteachers.[27] These dilemmas, which added to the stress of contemporary school leadership in England, will be examined in the following two chapters.

Notes and References

1   Chubb and Moe (1990, p.189).
2   *Ibid.*
3   Chubb and Moe (1992, p.4).
4   The publication of school 'results' in England has been expressed officially as: 'the results of National Curriculum tests and of public examinations for the age groups concerned will be published by schools and in comparative tables for every area. This will provide more reliable and useful information than ever before about school performance' (DES, *Choice and Diversity: a new framework for schools*, p.16).
5   See *Choice and Diversity*, 1992, pp.2–5.
6   Local financial management schemes were piloted in LEAs such as Cambridge, Cheshire, Lincoln and Solihull. A similar idea was pioneered in the 1970s by the Inner London Education Authority as the Alternative Use of Resources initiative.
7   In the dissemination of the potential benefits of local-site management, Caldwell and Spinks' (1988) text, *The Self-Managing School* was particularly influential. As the authors noted in 1992, 'we are fortunate to have been directly involved in change in a number of countries, largely through extended consultancies . . . We have been involved in these ways in Australia, Britain and New Zealand' (p.viii).

8   The 'winner–loser' syndrome was mentioned by many headteachers as an undesirable feature of the implementation of local management of schools in the area,
e.g.:

- My experience is that of somebody who is fortunate enough to be a
'winner'. Schools are 'winners' and 'losers' and we have a formula
funded budget which in fact would make us . . . the biggest winner
in the County. *(9)*

- The funding that has come with LMS has been inadequate to do the
job . . . We are very definitely the loser. *(21)*

- I can afford to be fairly positive about LMS because under LMS we
are a winner and I suspect that headteachers' views on LMS are very
much coloured by that. I regret very much that there should be winners
and losers under LMS. *(11)*

9   A number of headteachers pointed out that although a formal decision to make a
teacher redundant was taken by the school governors, in practice the governors
looked to the headteacher for 'guidance'. This gave heads the *sense* that they were
making teachers redundant and this was an unpalatable new managerial experience.

10   The new managerialism generated a number of dilemmas for the headteachers.
This one involved tensions between new conceptions of being involved in the
school's teaching culture. A more detailed examination of this and other dilemmas
will be undertaken in Chapter 8.

11   In a large-scale survey of 812 headteachers (primary and secondary) to examine
the impact of LMS, Arnott, Bullock and Thomas (1992) reported that 66 per cent
of their respondents felt that the demands of LMS had made them 'less familiar
with events in the classroom' (p.5). Further reports of the LMS Impact Project
based at Birmingham University will investigate whether or not this situation
changes with more experience of LMS.

12   Gillborn (1989, pp.77–8).

13   Wallace and Hall (1994, p.6).

14   Various conceptions of 'strong' leadership will be examined in Chapter 11.

15   Monck and Kelly (1992, pp.iii–1).

16   A typical headteacher's view was: 'I think that LEAs will have to slim down
because they won't have the money to spend on central administration'. *(7)*

17   There is no necessary link between local management of schools and the growth
of a market culture in education. However, it was clear to most of the participants
that such a link was being advanced by government policy. In other words, LMS
would not be operating in the future within the parameters of the local education
state but within the parameters of a market for schools.

18   These publications have been designed to establish moral justifications for the
market place and to counter the idea that markets are essentially amoral. The
Foreword of the 1993 publication argues that:

. . . neglect of moral issues has reinforced the tendency of churches to
view markets with suspicion, if not outright hostility. During the
Thatcher years when successive administrations, with solid popular back-
ing, sought to abandon collectivism and restore liberty in Britain, the
churches typically withheld their blessing, implying that market competition was at best morally dubious and possibly wicked. (p.vi)

19   For Chubb and Moe, an internal market for education is a situation of decentralized
management and enhanced choice for students and parents but operating within
a regulatory framework established by the government.

20 The institutional framework proposed by Chubb and Moe would involve, among other things, 'setting and administering rules for the chartering of new schools; seeing that information is provided (through personal contact) to all parents; setting up rules for the applications and admissions procedures to ensure that choice is open and fair; setting up rules and providing additional funding to ensure equal opportunities . . .' (pp.10–11).

21 A considerable educational consultancy and educational management enterprise movement has developed during the 1980s and 1990s. Aspirants for contemporary headship in England are being socialized by these agencies for their new roles and responsibilities.

22 See Barnes (1993) *Practical Marketing for Schools*, p.xii.

23 NAHT Memorandum, *The Marketing of Schools*, para 3.4.

24 Barnes (1993, p.138).

25 See Barnes (1993, pp.133–40) for a discussion of 'Marketing Schools and Codes of Professional Practice'.

26 This is not to say that competitive 'winning' was absent from their consciousness, only that they did not explicitly endorse the idea. Just as there could be invisible resistance to market culture in education, there might also be covert forms of its endorsement.

27 A similar conclusion has been reached by Bowe and Ball (1993, p.81):–
'the new elements introduced by LMS require schools to deal with different, expanded and contradictory sets of demands.'

Chapter 8

Moral, Ethical and Professional Dilemmas

Christopher Hodgkinson, in *The Philosophy of Leadership* (1993) and in other writings, has argued that administration *is* philosophy in action and that its central preoccupations should be with value judgments and with the attempted resolution of value conflicts in organizational settings. For Hodgkinson, educational leadership is especially involved with moral and ethical questions relating to various constructs of the good life. Within critical leadership studies, Foster (1989) has emphasized that educational leadership cannot be reduced to management or marketing because the educational leader has a responsibility to 'maintain an ethical focus . . . as a search for the good life of the community' (p.55).

Although the corpus of writings in education management studies has paid little attention to moral and ethical issues during the 1980s there is recent evidence that value issues are being recontextualized as appropriate matters for educational managers to consider. In texts such as *The Morality of the School* (1990) and *The Ethics of Educational Management* (1993) there is now a recognition that 'good management must stem from an appreciation of the ultimate purposes of the organization, rather than from the exigencies of crisis management.'[1]

This observation generates once again a question with a very long history, i.e., what are the ultimate purposes of the school? John White (1990) points out that this is a question for continuing debate and clarification among all the constituencies concerned with education. In that debate, value issues and value judgments are central but these are expressed from various perspectives. The discourse used in the debate also takes different forms. Historically, the ultimate purposes of English schooling have been expressed in a discourse of morality. This discourse has attempted to sanctify particular constructs of the 'good life' for the individual, the community and the whole structure of social relationships. These moral purposes of schooling have derived their inspiration mainly from the Christian religion and from the moral culture of its various denominational forms in English society. As argued in earlier chapters, this religious and moral culture of English schooling has been constituted in both direct and mediated categories. The direct and visible manifestation of religious and moral culture can be seen in the significant presence of state supported religious schools within the English educational system. However, this religious and moral culture is also powerfully present in apparently secular state schools where there are legal requirements for teaching religious education and for the daily organization of 'a collective act of worship'.[2]

Historically, therefore, the moral mission of English schooling has been the attempted transmission of mainly Christian values and morality to the young, either explicitly in schools of religious foundation or implicitly in state provided schooling. Such values and morality have been realized in the different moral codes of particular school cultures but they have all included certain key elements. Among these are teachings that spiritual considerations should take precedence over material considerations; that personal, social and sexual relations should be regulated in appropriate ways; that virtues of charity, love and compassion should be emulated; and that a quality of service to others should be, through acknowledged responsibility to the wider community, a high moral aim for schooling.

In recent decades, this religious and moral culture of schooling has undergone transformations arising from a variety of social and cultural changes.[3] The most fundamental of these has been the advance of a rational and secular culture which is not inclined to give any privileged place to Christian moral codes in the schooling process. As Christian commitment has become a minority commitment in English society, the value culture of modern schooling has become more open and more pluralist and a discourse of ethics has tended to replace the older discourse of morality *per se*. Ethics, with its emphasis upon principles regulating behaviour independently of any corpus of religious teaching, articulates more harmoniously with a rational and secular age. Ethical dilemmas arising from the conflict of value judgments (irrespective of religion) are seen to be appropriate matters for professional discussion in education and in a whole range of personal service professions. Therefore it is not surprising that with considerable transformations taking place in professional culture and with an apparent intensification of the range and nature of ethical dilemmas, value issues are now incorporated into 'management training'.

At the time of the research fieldwork, few of the participating headteachers had attended management courses where ethical dilemmas were on the agenda. However, many of them were encountering an intensification of value dilemmas as they sought to adjust to a rapidly changing educational, social and cultural context for schooling. In this chapter, the value dilemmas of headteachers in state schools will be examined and in the following chapter, for comparative purposes, the dilemmas of headteachers in Catholic schools will be examined.

Professionalism, Community and Self-Interest

The sharpest dilemmas for the headteachers in this inquiry arose out of their responses to the growth of a more competitive market culture in schooling which stressed individual survival and individual winning as *the* priority for school leaders. In essence the dilemma was, should they participate in a market culture for the material benefit of their schools and their pupils or should they remain loyal to their own personal and professional values at the risk of disadvantage for their schools? This dilemma of *professional community* versus *autonomous advantage* which was one of the outcomes of a market for schooling, was compounded by government incentives to all schools to opt-out of the control of the local state into a more autonomous grant-maintained status. It was widely understood by the headteachers that financial incentives were available from the government for those schools which voted for grant-maintained independence from the local education authority. Leadership from headteachers on this decision could result in a financial advantage for the school but at a cost of weakening the viability of the local education authority and of straining professional relations in the local education community (especially with other headteachers).

As was shown in Chapter 7, the early responses of the headteachers in the region to growing conflicts between professional community and individual self-interest in schooling was an attempt to strengthen the professional community by formal and informal 'support groups'. However, it was recognized that many factors now influenced the formation of individual school policies, among these the existence of empowered parents and empowered school governors. In other words, the conditions for the maintenance of professional solidarity and professional community had changed and head-teachers recognized its fragility in new competitive circumstances. The choice for institutional self-interest in a situation in which that self-interest was believed to be damaging to other schools and to professional colleagues was registered as a serious moral or ethical dilemma:

- If a neighbouring school has a threatened future, do I pamphlet its locality with details about my school? Do I openly advertise that I will accept transfers from students already on courses? There is a particularly heavy burden of moral dilemmas for those schools with surplus places. When moralities become uncertain, then you negotiate. You bring out 'mission' statements, you agree objectives . . . You then put aside your intuitive feeling for right and wrong and content yourself with your markers of success.
  (Male Secondary Head) (46)*

- My dilemma concerning marketing the school in a competitive arena is that my distaste for the need, rationale and outcomes which surround the idea is virtually total . . . Am I indulging my own values at the expense of my school by not image making at every opportunity?
  (Female Primary School Head) (48)

---

* *Note* Numbers in brackets used after quotations refer to the code numbers of the headteachers' accounts.

- Do you market your school in the hope of getting extra pupils, knowing that another school may suffer as result? After much deliberation this school is now being much more 'pushy'. *(Male Primary School Head) (52)*

There was evidence from this study that despite the 'distaste' which marketing the school created for some headteachers and despite the moral and professional dilemmas which they perceived and experienced, there appeared to be an iron law of inevitability about market intensification in certain localities. In these circumstances, institutional survival was at stake, and the headteachers understood this.

This was much less true about decisions to opt-out of local education authority control and to seek autonomous advantage in a decision for grant-maintained status. The political and educational culture of the region was resistant to such an overt attempt to divide state schools and to weaken the local education state. However, all the headteachers, and perhaps more significantly the school governors and the parents of the region, had been subjected to a sustained political and ideological campaign from the Department for Education and other agencies which had stressed the explicit financial advantages and the implicit social status advantages of opting-out. There was evidence that pressure was increasing on some headteachers to give leadership for the grant-maintained option. Simon and Chitty (1993), in a strong critique of these developments, have argued:

> By far the largest section of the 1988 Act is concerned with opting out, comprising over fifty separate clauses, and this was certainly the most radical and crucial feature of that Act . . . By these means the school is removed totally from the local authority's control, guidance (or assistance). It becomes, in Thatcher's memorable, if contradictory words, a 'state independent school'. This means that the school is 'independent' from the LEA but is now directly subject to the state . . .[4]

From this perspective the whole opting-out strategy for English state schooling in the 1980s and 1990s has been part of a larger political strategy to undermine and weaken local education authorities largely under the control of Labour administrations.

In contrast to this interpretation, Chubb and Moe (1992) have celebrated opting-out as the most fundamental and the most essential of all the education reforms facilitating greater choice in schooling:

> If enough schools were to follow this path, the existing system would collapse and a very new and different one would take its place—a system whose hall mark is the foundation of effective education: school autonomy.[5]

Chubb and Moe have also argued that headteachers in England should give 'strong leadership' to school governors and to parents to support this most important restructuring of the school system.

The headteachers of the region, despite the existence of local political and cultural insulations from these innovating messages, were beginning to experience this major issue as a leadership dilemma. Should they provide strong leadership for apparently greater autonomy (and material resources) or should they support a concept of local education community as expressed in the LEA and in their existing network of professional relations with other local headteachers? For Chubb and Moe (1992) the issue is clear cut:

> Largely because of its experiment in opting out, Britain has already broken with tradition and moved boldly toward a choice-based system of public education. (p.45)

For the headteachers in this study, facing the issue as an emergent dilemma in their particular locality, there was a greater sensitivity to what was at stake in breaking 'with tradition' (i.e., ideas of educational community and professional collegiality) and a greater awareness of the social and educational consequences of 'boldly' opting-out:

- Opting-out is really opting *in* to increasingly centralized government control—*but* it brings in the money! What do heads do if they and their schools are not to be left behind?
  (Male Special School Head) (47)

- The greatest moral struggle in the opting-out scene is the struggle of the headteacher to hold on to a belief that education has any moral basis.
  (Male Secondary Head) (46)

- The major moral dilemma of GM status is the possibility of depriving other schools to one's own personal advantage . . . How far can the individual school seek to promote its own well being and development without being seen to impinge upon other institutions?
  (Male Secondary Head) (45)

- Part of me feels that opting-out of local authority control might not be a bad idea. After all, what is left of them? The dilemma is that I have been supported and facilitated by my LEA and I would like to maintain a city-wide corporateness.
  (Male Primary School Head) (59)

In the ideological and value struggles between professional community and autonomous advantage, the participants were, in the main, remaining loyal to an existing culture which emphasized the former. For some, the enhanced autonomy of local management of schools was a sufficient indicator of 'progress', without the need for the destruction of local education networks. What could not be predicted, however, was the extent to which school leadership on this issue might emanate from school governing bodies or organized groups of parents. In other words, headteachers could be faced in the future with leadership initiatives on grant-maintained status arising from active governors or parents. Such circumstances would have the effect of making explicit the leadership dilemma for headteachers as well as making explicit the power relations of leadership in a situation of proposed radical reform. Would such an issue be a resigning issue on principle, or could a decision for opting-out against the advice of the headteacher be legitimated as a valid expression of local democracy?

Value dilemmas relating to professionalism, community and self-interest in schooling reform are becoming sharper in England for both governors and headteachers. In their own staff development courses, the headteachers in this inquiry felt that they had been 'trained' (with varying degrees of effectiveness) to deal with the logistics of finance, management and marketing. However, they felt that they had not had sufficient opportunities to reflect upon and discuss collectively the moral, ethical and professional dilemmas that they faced as contemporary school leaders. Both local education authority provision of 'managing change' courses and the provision of other agencies had been primarily technical whereas the heads were also interested in courses or study opportunities where professional dilemmas and principles for their resolution were a prime focus.

These observations legitimate Greenfield's (1993) assertion that, 'with the elimination of values, consideration of the conduct of organization is reduced to technicalities' (p.146). In the new conditions for English schooling, the headteachers appreciated the technical assistance which they had received to help them with the requirements of a new managerialism. But headteachers also faced important value issues, which they expressed as moral, or ethical, or professional dilemmas. They were aware of expectations that they should give leadership to governors, teachers and parents on such dilemmas and how they might be appropriately resolved. They were also aware of their own professional support needs for dealing with leadership in the domain of values.

The Economy of Teacher Employment

In a text which is largely a celebration of leadership in the self-managing school, Caldwell and Spinks (1992) claim that the new empowerment of school leaders offers the 'promise of a richly fulfilling career',[6] but acknowledge that 'the task of leadership will be difficult in the case of large-scale restructuring'.[7]

None of the headteachers in this research were faced with large-scale restructuring of their schools as a result of the new conditions for schooling but a number of them were encountering an emergent culture of 'restructuring'[8] which was affecting both staff recruitment and staff retention. What might be called the *economy of teacher employment* had become a central preoccupation of all headteachers, given that teacher costs represented the largest sector of the devolved school budgets for which they had the responsibility (with the school governors).

For some headteachers, however, the culture of restructuring was beginning to express itself in changed criteria regulating the appointment of teachers to the school. School governors anxious to demonstrate prudent budgetary control over staff costs were, in the opinion of some heads, beginning to place 'cheapness of appointment' before 'quality of appointment'. The dilemma for headteachers in these situations was that as the leading professional they understood their first commitment to be to the quality of the proposed appointment but with new budgetary categories which could result in deficits, they had also to recognize that budgetary control was essential. These dilemmas were beginning to emerge and a process of restructuring of expectations for appointments could be detected in some school governing bodies from this perspective:

- We did an appointment recently and at the end of the day the best candidate turned out to be a probationer . . . One reaction to this was, 'Well, great, it's going to be a cheap appointment.' Now that is a dreadful thing to hear . . . I said, 'I don't care what it costs. We want the best person from the candidates who present themselves.'
  (Male Secondary Head) (2)

- We no longer appoint staff on experience and excellence but upon salary level . . . I am very jealous of headteachers with surplus [budget] situations. If I am not careful the whole outlook of my job will see money first and children last.
  (Male Primary School Head) (55)

If some heads faced dilemmas about whether they could afford to appoint quality (but expensive) teachers in the best interests of the pupils, others faced even sharper dilemmas about teacher redundancy. It could be argued that the culture of restructuring in self-managing schools has two dimensions. The restructuring of expectations for teacher appointments is a relatively invisible dimension in that the criteria used at the actual point of decision making are rarely made public and may in fact operate at an implicit and covert level. The restructuring of staff establishment, on the other hand, is a visible dimension and is made explicit in proposals for teacher redundancy.

Headteachers of schools who began their responsibilities for local management with a deficit budget position had to face staff restructuring. Whether they found this experience of leadership in the self-managing school part of the 'richly fulfilling career' promised by Caldwell and Spinks (1992) seems improbable. In fact, the evidence from this study suggests that teacher re-dundancies were experienced as a major professional dilemma for those headteachers involved:

- The LMS man[9] told me that I can't save on minor things—I've got to look at salaries . . . Now I have built up over the years in this school a super staff. We do everything together. Our staff meet-ings are devoted to planning our work . . . what the children are going to do, and everybody works well when they get back into classrooms. Now he's asking me, after all these years, to say to one of my staff, 'Sorry, I can't afford to pay you any more.' To me, that's not on, it's wrong in an area like this where more than half of our children have free meals.[10]
  (Female Infant School Head) (15)

- Heads are faced with problems never imagined, e.g., redundancy. How could I make a colleague of long standing redundant? Why should I have to do it ?
  (Male Primary School Head) (61)

- There is considerable moral conflict when it comes to teacher employment or redundancy. I have responsibility to the gover-nors for the effective management of the budget . . . I am acutely sensitive to the feelings of redundant teachers and to the vagaries of selection of those to be made redundant.
  (Male Secondary Head) (44)

- There is a conflict between a wish to retain a 'good' teacher for professional reasons and not being able to, because of cuts in central government funding. External pressures and legalities *force* unprofessional decisions.
  (Male Special School Head) (47)

There was evidence that all of the local education authorities in the north-east region had, before the Education Reform Act, operated funding policies which took account of economic and social disadvantage in particular school localities. Under the new formula funding regime, many of these schools were now designated as 'over staffed' and in budget deficit positions. The new managerialism required that staffing levels should be cut in order to produce 'financial balance'. For the headteachers involved, this was a betrayal of their pupils, the local community and their teaching colleagues. They were faced with the dilemma of responsibility for financial probity on the one hand and professional value judgments and commitments on the other. Such headteachers, as school leaders in a decentralized system of schooling, did not find these situations 'richly fulfilling'. It is instructive to note that Caldwell and Spinks' (1992) celebratory text, *Leading the Self-Managing School* has no index category for 'teacher redundancy', although there is a category for 'restructuring'.

Caldwell and Spinks (1992 p.177) recommend that in situations of school restructuring there should be a policy of 'caring and cushioning'. For the headteachers in deficit budget positions in this study, 'caring and cushioning' appeared to be a hollow management rhetoric given the circumstances in which teacher redundancy was actually taking place in their schools and communities, and to their own colleagues. This obvious disjuncture between the discourse of education management and leadership texts and the practical realities which school leaders face in particular locations provides yet another argument for a corpus of policy scholarship studies. Such scholarship attempts to examine comprehensively and without proselytizing zeal the actual outcomes of schooling reform by, among other things, close attention to the 'voice' of those involved.

Headteachers, Pupils and Parents

In writing about the complexities of relations between education and the good life, John White (1990) has observed:

> It is not surprising that many of us are confused about how, or why, we should lead a moral life, or about how as teachers we can set about devising moral education programmes in school. The confusion in-side ourselves is an internalization of the fissures in our culture. (p.45)

The participants in this study were school leaders who recognized that they had responsibilities to provide some form of moral education for their pupils. At the same time they recognized that attitudes to moral behaviour were diverse and changing and that many of the moral certainties of the past were being questioned or rejected by both the pupils and the parents in the community. To know what was the right educational response to fast-changing moral, social and cultural mores, in which the hegemony of Christian moral codes had been weakened, constituted an important dilemma for the headteachers. Unlike headteachers in schools of religious foundation, the headteachers of state schools had no access to a formal moral charter to guide their decisions on moral dilemmas and moral education.

The moral dilemmas of school leadership in the sector of pupil and parent relations and behaviour had two dimensions, intrinsic and extrinsic. Intrinsic dilemmas were those aspects of pupil and parent behaviour which headteachers believed were undermining moral conceptions of the good life and in relation to which they felt the school must take some countervailing action. Extrinsic dilemmas arose out of the fact that if such problems were made visible and if public action was taken about them, the outcome could be that the school's reputation would suffer and its position in a competitive market for pupils might be weakened. While such dilemmas have always existed for headteachers, concerned on the one hand with appropriate moral and social conduct and on the other hand with the school's reputation and image in the community, the effect of market culture in schooling has sharpened these dilemmas considerably.

In the paradigm case of youthful drug taking, Frank Coffield (1994) has argued:

> . . . the market which pits school against school in the competition for pupils and funding has resulted in heads being unwilling to admit that their school has a drug problem in case its reputation is damaged. And yet each of the 29 schools in my study in the north-east of England had a significant number of pupils taking soft drugs . . . (p.21)

These observations about 'unwillingness to admit' are confirmed by the present study. Only one headteacher in the sample made explicit reference to the dilemmas created by a growing drug culture in the region and of difficulties in finding the educationally right response to it:

- Some of our pupils have exhibited tremendous mood swings consistent with drug or substance abuse. It is difficult to elicit appropriate responses from parents. Most do not want to believe it and are aggressive towards the school for suggesting the possibility . . . It is difficult to find a suitable response from the school. *(Male Secondary Head) (44)*

In one sense, the silence of the other headteachers on this issue also spoke. It spoke of the considerable difficulty which they faced in the tension between open admission of a school and community 'problem' and the market consequences of such an admission. This had not been part of their management training courses.

In addition to this, the impact of changing moral, social and employment conditions in the wider community was being registered by some headteachers as a further intensification of the pressures upon them as school leaders both in primary and in secondary schooling:

- Nowadays an increasing number of children come into school without obvious awareness of what is and what is not 'acceptable' . . . Are headteachers/teachers out of step with society? Even children from so-called 'good' homes can be demanding, aggressive, rude and unable to work/play cooperatively. *(Female Primary School Head) (56)*

- The major change in the role of a headteacher has been the impact of the change of our society which, although gradual, seems to

have been affected more by developments since 1979. Children are now much more aware of their rights; parents are aware of their rights; there are more single parent families, Aids, drugs, sex videos etc. These have impacted quite significantly on young people and this clearly has had an impact upon the school.
(Male Secondary Head) (35)

- Unemployment leads to a variety of social and domestic problems which very definitely and very clearly are spilling over into school . . . The amount of time that is being spent in dealing with that is going up by the term.
(Male Secondary Head) (21)

It is important in this analysis not to become locked into a 'present crisis' perspective and by implication to glorify and romanticize a past golden age of schooling and society. State schools, by reason of their service to a comprehensive social constituency, have always encountered moral and social problems among their pupils and problems of poverty, deprivation and hopelessness. Headteachers of such schools have historically been expected to give moral and professional leadership in responding to these problems. What has changed, however, are the moral codes and moral certainties which headteachers could invoke in constructing a response to the value dilemmas of school leadership.

Issues related to the exclusion of pupils from the school for unacceptable behaviour were a further source of dilemma for the participants in this study. Headteachers found themselves attempting to balance the individual care and welfare of particular pupils with considerations of the general welfare of the majority of the pupils. This dilemma was compounded by the headteachers' understanding that their classroom teachers expected 'strong leadership' about, and 'protection' from, disruptive and challenging pupils. At an implicit level, headteachers were aware that their colleagues expected them 'to deal with', 'get rid of' or otherwise resolve problems related to disruptive pupils. Thus accepting excluded pupils from another school was viewed by classroom teachers in many cases as betraying the 'staff protection and support' role which they expected of a headteacher.

In the heightened market conditions for schooling following the Education Reform Act 1988, the question of pupil exclusions had become a much more difficult issue for headteachers. On the one hand, excluding pupils seen to be disruptive could enhance a school's reputation for maintaining standards of discipline and might have beneficial effects upon its learning culture and ultimately on its league table ranking of examination and test results. On the other hand, too many exclusions might begin to construct a community image of a difficult, and possibly failing school. These dilemmas, involving as they did the school governors, the parents and social services agencies, were becoming sharper for some headteachers:

- If an excluded child cannot return to the school which has excluded him, then another school must take him. If I am that school concerned, how do I protect my staff from the severe failure of other schools? How do I help the child?
  (Male Secondary Head) (46)

- This is a caring school which, in such circumstances, would wish to build the self-esteem of a damaged child and demonstrate that gaining attention is not dependent on antisocial and aggressive behaviour. This approach has to be balanced against the need to provide a safe and productive working environment for the rest of the pupils.
  (Male Secondary Head) (44)

- Is it [exclusion] all we have left? If we exclude, this goes against everything I believe in. How can I help a child who is not in school? If parents do not value school then has exclusion any value?
  (Male Primary School Head) (58)

There was also a moral and professional dilemma—or a series of dilemmas for headteachers when considering pupil exclusion. Headteachers generally recognized that disruptive and antisocial behaviour arose out of difficulties in the pupil's family circumstances caused by complex interpersonal, social and economic conditions. Care in the school might be one of the very few sources of support for such 'damaged' pupils. Exclusion from school would therefore be, from the viewpoint of the pupil, another experience of rejection. However, in the institutional conditions of a school the principle of unconditional care which might operate in individual counselling situations was not an option for the headteachers. There had to be conditions (moral, social and interpersonal) for continued membership of the school as a community. The dilemma for the headteachers was that leadership in defining these conditions for membership was expected of them by the governors, the teachers and the pupils in the school. For those headteachers who were particularly sensitive to the personal care of their pupils, this was a heavy responsibility.

The moral fissures in contemporary culture to which White (1990) has referred, make the responsibility for giving moral and social leadership a more difficult enterprise for modern headteachers. It is obviously tempting in these circumstances to retreat from the moral aspects of school leadership and concentrate instead upon school finance, managing and marketing—the visible performance indicators of success. Problematic aspects of pupil and parent behaviour can be devolved, at least in secondary schools, to specialist professionals in pastoral care and home-school relationships.[11] Some headteachers, however, remained confident that the traditional moral and spiritual responsibilities of their role could and should be maintained in changing circumstances:

- Headteachers have indeed a responsibility to ensure the moral and spiritual development of young people. This is not new. It has always been understood and was formally enshrined in the 1944 Act and re-affirmed in the 1988 Act.
  (Male Secondary Head) (36)

Such confidence however was not typical of the majority of headteachers. While they could all cite evidence of the moral and social positives of pupil and parent attitudes and behaviour,[12] this was balanced by evidence of the negatives. Such negatives included an awareness that individual self-interest on the part of a sector of pupils and parents was on the increase. How headteachers should respond to this, given the absence of any consensual moral codes about community and public good in the wider society, posed a value dilemma for them as school leaders.

The constituents of social and moral solidarity appeared to be weakening in many localities, from the perspective of these headteachers, often as the economic base of the community was collapsing or weakening. In these situations it was apparent that headteachers in state schools faced greater difficulties than their colleagues in schools of religious foundation. As will be seen in the next chapter, headteachers of Catholic schools in particular believed that the core values of Catholic schooling remained an important base for moral cohesion in difficult times.

On the Moral and Ethical Education of State School Leaders

Headteachers in English state schools have been the heirs of a moral and religious culture of school leadership formed over a long historical period. To adapt Bourdieu and Passeron's (1977) concept of cultural capital, it could be said that English school headship has traditionally been endowed with a moral and spiritual capital derived from the past. In the period of Christian hegemony, headteachers, in both their personal and professional formation, were socialized into the spiritual and moral codes of various religious denominations. They carried forward their own educational experience which in turn informed their professional activities as the chief agents of spiritual and moral transmission to the next generation. In more secular times, these processes of socialization and formation of headteachers as school leaders have become more pluralist and differentiated. In addition to moral and ethical codes derived from various religious and humanist cultures, many contemporary headteachers have been educated in value questions in schooling through the medium of courses in teacher education concerned with 'principles in education', 'moral education', 'ideas of great educators', 'value issues in education' and courses in the philosophy of education.

There is now a sense in contemporary English state schooling that the moral and spiritual capital of leadership which has been a cultural resource for school leaders in the past is weakening because the sources for its renewal are also weakening. The cultural inputs from religious tradition and commitment are now more limited in scope. Reforms in teacher education, which have on the one hand reduced the number of colleges of religious foundation and on the other hand have excised 'theory' in favour of 'competencies' in all teacher education institutions, have resulted in a depowering of the values education of the next generation of school leaders. The irony in this situation is that moral, ethical and professional value dilemmas in school leadership have probably never been as sharp and complex as they are now.

In preparing individuals for school headship an emphasis upon finance, management and marketing is clearly insufficient, if society expects schools to have moral and ethical purposes. The difficulty in the present situation is that a new generation of school leaders is coming to power having had much less exposure to a moral and ethical cultural tradition or to a professional education which focuses seriously upon these questions. The socialization of competency-based courses of teacher 'training', followed by subsequent courses in management 'training' represents a serious and literal devaluation of the moral and ethical preparation of future and current headteachers.

Fullan (1993) has argued that a sense of moral purpose has to be recovered in schools but that certain skills and forms of professional development are necessary for the effective realization of this:

> Without moral purpose, aimlessness and fragmentation prevail.
> Without change agentry, moral purpose stagnates.[13]

The headteachers in this research recognized a need for professional support in dealing with value issues and issues of moral purpose in school leadership. For some headteachers, courses with a 'values' focus seemed appropriate:

- Would certainly appreciate a course on moral philosophy coupled to analytical sessions examining my own dilemmas and those of others.
  (Male Primary School Head) (62)

- Something which allowed the examination of pluralist viewpoints and focused on a critical analysis of those viewpoints . . . would enable heads to crystallize their own value-judgments and enable them to resolve moral conflict as an intrinsic part of their role.
  (Female Primary School Head) (48)

- There is a need here to set up courses for headteachers and policy makers to help to develop a common understanding of the dilemmas and possible ways out.
  (Male Secondary Head) (53)

In addition to continuing professional development in the form of courses provided by higher education institutions, LEAs and other agencies, head-teachers wanted more opportunities and spaces for discussion and reflection with their colleagues. There was evidence throughout this inquiry that head-teachers valued the support which they had received from informal groupings or clusters of headteachers in various localities and from their own professional associations.

In analyzing the culture and work conditions of teachers and headteachers in English schooling at this time, a particular irony and contradiction is detectable. Work intensification for teachers and headteachers has increased dramatically and yet at the same time, the notion of the 'reflective practitioner' has emerged as the desired goal of both initial teacher education and continuing professional development. Everard and Morris (1990) recommend that 'every manager should constantly reflect on the ethics of his or her conduct'.[14] For the headteachers in this study the problem was to find the time and the spaces for such reflection. Many headteachers asserted that the intense work pressures of contemporary school leadership (even with the support of a senior management team) had resulted in a deterioration of the quality of their personal lives and had led to a neglect of their own family and domestic responsibilities.

The headteachers in state schools, in general, did not feel well equipped to deal with the range and complexity of the moral and ethical dilemmas which confronted them. If leadership was expected of them on these matters they were less sure that they had the professional resources to make appropriate responses but they were certain that the necessary spaces for discussion and reflection on these issues were not available to them. If this situation is placed in a socio-historical and socio-cultural perspective, a remarkable transformation in the nature of school leadership in England becomes apparent. From a position in which school leadership was primarily defined in terms of its capacity to give moral and ethical direction and was culturally and professionally resourced to do so, contemporary school leadership appears weakened on both counts. It is now much more difficult in a pluralist and secular society to give leadership on moral and ethical questions. If, at the same time, headteachers are not academically and professionally resourced to deal with such questions then the problematics of the situation are compounded. School leadership has become in an important sense, devalued. The combination of management and market preoccupations when placed alongside this change in the domain of values, may result in the final triumph of commodification over moral purpose in schooling. It may result in the dislocation of English state schooling from its originating religious and moral culture and its relocation within the instrumental and amoral culture of the market place.

Many contemporary texts on education management and leadership use a discourse of 'leadership', 'vision' and 'mission'. Bottery (1993) lists the characteristics of the educational leader as 'critical, transformative, visionary, educative, empowering, liberating, personally ethical, organizationally ethical, responsible' (p.186). Beck and Murphy (1993, p.199) argue that American school principals 'must lead in complicated environments and complex situations in which actions have far-reaching, long-term political, social, cultural and moral implications.' The rhetoric of the qualities which headteachers and school principals should display, especially on matters to do with values, is becoming part of the check-list culture of education management studies. Bottery's listing of these qualities constitutes a description not only of the ideal school leader but also of a person who must be seriously considered for canonization as an educational saint.

Listing the virtues of the transformative or moral school leader is one thing. Analyzing in detail the moral, ethical and professional dilemmas which they face in their work keeps this listing activity grounded in reality. The most fundamental stage in the analysis, however, is to ask questions about the cultural and professional resourcing of such virtues. How do school leaders form and sustain qualities such as vision, professional responsibility, educative potential, moral purpose, and ethical integrity? What are the sources of their own ability to give leadership on complex value issues? Unless one subscribes to a doctrine of essentialism, that leaders are simply born and not made, then questions to do with the moral and ethical resourcing of school leadership have to be faced.

Schools of religious foundation provide one context for pursuing some of these questions. If a cultural transformation is taking place within English state schooling and if there are new challenges for school leaders in those settings, to what extent are formally religious schools affected by the same developments? Are the leaders of such schools in a qualitatively different position because of the existence of more strongly defined and consensual religious and moral codes? Do they have more sources of support to deal with contemporary value dilemmas in schooling? The following chapter attempts to answer some of these questions by analyzing the accounts of headteachers of Catholic schools who participated in the research.

Notes and References

1   Bottery (1993, p.1).
2   Chapter 8 of the Government White Paper, *Choice and Diversity* (1992) reiterated the importance of spiritual and moral development as aims for all maintained schools in England and Wales: 'religious education and collective worship play a major part in promoting the spiritual and moral dimension in schools' (p.37).

   The renewed emphasis of the Secretary of State for Education that this collective act of worship should be primarily Christian in character provoked controversy in 1994 and objections from Jewish and Muslim communities. See *Times Educational Supplement*, 17th June 1994, No.4068. Headteachers of schools in multi-faith areas faced considerable dilemmas arising from legal requirements for daily acts of Christian worship when, in many areas, multi-faith celebrations had emerged as the appropriate multicultural response.

3   The particular impact of Muslim religious and moral culture may be noted here. Many Muslim communities in England have insisted on priority for religious and moral teaching which recognizes the integrity and importance of Islam.

4   Simon and Chitty (1993, pp.28–9).

5   Chubb and Moe (1992, p.28).

6   Caldwell and Spinks (1992, p.203).

7   *Ibid.*, p.182.

8   In the discourse of the new managerialism, restructuring is a favoured description for processes which often result in redundancy.

9   The 'LMS man' was an official sent by the County Treasurer's Department to advise headteachers in small primary schools about the new budgeting realities of devolved management.

10 In the English school system, the number of children receiving free school meals is taken as an indicator of poverty in the locality. This school served a community with high levels of poverty and unemployment.

11 Devolution of responsibility for moral issues in schooling, like devolution of budgeting responsibility, can have positive and negative consequences. The positive consequences of having a team of staff concerned with moral and social welfare of the pupils is clear. The negative consequence may be that the position of school leader becomes distanced from these issues as central concerns of education.

12 These positions included work in the community, commitment to charitable causes and evidence of environmental concern. An awareness of international poverty and distress was apparent and, in general, there were generous responses to these situations from pupils and parents.

13 Fullan (1993, p.18); Fullan also defines change agentry as 'being self-conscious about the nature of change' (p.12).

14 Everard and Morris (1990, p.9). However, they also observe that 'this is not a book about educational and managerial philosophy and ethics: it is about effective practice' (p.11). This illustrates very neatly the technism of education management texts which suppose that 'effective practice' in education *can be* separated out from philosophy and ethics.

Chapter 9

The Dilemmas of Catholic Headteachers

Bryk *et al.* (1993), in a major study of the culture of Catholic schooling in the USA, have argued that such schools are informed by 'an inspirational ideology' (p.301) which makes them qualitatively different from public (state) schools. This inspirational ideology celebrates the primacy of the spiritual and moral life; the dignity of the person; the importance of community and moral commitments to caring, social justice and the common good. Vatican II, in the view of Bryk *et al.*, produced not only a new role for the Church in the modern world, but a new conception of the Catholic school and of Catholic education in which enhanced importance has been given to respect for persons, active community and a strong social ethic of citizen responsibility in a national and an international sense. The argument of *The Catholic School and the Common Good* is, among other things, that Catholic schools are culturally and morally distinctive as educational institutions:

> Two important ideas shape life in Catholic schools, making them very different from their organizational counterparts in the public sector: Christian personalism and subsidiarity. Christian personalism calls for humaneness in the myriad of mundane social interactions that make up daily life . . . it signifies a moral conception of social behaviour in a just community . . . subsidiarity means that the schools reject a purely bureaucratic conception of an organization . . . Decentralization of school governance is not chosen purely because it is more efficient . . . rather decentralization is predicated in the view that personal dignity and human respect are advanced when work is organized in small communities where dialogue and collegiality may flourish.[1]

These at least are the commitments of the formal inspirational ideology of the new Catholic schooling in America, although the extent to which these virtues are actually realized will, it is acknowledged, vary from school to school.

The critical agents for the translation of these formal commitments into lived school experience are, in the view of Bryk *et al.*, the school principals. Catholic school principalship in American has been strongly influenced by the spiritual and moral capital of the various religious orders which have provided most of the leadership positions until recently.[2] There are therefore also qualitative differences in the nature of school leadership:

> Although much of the work of Catholic school principals is similar to that of their public school counterparts, we conclude that the nature of school leadership has a distinctive character here. Both public and Catholic school principals value academic excellence and students' educational attainment. For principals in Catholic schools, however, there is also an important spiritual dimension to leadership that is apt to be absent from the concerns of public school administrators. This spirituality is manifest in the language of community that principals use to describe their schools and in their actions as they work to achieve the goal of community.[3]

Although lay Catholics are increasingly taking over school leadership positions, such lay principals are the heirs of a tradition of spirituality established by religious orders and it is not uncommon for them to have received their own education and professional formation in institutions provided by such orders.

The distinctiveness of Catholic schooling culture and of its educational leadership has been commented on, in a variety of contexts, by Hornsby-Smith (1978), Flynn (1985), Egan (1988), Angus (1988), O'Keeffe (1992) and McLaren (1993). In all cases these analyses have noted the tensions and dilemmas that occur when Catholic schooling values (which are themselves in a process of change) encounter situations of rapid social, cultural and ideological change. The Catholic schooling system has been historically relatively insulated in various ways from the changes in secular culture in America, Australia and Britain. Catholic schools in these societies were constructed as defensive citadels for minority communities anxious to preserve the transmission of the faith and of its spiritual and moral codes and symbols. How this relatively insulated educational tradition is responding to the challenges of individualism, competitiveness, new managerialism, market culture and the commodification of knowledge is a matter of considerable research interest. For McLaren (1993) the issues are clear:

> It is crucial that we continue to explore how Catholic schooling, by virtue of its ineffably vast and unique universe of signifying structures, plays a fundamental role in the socialization of students[4] . . . A pedagogy that is not grounded in a preferential option for the disempowered and disenfranchised—'the wretched of the earth'—only transforms students into vessels for the preparation of new forms of fascism and a grand epic of destruction.[5]

In referring here to the preferential option for the poor, McLaren is emphasizing the historical commitment of Catholic schooling to the service of poor immigrant and ethnic minority communities and to its particular mission in inner city localities in a number of societies. However, the Catholic population in various contexts has become more prosperous and socially differentiated over time so that the mission of Catholic schooling is less focused and unitary than it once was. As Catholic schools respond to contemporary market values in education and to the issues of institutional survival which they generate, a conflict of values is likely to result. Stated in the starkest form, it could be argued that there is little market yield or return for schools which continue to operate a preferential option for the poor. In a market economy for schooling the imperatives of visible and measurable success, financial balance and good public image all combine against commitment to 'customers' who are lacking in both cultural and economic capital. How will the leaders of Catholic schools respond to this dilemma? Will headteachers and school principals work to maintain the integrity of Catholic schooling values and commitments in the new market place for education? Will they be able to balance moral purpose and institutional survival?

In examining the British Government's 1992 White Paper, *Choice and Diversity*, Richard Pring (1993) has argued that its philosophy is incompatible with the distinctive Catholic idea of the nature and purpose of schools. In particular, in placing the market and individual self-interest at the centre of educational arrangements, the reforms undermine Catholic educational values and practices which emphasize the importance of community and of concern for the common good:

> The point is that the market model of individuals all pursuing their own respective interests leads not to an improvement of the general good but only to an improvement of the positional good of some vis-à-vis other competitors and also to a deterioration of the overall situation . . . (p.8)

The thirty-four Catholic headteacher accounts which were generated during the fieldwork for this study represented the responses of fifteen headteachers in the north-east region and nineteen working in other regions. These headteachers were asked, with varying degrees of explicitness, to indicate their responses to the changing culture of English schooling in relation to the 'special mission' of the Catholic school. In order to provide the appropriate value framework in which these responses could be located, the participants were first invited to make explicit, as school leaders, their understanding of the distinctive objectives and commitments of Catholic schooling.

The Special Mission of the Catholic School

Writing of Catholic schooling, Bryk *et al.* (1993) have asserted that 'the underlying values of the institution—shared by its members—provide the animating force for the entire enterprise' (p.279). This formal position was endorsed by all of the Catholic headteachers but from a research viewpoint what was more significant was the way in which these Catholic school leaders articulated and defined 'the underlying values'. The predominant view was that the special mission of Catholic schools was expressed in three interrelated features, i.e., Gospel values, the teachings of Christ and the nurture of community. These features were articulated by primary and secondary school headteachers:

- We represent the only 'face of Christ' for many pupils. We are the new Church—and possibly the Hope of tomorrow . . . [against] a vast depressive value-for-money culture being focused on our pupils. Catholic schools are about evangelization and mission. They are about community . . . 'our' school is a protector of the real values. RC schools must uphold such commitment.
  *(Male Secondary Head) (63)**

- The special mission of a Catholic school is to have Christ at the centre of all we do in school and to give the pupils in our care opportunities to take part in spiritual growth . . . in a living, worshipping community . . . I firmly believe it is my prime responsibility to keep God at the heart of our school, permeating everything.
  (Female Primary School Head) (64)

- To change and challenge society's norms and ideals based on Christ's teaching and example . . . To work with Catholic parents and the parish to provide an education compatible with Christian principles.
  (Female Primary School Head) (68)

- To demonstrate that Christian values and beliefs are relevant and of use in the modern world. To help young people have a sense of justice, rights and responsibilities which transcends pragmatism . . . To help them towards a knowledge that there is a God who loves them and gives them worth.
  (Male Secondary Head) (71)

In these terms, the underlying values of Catholic schooling were defined formally by many of the headteachers in this inquiry. However, all of them recognized that this was a *discourse of mission*. The realization of this mission was not straightforward but dependent upon: their own leadership qualities; support from parents, governors and the parish; the commitments of teachers,

* *Note* Numbers in brackets used after quotations refer to the code numbers of the headteachers' accounts.

not all of whom were Catholics; and, the response of pupils, many from nominally Catholic homes and an increasing proportion from non-Catholic backgrounds. At the same time some of the headteachers believed that wider social, cultural and ideological changes in English society were antithetical to the special mission of Catholic schools.

In addition to the prime value commitments already indicated, many of the participants saw a social ethic of 'serving others' as central to the mission of the Catholic school. In many accounts this social ethic was implicit in the strong discourse and imagery of educational community and wider community. In other accounts, it was explicitly referred to:

- To find God in all things and to serve others are at the heart of what we try to do.
  (Male Secondary Head) (72)

- To provide an overtly Christian education within an overtly Christian environment and with particular concern for the 'poor' [of all types].
  (Male Secondary Head) (76)

- The total development of individuals to full potential—spiritual, intellectual, social, moral, physical. It is not self-fulfilment but the development and use of our gifts to serve God through others.
  (Male Secondary Head) (73)

There was a division of opinion among the Catholic headteachers participating in this study as to whether or not the realization of the special mission of the Catholic school was becoming more difficult to achieve in contemporary conditions. Some headteachers took the view that the challenges that Catholic schools faced had resulted in more explicit discussion and clarification of underlying values and mission and that the schools were stronger in their identity from these processes. An enhanced culture of partnership with governors, parents and the parish was also seen to have reinvigorated and empowered the schools in respect to their spiritual and moral purposes. A sense of confidence existed among some of these Catholic school leaders who believed that the defined spiritual and moral commitments of Catholic education were attractive to a wide constituency of parents, i.e., not only to Catholic parents. Other headteachers were less confident that their schools were actually realizing their special mission in terms of real effects upon the beliefs and practices of their pupils. They recognized considerable contemporary impediments to the successful translation of formal mission into lived practice. For these headteachers such impediments were located both within Catholic schools and in the wider society. The participants, however, whether confident or less confident on this issue, were largely in agreement that Catholic school leaders faced a whole range of moral, ethical and professional dilemmas of a kind not encountered by their predecessors. These dilemmas ranged from the specifics of individual moral behaviour to wider cultural, structural and political issues. Taken together they provided considerable challenges to Catholic headteachers as school leaders.[6]

Catholic School Leadership and Changing Moral Codes

Referring to a new culture of religious and moral teaching in Catholic schools, Bryk *et al.* (1993) have argued that:

> The spirit of Vatican II has softened Catholic claims to universal truth with a call for continuing public dialogue about how we live as people . . . This principle implies a very different conception of religious instruction. In contrast to the pre-Vatican II emphasis on indoctrination in the 'mind of the Church', contemporary religion classes now emphasise dialogue and encounter. Drawing on systematic Christian thought, teachers encourage students to discuss and reflect on their lives . . . (p.302)

While many liberal Catholic educators and school leaders have welcomed this greater openness about religious and moral questions, this new culture also generates its own problems and dilemmas. In a pluralist and secular society, the existence of an absolute and clear-cut religious and moral credo provides an anchor for teaching and for moral decisions. Where the credo is less absolute and clear cut, the dilemmas for teachers and parents become more challenging. This situation is no longer about the application of an absolute moral code to a given human situation. School leaders, teachers and parents have to engage in principled moral reasoning about different human dilemmas in which some degree of personal autonomy and situational adjustment is expected by the participants.

At the level of the Catholic school, leadership on these complex issues is looked to from the headteacher, among others. The headteachers in this study had encountered dilemmas of moral behaviour relating to pupils, parents and teachers. They were aware that some form of moral leadership was expected from them but they were now more uncertain than in the past about the nature and direction of that moral leadership.

Many of the dilemmas which the headteachers faced arose from a disjuncture between official Catholic moral teaching and the mores of contemporary society:

- The gap between traditional Catholic images of 'the family' and the reality of children's experience of single parents, violence, abuse, crime.
  (Female Primary School Head) (66)

- Increasingly, Catholic staff are divorced, separated or living together. As a leader of a Catholic community where do I draw the line between the church's teaching and my compassion as a Christian?
  (Female Infant School Head) (75)

- Trying to reason with 6th formers who are active sexually—trying to give any moral teaching when the answer comes back, 'My mother can have her boyfriend at home but won't let me bring mine home.' The double standards of parents who expect us to preach morality but do not give the example.
  (Female Secondary Head) (80)

- The church's teaching on sexual behaviour and values is promulgated within the school so that contraception, as discussed openly in society in general, is not really addressed. Inevitably, youngsters at the school become pregnant—and some have abortions. Others go on to produce more children (in or out of marriage) without consideration of the long-term demands of parenting and often beyond their capacity to cope.
  (Male Secondary Head) (77)

While it was open to these Catholic headteachers to try to displace such sharp moral dilemmas to the school governors, the priest or school chaplain or to religious education teachers and pastoral care staff, their own professional conception of school leadership prevented this from being an easy way out. The community of school parents who might have been looked to as a source of support in coming to a reasoned and consensual position on these moral dilemmas was not an unproblematic ally. Parents' own double standards and disagreements about the appropriate 'Catholic' response to particular situations were complicating factors. In particular, some headteachers noted that community, partnership and dialogue approaches to trying to resolve difficult moral and behavioural situations were being threatened by parents' more assertive use of legal procedures:

- Parents' knowledge of, and awareness of, their legal rights is in conflict with the concept of working together and ideas of mutual support and reconciliation.
  (Female Primary School Head) (66)

- Parents who have become aware of legal procedures and approach solicitors without first attempting dialogue with the school—increasing in respect of racial issues and serious behavioural issues.
  (Female Secondary Head) (69)

It became apparent during the course of this study that 'community' as a central value and symbol of Catholic schooling was under attack from the ethic of possessive individualism, from market forces and from a customer culture reinforced by quick recourse to legal procedures.[7]

In his ethnographic study of the conservative Catholic school of St Ryan, McLaren (1993) noted that:

> In essence, the teacher defined—in fact, *created*—a moral order. The parameters that defined Catholic behaviour were thus drawn up and the students now had a criterion with which to judge subsequent behaviour as right [Catholic] or wrong [non-Catholic]. (p.107)

These certainties were no longer available to the Catholic headteachers participating in this study. Both the spiritual and moral orders of the schools were now open to discussion and dialogue among pupils, parents and teachers. For most of the research participants, who were lay Catholics rather than priests, or religious leaders, spiritual and moral leadership in these circumstances was demanding. They were aware of their own professional needs for staff development and support in dealing with changing moral codes and such support was looked for in courses provided by the Diocese, the Catholic Education Service and professional organizations such as The Association of Catholic Schools and Colleges.[8] The headteachers also recognized the strategic importance of 'good priests' and 'good school chaplains' in assisting to find a basis for dealing with the moral dilemmas of school leadership. In these cultural support networks, Catholic headteachers had access to resources for dealing with the challenges of moral leadership and in this sense they were in a relatively stronger position than their colleagues in state schools.

Bernstein (1990) has suggested that 'Christianity is less a religion of certainty [faith cannot be taken for granted, it must be continuously won] than a religion of ambiguity and paradox' (p.149). The culture of traditional Catholicism had been constructed to reduce ambiguity and paradox by the strong framing of its teaching. Post Vatican II Catholicism has resulted in greater realizations of ambiguity and paradox in moral codes. Leadership in Catholic schools has therefore involved headteachers in a continuing struggle with these ambiguities.

Catholic Schools and Community: Admissions and Exclusions

> As Christians we aim to create a loving, worshipping community where joys and sorrows, successes and set-backs will be shared . . . We aim to provide a curriculum permeated by the Gospel spirit . . .

This statement, taken from the mission document of one of the participating Catholic schools in this inquiry,[9] represents important elements of the 'inspirational ideology' of Catholic schooling. A high aspiration for the creation of a loving and worshipping community is set forth as the educational ideal to be worked for.

On trying to realize this ideal in their particular school settings, Catholic headteachers had to face many impediments and dilemmas. Among these were the difficult issues of school admissions and exclusions. Such issues were fundamental to the constitution and nature of the Catholic school as a community. Admission decisions regulated who might be allowed to join the community and to benefit from its academic, spiritual and moral culture. Exclusion involved painful decisions about temporary or permanent 'excommunication' from the school community.

Dilemmas of admission related to conflicts in wishing to be 'open' to the Catholic communities and to other faith communities in the locality without weakening the Catholic ethos of the school.[10] While this was the ostensible issue, it also encoded a whole range of other issues relating to the social class and ability characteristics of pupils and issues of race and ethnicity. In other words, a tension existed between a relatively open and comprehensive policy on school admissions and an awareness that certain amounts of selectivity by faith commitment, social class and ability level would be in the long-term interests of the school in a competitive market for schooling.

The disjunctures between the principles of formal mission statements and the realities of admissions policies were clear to a number of the participants:

- When rejecting admissions applications are we displaying Gospel values?
  (Male Primary School Head) (67)

- Coping with increasing numbers of SEN pupils in mainstream school (especially behavioural/emotional needs) creates much tension and moral dilemma. We are under-resourced and inappropriately trained and skilled to cope. The mission is under threat.
  (Female Secondary Head) (82)

- Preference in admissions at Year 7 is sometimes given to the most able rather than the most deserving, in order to maintain good results.
  (Male Secondary Head) (77)

If dilemmas of admissions exercised the moral and professional conscience of Catholic school leaders, issues of exclusion from school were even sharper. Catholic headteachers could find themselves torn between a 'prodigal son/daughter' imperative with its implications of forgiveness and reconciliation and a responsibility to the whole community imperative with implications for firm discipline and hard decisions if necessary. The act of exclusion has powerful symbolic and cultural meanings within Catholic schooling. To the extent that such schools explicitly represented themselves as loving and caring communities permeated by Gospel values, the act of pupil exclusion, as an act of apparent rejection, was discordant with this value culture.

Bernstein (1977) and McLaren (1993) have pointed to the significance of consensual rituals of various types in constituting and renewing the moral and social orders of schools and in reaffirming the idea of the school as a community of shared values and practice. Catholic schools in general have an educational culture strongly marked by ritual and symbolic forms derived from the symbolic capital of Catholicism as a religion. Permeating such schools in the practice of the faith is a discourse and an imagery of fall and reconciliation, of sin and forgiveness, and of justice and mercy. But just as the Catholic Church has rituals of inclusion and acceptance as well as rituals of exclusion and rejection, so too do Catholic schools. The modern and enlightened practice of both the church and the schools has been to place the emphasis upon the former, but the latter still exists and may be used if the circumstances require it.

Some of the Catholic headteachers in this study were finding that the circumstances in their school and localities were requiring the serious consideration of exclusion despite the negative spiritual, moral and cultural associations which it carried. With the removal of certain forms of traditional disciplinary sanction in Catholic schools, the act of exclusion had taken on a new significance but at the same time challenged school leaders who claimed that community informed by Gospel values was a defining feature of Catholic education. Because such headteachers had a keen awareness of this dissonance and because they realized that most cases for the exclusion of individual pupils arose out of wider interpersonal and social difficulties in the life of such pupils, they encountered moral and professional dilemmas. These dilemmas were sometimes compounded by pressure brought to bear upon headteachers by groups of parents or groups of teachers who claimed that the exclusion of certain pupils was necessary for the common good of the school. In these circumstances such headteachers felt a leadership responsibility as the guardian of the school's moral and spiritual integrity in making judgments about individual deviance and the common good:

- Exclusions are a very difficult area especially for Roman Catholic schools because by exclusion we put a child out of our pastoral care and the Church itself is 'opportunity for forgiveness'. However there is also the claim of Justice and Peace for others in the community, other pupils and the staff. Staff feel that we don't support them if we hold on to their problems.
  (Female Secondary Head) (82)

- There is a danger of casting a child adrift. Those excluded often lack parental support/control in any case.
  (Male Secondary Head) (78)

- The dilemma is care for the individual pupil versus showing the pupil that there must be boundaries . . . There is the dilemma of the racial imbalance in exclusions (e.g., black pupils are 10 per cent of the school population but 20 per cent of exclusions). *(Male Secondary Head) (76)*

It was noted in Chapter 8 that even within the confidential and confessional context of the research inquiry, headteachers were silent on some issues which were known to be real problems in their schools and localities. For the sample of schools in the north-east region, drug-taking was a paradigm case of headteacher silence. The sample of Catholic schools was a national one (*albeit* small) including major metropolitan areas as well as small town and rural areas. Despite this wider social and cultural constituency it is remarkable that very few references were made to racial or ethnic issues as those which posed dilemmas for Catholic school leaders. The explicit acknowledgment of the racial imbalance in pupil exclusions in an urban Catholic school, given in account 76 above, broke this culture of silence.

The culture of silence on racial issues in the participating Catholic schools might be explained in various ways, including the stance that for Catholic headteachers there is 'no problem here'.[11] However, as O'Keeffe (1992) notes:

The demographic changes which have taken place in British society are manifested in all aspects of British life including the pupil population of Catholic schools . . . Catholic schools face the need for development of good practice in multicultural education, the adoption of anti-racist stances and the demands of a multi-faith intake. (pp.42–3)

It seems improbable that Catholic urban schools are insulated from problems of locality racism or institutional racism and therefore another explanation for the silence on these issues might be that Catholic headteachers find it a discomforting issue. Official Catholic teaching is quite clear that racism, in all its forms, offends against Christian values, ideas of community and respect for persons, and Catholic schools have been exhorted to generate an educational ethos which resists racism. The relative silence of the Catholic school leaders on this issue does, however, suggest that there must be more than exhortation if an effective anti-racist stance is to become a priority commitment for Catholic headteachers. Mukherjee (1984) in a challenging statement to all white educators has stated that 'your racism has been your silence . . .' (p.6).[12] To the extent that such an observation is true for this present study it would imply that Catholic school leaders (and other school leaders) must be prepared to 'give leadership' in breaking the culture of silence about racism.

Catholic Schools and Community: Grant-maintained Status

The Education Reform Act 1988 and Education (Schools) Act 1992 have set in train a transformation of our school system. They have created more choice and wider opportunities as a springboard to higher standards. Central to this has been the development of school autonomy, both within schemes of local management and increasingly as GM (grant-maintained) schools outside local government.[13]

The official discourse of the government White Paper, *Choice and Diversity: a new framework for schools* (1992), made it quite clear to all governors, parents and headteachers that a strong political imperative existed to encourage maintained schools to opt-out of local government jurisdiction and to choose 'autonomous', grant-maintained status. To add economic incentives to these political imperatives, parents and governors were assured in 1993 that the grant-maintained school 'received extra money to reflect its particular circumstances and responsibilities compared with other schools'[14] and in 1994 large scale newspaper advertising was undertaken by the Department For Education with headings such as 'Three-quarters of grant-maintained secondary schools have employed additional teachers'[15] and 'The majority of grant-maintained schools have increased spending on books and equipment'.[16]

For Catholic school governors and parents, the financial incentives associated with the option for grant-maintained status constituted a particular form of educational temptation. As Simon and Chitty (1993) noted:

> The most decisive of financial inducements so far offered lies in capital grants (for new buildings etc.). Several years' experience have now made it abundantly clear that schools becoming GMS have been treated far more generously than county schools. In 1991 for instance GMS schools got an average four times as much in the way of capital grants than mainstream county schools . . . (p.44)

As the Catholic community in England and Wales had significant financial responsibilities for the capital costs of the Catholic schooling system, the grant-maintained option became a major focus for debate in the 1990s. For some Catholics, the grant-maintained option appeared to be a form of manna from heaven, providing extra resources to build upon and expand the excellences of Catholic education. For other Catholics, the financial inducements were the equivalent of thirty pieces of silver,[17] encouraging Catholic schools to abandon community values for individual self-interest. In other words, the Catholic educational community in England was deeply divided as to what course of action would be in the best interests of the pupils, the future of Catholic schooling and of the integrity of its special mission.

In order to give educational leadership in this contested situation, the Catholic hierarchy through the agency of the Catholic Education Service gave its formal response to the White Paper. This response took up the moral and professional dilemma of common good versus individual self-interest and implicitly criticized the GMS option for advancing the latter:

We do not in principle oppose increased independence and self management for schools. However, the GM option is more than this. It intensifies financial and curricular inequalities between schools and creates new inequalities. It also supposes that schools derive their strength from their own autonomy, without any sense of having a wider responsibility (the common good). Moreover there is no reason to believe that the growth of the GM sector will do other than undermine the financial viability and reputation of those schools which remain outside the GM sector.[18]

The official discourse of the Catholic hierarchy, although coded in diplomatic forms, made it clear that they had grave reservations about the autonomous advantages of grant-maintained schools and perceived serious moral dilemmas arising from conflicts between Catholic community values and the values of the GMS option.[19] However, as James Arthur (1994a and 1994b) has demonstrated, Catholic parents and school governors in England were not prepared to accept the voice of the hierarchy as the definitive voice on this issue. Some parents and governors took the view that it was for Catholic parents by a democratic process of balloting to adjudicate the GMS option in particular localities and for particular schools. The ideology of parent power had produced some significant transformations within Catholic schooling culture. In a culture which had been historically characterized by deference to the teachings and advice of an ecclesiastical hierarchy on matters spiritual, moral and social, the 1980s and 1990s had produced a more assertive and differentiated Catholic community.

The headteachers of Catholic schools were caught up in this struggle between hierarchical counsel and parental assertion, and in the dilemmas arising from conflicts between a construct of special mission as community values and a construct of special mission as providing the best educational resources for Catholic pupils. The most characteristic response of the participants was a recognition of the moral and professional dilemmas posed by the GMS option without much indication of how they, as school leaders, thought that these dilemmas should be resolved:

- The option of GMS presents a major philosophical dilemma. If a school opts out, does it benefit to the detriment of others; if the school stays with the LEA are the pupils not receiving their due desserts?
  (Male Secondary Head) (40)

There were few robust condemnations of the GMS option by these Catholic headteachers and where indications of personal disapproval were given, they were signalled in a qualified and tentative way:

- I feel there is a danger of enjoying and capitalizing on the different image and possible more elite image which GMS would probably

bring with it. This would be giving in to and going along with an essentially competitive rather than cooperative approach.
(Male Secondary Head) (78)

- Grant-maintained status has my gut reaction of, no way! However, faced with the question, would I resign as head if there was a vote to opt-out, I have to admit that I would stay.
(Female Primary School Head) (64)

- My beliefs are opposed to GM status but I realize that if and when other schools in the locality opt for GM status, I will be left with no alternative.
(Male Primary School Head) (67)

It seems clear from these responses that many of the Catholic headteachers, while fully recognizing the moral dilemmas posed in the option for grant-maintained status, also recognized the power relations in which such a decision was structurally located. If the authority of the Catholic hierarchy had been opposed by groups of parents and governors on this issue, then the authority of the headteacher as school leader could similarly be challenged if the head was explicitly opposed to such a change. The dilemma for the headteachers was that they were aware of expectations for leadership on this major policy issue and yet they were cautious about giving such leadership if this meant expressing an authoritative professional and moral stance. Formally, this was a decision for the parents and therefore it was possible to say that constitutional leadership involved facilitating the correct procedures for parental decision making rather than articulating a personal professional preference.

In a difficult policy dilemma position such as this, Catholic intellectual and cultural capital could provide resources for headteachers in a mode of analysis popularly designated as Jesuitical reasoning. This cultural resource was used, to good effect, by one participant who not only recognized the dilemmas of the grant maintained option but wished to resolve them in terms of valid Catholic practice:

- The major criticism of GMS must be that it can only be introduced into an individual school by disadvantaging some other part of the service. This must represent a serious moral dilemma—particularly when there are significant funding and educational advantages on offer to the school that successfully obtains grant-maintained status—and those advantages must be at another school's expense . . . There is also, of course, a moral dilemma for the Bishop of a Diocese in terms of grant-maintained schools because, in Canon Law, it is incumbent upon him to provide for the Catholic community education which is at least as good, or better than, alternative education that is available in the area. A criticism of the

grant-maintained principle has been (or is) that it creates a two tier system—presumably based on one tier being better than the other. If the better education is provided by grant-maintained schools and if, under Canon Law, it is incumbent upon the Bishop to provide education comparable with the best, then he would appear to be obliged to support grant-maintained schools—despite the damage that it might cause to other parts of the service.
(Male Secondary Head) (77)

This argument, that the prime responsibility of Catholic educational leaders (bishops, school governors and headteachers) was to ensure that the best possible educational resources were available for the education of Catholic pupils, was echoed by those headteachers who saw no dilemma in the grant-maintained option. Although a minority of the participants in this inquiry, such headteachers took the view that the Catholic schooling system in England included independent and private schools and therefore, by logical extension, the creation of 'state independent schools' in the GMS option presented no major moral or professional dilemmas for Catholic educators.

Catholic educational leadership in the 1980s and 1990s in England has had to face, once again, fundamental dilemmas between notions of the common good and of autonomous advantage. These dilemmas have been crystallized particularly by the specific policy issue of grant-maintained status and by a general increased salience of market values in schooling. The Catholic community appears to have been as divided on these issues as the non-Catholic constituency. In the most recent review of these divisions, James Arthur (1994a) concludes:

The Church's dispute with both government and some of its own members can be located in the differing interpretations of parental rights. The government's stress on parental involvement and choice gives predominance to 'the market' and emphasises individual rights over the rights of the community as a whole. By contrast, the Church's distinctive mission places greater emphasis on the right of the whole Catholic community in determining the future of Catholic schools. The Church does not recognize that the rights of parents and pupils already placed in Catholic schools can override the rights of the whole Catholic community. (p.188)

There are considerable theoretical paradoxes and contradictions which are generated by this situation. On the one hand, an essentially authoritarian and hierarchical leadership claims to speak for the good of the whole Catholic community on educational policy matters. On the other hand groups of school governors and parents claim, through the process of a ballot, to be the democratic voice of the community on a key issue such as grant-maintained status. Objections to the validity and legitimacy of both sets of claims can be made.

What is missing in this contested area of educational policy is the active democratic involvement of the whole Catholic community,[20] informed by a balanced representation of the arguments. Without such involvement, Catholic headteachers as school leaders find themselves, in general, trapped in a network of contradictions.

Catholic Values and Market Values

Bryk *et al.* (1993) have argued that Catholic schools in the USA have historically been engaged in a cultural struggle to balance market concerns (critical to survival) with Catholic values (critical to mission). In other words, Catholic schooling in America has been powerfully shaped both by the influence of market forces and by the influence of an inspirational ideology of Catholic schooling. The sensitivity of American Catholic schools to market values has been the inevitable result of receiving no financial support from public funds. American Catholic schools, unlike their English counterparts, have not been culturally and financially insulated from the market and they have had to demonstrate a responsiveness to clients in a competitive situation. However, Bryk *et al.* (1993) concluded in their major research inquiry:

> Even so, the control of Catholic school operations involves considerably more than market responsiveness to clients. Many important observations about these schools cannot be reconciled in these terms. Market forces cannot explain the broadly shared institutional purpose of advancing social equity or account for the efforts of Catholic educators to maintain inner-city schools (with large non-Catholic enrolments) while facing mounting financial woes. Likewise, market forces cannot easily explain why resources are allocated within schools in a compensatory fashion in order to provide an academic education for every student. Nor can they explain the norms of community that infuse daily life in these schools. (p.300)

The detailed research reported in *Catholic Schools and the Common Good*, while it celebrates the balance achieved between market and mission in Catholic schooling, concludes in sombre terms. Contemporary conditions in America are beginning to demonstrate that market forces, market values and the inexorable circumstances for institutional survival and financial solvency are threatening the historical mission and values of Catholic schooling.

For English Catholic schools in the maintained sector of education this encounter with market forces and market values is a much more recent phenomenon, an experience of the 1980s and 1990s. Previously insulated to a large extent from market forces by state and Diocesan funding, by the historical loyalty of local Catholic communities, and by large pupil enrolments resulting from large Catholic families, Catholic schools were the possessors of a relatively autonomous zone of influence. Within this autonomous zone, Catholic school

leaders could articulate a distinctive mission and set of Catholic values independently of market culture and market values. Bernstein (1990) has pointed
to the crucial importance of structural and cultural boundaries and insulations
in the maintenance of a distinctive mission or voice for cultural institutions
and their agents. However, such boundaries and insulations are in a constant
process of change and:

> It follows that, as the strength of the insulation between categories
> varies, so will the categories vary in their relation to each other and
> so will their space, their identity and 'voice'. (p.24)

This precisely describes, in formal theoretical terms, the changing relation between Catholic schools and the market place. These two categories, previously
with strong insulations from each other in English schooling have, as a result
of the education reforms of the 1980s, been brought into a much closer relationship. With local management of schools, open enrolments, a more
differentiated Catholic community, and a lower Catholic birth-rate, such
schools have to operate in a competitive market in education. In other words,
the space, identity and voice of contemporary Catholic schooling is now more
directly challenged by market values then ever before in its history. In these
circumstances the critical question for Catholic school leaders is, can a balance
be found between Catholic values and market values, or will market forces
begin to compromise the integrity of the special mission of Catholic schooling?
Can Gospel values survive in the face of a more direct relationship with the
market place?

McLaughlin (1994) has argued that there are important moral limits to
the extension of market culture into schooling. Among these are considerations about the generation of civic virtue and about the provision of fair
educational entitlements for all pupils. In short, McLaughlin is arguing that
central elements of market culture are in conflict with Catholic values in
education. However, a minority of the Catholic headteachers involved in this
inquiry were confident that, with appropriate school leadership, the integrity
of Catholic values in education could not only be maintained but extended in
its range of influence:

- Heads of Catholic Aided schools might experience fewer dilemmas here than County colleagues . . . The apparent decline of moral
  and spiritual functions in schools might explain why Church schools
  are quite attractive to a wide community.
  (Male Secondary Head) (40)

- There is support from parents for a stance which is overtly counter to the prevailing market values. Parents do want good exam
  results but not at all costs and an education which is balanced and
  Christian has attractions.
  (Male Secondary Head) (72)

- The voluntary aided sector is prominent here and still under the control of the Diocese, so most headteachers in this sector are aware of a need for moral controls.
  (Male Secondary Head) (37)

This confident minority of headteachers took the view that not only were the spiritual and moral resources of Catholic schooling strong enough to resist possible corruption or pollution by market values in education but that, ironically, these moral resources were being recontextualized as potent market assets in the competitive appeal for parental choice of schools in a wider constituency. In other words, demonstrable moral leadership would ensure the success of Catholic schooling in the new conditions of the educational market place.

While not denying that Catholic schools had moral and spiritual strengths which could be viewed as assets in a competitive situation of parental choice, the majority of the headteachers had reservations and dilemmas about the impact of market values upon the special mission of their schools:

- Catholic values and market values appear to be ever in conflict— an obvious example is the funding available for religious education and for spiritual and moral experiences, e.g., residential courses.
  (Female Secondary Head) (69)

- I would rather see the school shrink in size but remain true to its ideals and faith commitment. I do not see a child as a £1000 through the school gate.
  (Male Primary School Head) (42)

- Catholic schools really must keep the explicit link between Christ and person-centred education . . . How do we square our vocational vision of pupils as persons, with the market vision of economic units? How does this affect our treatment of special educational needs? How does this affect our admissions policy?
  (Female Secondary Head) (82)

For the Catholic headteachers who took seriously those aspects of the special mission of Catholic schools which related especially to service to the poor and the disadvantaged, there were dilemmas. Such headteachers realized that a new set of strategies known as 'playing the market' was emerging among some school leaders in their localities. In essence, playing the educational market[21] involved selecting the most able pupils from the most educationally supportive homes in order to maximize the output of measurable success on league tables of performance. In this way, a public image of an 'excellent', 'successful' or 'effective' school could be constructed and the cultural capital of success once acquired could be further strengthened. Failure to engage in this market strategy could lead to a school's decline and to the creation of a 'sink school' image.[22] The moral dilemma for educational leaders (as opposed to simply managers), however, was constituted by a recognition that 'playing the market' made it much more difficult to serve the poor and the powerless. Success could be achieved with the poor and the powerless but at a greater cost in terms of time, resources, staff commitment and educational support. It was precisely the questions of 'cost' and 'cost effectiveness' which were preoccupying all headteachers in the market conditions for schooling.

Challenges for Contemporary Catholic School Leaders

Catholic school principals and headteachers are being exhorted to defend the historical commitment of Catholic schooling to the service of disadvantaged communities in America and in Britain. McNamee (1993), in reviewing the challenges for Catholic schools in the USA, concludes:

> What can Catholic schools do to meet current and future challenges presented by Hispanics, new immigrants and the poor? First, the Church must make a commitment to increase the access of these special populations to Catholic schools. (p.17)

As this study has shown, the growing influence of market culture upon Catholic schooling makes the realization of this educational ideal more difficult than in the past. Also, as a result of wider cultural and religious change, it is much less certain that 'the Church' as an entity can make such a commitment in an era of devolved school-site management and of increased parental choice and assertion. In a similar way, O'Keefe (1993) argues that:

> The rationale and current status of Catholic schools for the poor in the United States present a powerful challenge to the Catholic community. (p.14)

Despite an analysis which calls for a new belief in education for the common good, O'Keefe is forced to acknowledge 'the reluctance of white, middle class suburban Catholics to see themselves in communion with poor, urban minorities.'

In Britain, John Haldane (1993) has asserted that:

> Catholic education must establish a social conscience as well as one concerned with individual well-being . . . the first task for a Catholic philosophy of education is to identify the good. The social good is only a part of that but it is a sufficiently large and central part to justify making it a focus of attention . . . (pp.11–12)

At the same time as he sets this mission for Catholic education, Haldane recognizes that liberal individualism is politically and ideologically in the ascendant in Britain and elsewhere rather than forms of social communitarianism with commitments to the social good.

These are the fundamental dilemmas and challenges for Catholic school leaders in contemporary conditions. While there have always been tensions between the educational pursuit of the common good and the educational pursuit of individual interest, these tensions have at least been held in a position of ideological balance. There has been an educational settlement or compromise based upon a recognition that both common good and individual interest have their legitimate claims in educational theory and practice. The ideological changes of the 1980s and 1990s, in particular the influence of New Right agencies in both America and Britain, have broken that historical settlement by, in effect, denying the existence of constructs such as 'society' or of 'common good'.

The apparent triumph of liberal individualism as a decisive political, economic and cultural doctrine and its implementation in terms of educational policy and practice provided the majority of Catholic headteachers in this study with the greatest challenge they had yet faced in their careers as school leaders. These headteachers might look for guidance or leadership to 'the Church' on these contested matters, but in a post-modern age what 'the Church' was and what its voice on these issues might be lacked the definition and certainties of the past. There were therefore no *ex cathedra* statements or absolute moral codes which could give instant guidance on these social, cultural and professional dilemmas.[23]

Notes and References

1   Bryk *et al.* (1993, pp.301–2).
2   Bryk notes that 'the majority of principalships in Catholic high school (61 per cent in 1988) still come from religious orders, an arrangement that provides schools with some distinct benefits' (p.157).
3   *Ibid.*, p.156.
4   McLaren (1993, p.254).
5   *Ibid.*, p.290.
6   It must be noted here that the participating headteachers represented a very limited sample of the Catholic school system in England and Wales which consists of 1886 primary schools and 407 secondary schools. Catholic provision is approximately 10 per cent of the public education service (Catholic Education Service data).
7   However, it is important not to romanticize concepts of community in schooling. Community can be appropriated for oppressive and unjust processes and recourse to legal and bureaucratic procedures may be necessary in the interests of justice for individuals.
8   It can be noted that all of these agencies are giving much more attention in the 1990s to courses on school leadership rather than simply school management and that such courses are addressing spiritual, moral and value issues in Catholic schooling.

9   See headteacher, Account 39.
10 This major dilemma permeated many of the headteacher accounts. Demographic changes were affecting Catholic schools and school closures were becoming a feature of the system (356 schools closed between 1978 and 1991). The percentage of Catholic teachers in Catholic secondary schools has fallen from 66 per cent in 1978 to 58 per cent in 1991. Non-Catholic pupils have increased from 3 per cent of the school population to 14 per cent in 1991 (Catholic Education Service data).
11 The 'no problem here' response is characteristically given in schools and localities which have no significant ethnic diversity or in situations where it is claimed that racism may feature in the community but not in the school.
12 Mukherjee, quoted in Troyna (1993, p.92).
13   White Paper, 1992, p.19, para. 3.1.
14 *Grant Maintained Schools: Questions Parents Ask*, DFE booklet, November 1993, p.5.
15 *The Guardian*, 4 February 1994.
16 *The Times Educational Supplement*, 4 February 1994.
17 This classic phrase was used by some headteachers during the course of this inquiry.
18 Catholic Education Service: *A Response to the White Paper*, 24 September 1992, p.7.
19 The Catholic response can be compared with the much stronger criticism of grant-maintained policy emanating from the Muslim community in Britain. *The Times Educational Supplement* for 1 July 1994 carried a front page report under the heading 'Muslims condemn "unfair" GM Policy'. Leading Muslim educators argued that 'it's not acceptable and it's not Islamic to disadvantage the majority for the benefit of the privileged minority'.
20 Despite a Vatican II discourse of involvement of the 'whole people of God' in the life of the Church, active democratic involvement is radically at odds with the hierarchical and authoritarian traditions of Catholicism.
21 These strategies are indicated by a growing discourse in education using constructs such as 'the major players' or 'the stakeholders'.
22 As one head noted, 'once a school is on a downward spiral it is going to be much more difficult than in the past to build it up'. His argument was that the removal of LEA support and greater dependence on market forces would cause this difficulty. See account (10).
23 The categorical teaching of Catholicism on the regulation of sexual behaviour can be contrasted with a much greater degree of ambiguity on social, economic and political matters.

Chapter 10

Women and Educational Leadership

This chapter builds upon and extends the discussion outlined in Chapter 3, in which a literature generated by women academics, in the main, has raised fundamental questions about the gender relations of educational leadership. In that literature, Shakeshaft (1989) has suggested that there is a distinctive female culture of education management and Blackmore (1989) has called for a feminist reconstruction of the concept of an educational leader which will move away from patriarchal concepts of power and control over others. Grundy (1993) has argued that educational leadership, informed by feminism, can be a form of 'emancipatory praxis'[1] which provides an alternative to traditional male hierarchical and bureaucratic approaches to leadership and management.

There is a general recognition that theoretical analysis and educational practice on gender and leadership issues must be brought into a closer relation (Yates, 1993) and that more research which links the two should be undertaken. In developing such research, Ozga (1993) emphasizes the collection of accounts from women with leadership responsibilities in education and Adler *et al.* (1993) stress the importance of analytical distinctions between women in management and feminists in management. As Arnot (1994) expresses it, 'research must capture the unity and the diversity of the educational lives of women' (p.101).

The present study has focused upon headteachers as educational leaders and it has used accounts as its basic data source but it has to be acknowledged at the outset that women headteachers were not strongly represented in the total sample. Of the eighty-eight headteacher accounts available for analysis, only twenty-four were from women headteachers who had been asked with varying degrees of explicitness[2] to comment upon the changing nature of school headship in England. Valerie Hall (1994), in reviewing empirical research in Britain, has concluded that there has been:

> [a] failure of research based literature on educational management in Britain to address issues relating to women as managers and their contribution to the practice of school management (Hall, 1993) . . . Theories of educational management and administration in Britain continue to be based largely on research into men as school leaders . . . Such studies have tended to use 'no differences' as a rationale for not focusing on gender as a potentially significant factor in understanding educational leadership. (p.1)

In reporting her own closely focused qualitative study of six women headteachers (three secondary, two primary, one infant school) Hall found that while none of the women endorsed or sharply exemplified a feminist approach to educational leadership, some qualitative differences from conventional male practice could be observed. These included a strong commitment to teamwork and professional consultation and an ambivalence about power issues, i.e., 'they enjoy the power to make things happen but fear the potential for abusing power'.[3]

The analysis of the accounts of the twenty-four women headteachers participating in this study largely confirmed these findings. Relatively few of these women educational leaders made explicit reference to feminist perspectives, to equal opportunity questions or even to ideas about a female style of educational management. For whatever reason, these matters were not central to their discourse.[4] The majority took the view, either explicitly or implicitly, that while there were differentiating features in leadership styles between power focused and power sharing, and between line executive and team consultative modes, gender was not of itself a simple predictor of these. In other words, their view was that some men and women headteachers operated relatively democratic and participatory decision-making regimes and some men and women did not. The critical factor here was a principled commitment by a headteacher and not simply the gender of a headteacher. These views were based, in the main, upon their own professional experiences in schools before they became headteachers and upon their own current experiences, and that of their female colleagues, as headteachers. Some recognized that this base of experience was perhaps too limited to make a definitive statement about whether or not a female style of educational leadership did exist. Particularly in areas of strong male domination, it was difficult to make such comparative judgments:

- I do not know if there is a female style of leadership/management. There are so few of us [women] in the northern region!
  (Female Secondary Head) (86)

In only one case did a woman headteacher assert explicitly that gender issues were important in educational leadership and that a distinctive female style of management could be discerned:

- Texts on managerial style and models simply do not pay heed to anything other than male roles . . . As an observer of the male culture of educational leadership and management . . . I am aware that my approaches are frequently totally different from the one view of 'cut and thrust' management displayed by colleagues . . . The female style of management does exist but it is more complex than that of the male . . . Female style is rounded, complex, caring, developing, allowing for growth in others, sharing

> but leading, central in staff teams, a hands on approach but not in
> a hierarchical sense—acting as a catalyst—openness in recognizing
> other points of view.
> *(Female Primary School Head) (85)*

This account was exceptional in its eloquent and developed thesis that a
female style of educational leadership existed. However, it cannot simply be
dismissed as the ideosyncratic account of one headteacher since analysis of
other accounts demonstrated that the qualities claimed for a distinctive female
leadership in this account were echoed and reproduced in other accounts by
women headteachers without the process of explicit social labelling.[5] In other
words, there were distinctive emphases within women's accounts of school
headship issues which were qualitatively different from those of most of the
men headteachers.

Care for pupils and teachers and care about social relationships with pupils
and teachers, for instance, was strongly evident in the accounts of the women
headteachers:

- I do believe that secondary women heads place the child and
  meeting its needs at the centre of their concern and are therefore
  more likely to address behaviour from staff which damages that
  (e.g., aggressive behaviour to pupils etc.).
  (Female Secondary Head) (86)

- I would say that our great strength in this school is being able to
  talk together and sharing, therefore we can share our problems.
  You have somebody with a sympathetic listening ear.
  (Female Infant School Head) (20)

- Normal relationships, I think, are good in that we discuss everything together. I have always talked over the work with the staff.
  Now the staff meetings will probably seem to someone on the
  outside, something like a jumble because we have all got bits of
  paper spread out on the table and people are jotting things down
  and people interrupting. It's not a formal staff meeting as such
  . . . I've never seen it as a power game.
  (Female Infant School Head) (15)

Valerie Hall's observations about women headteachers' ambiguous relation to power was exemplified in this inquiry. When speaking about the new
empowerment of local management of schools and the emergence of managerial styles of school headship this ambiguity was clearly apparent. Women
headteachers appreciated the potential of local management of schools (LMS)
for 'making things happen' and they were generally determined to show that
women were as competent in forward planning and financial control as men,

but they had a greater awareness of the dangers of managerial culture. In particular they were sensitive to the distancing effect which managerial pre-occupations could exercise upon their direct and fundamental educational and social relations with pupils and teachers and classrooms.

These interpersonal and educational sensitivities were more salient in the accounts of the women headteachers and with these sensitivities came a greater caution about the new managerialism and the creation of new hierarchies associated with it. While commitment to team work and a culture of con-sultation could be found in the accounts of both men and women headteachers, the discourse of the women school leaders more frequently took teamwork to be a normal and organic process whereas men referred to 'their' creation of teamwork as an important innovation in the culture of a school.

These qualitatively different leadership sensitivities extended also to re-sponses to the growth of a more competitive and market orientated culture of schooling in the 1990s. As the analysis in Chapter 7 demonstrated, the responses of male headteachers were in part affected by the existing strength of their schools in terms of reputation and their assessment of the likelihood of win-ning or losing in more competitive conditions. This discourse did not feature in the accounts of the women headteachers. The potential 'cut and thrust' of the educational market place was not celebrated in these accounts and the notion of 'winning' did not feature as an important concern of women headteachers. This is not to say that the participants were unconcerned about the relative achievements of their schools or about the creation of a good image in the eyes of the parents, but their aspirations were expressed in a language largely devoid of market values. It was apparent, however, that the increasing emphasis which was being placed upon indicators of visible and measurable success in a competitive market situation for schooling would bring new pressures to bear upon women headteachers in particular. Some of them indicated experiences of existing pressure arising from the expectations and prejudices of a male dominated leadership culture:

- I do think that governing bodies tend to think of heads as male. My own Chair of Governors (after I was appointed) explained that he needed a *strong* head who would get on with the job and 'lead from the front' . . . I think there is probably an interesting study to be done on women heads who have taken on urban schools with a very male dominated repressive ethos . . .
  (Female Secondary Head) (86)

- The feeling I hold is that I must always fight to prove my capa-bility on gender stances and strive to exhibit that I am not only as good but better than the male.
  (Female Primary School Head) (85)

The traditional male expectations about women as educational leaders and managers in English schooling culture has tended to focus on their capacity to give 'strong' leadership in disciplinary and social control terms. In other words, the mediated forms of the headmaster tradition with its associations of dominance and discipline have continued to be a real force in the selection and evaluation of women headteachers. Contemporary reformulations of strong leadership as strong market leadership seemed likely to generate new forms of pressure for women school leaders. Insofar as market forces were a cultural realization of masculine competitiveness and insofar as women attempted to implement alternative values in education then growing conflict seemed inevitable.[6]

Some of the participants believed that the position of headteacher could become less attractive to women applicants because of the transformations which were taking place in the nature of school leadership. These transformations included the effects of the new managerialism, an increased competitive and market ethos in schooling, and the intensification of work pressure and its effects upon personal and social life:

- I think that the position of Headteacher [secondary] is becoming less attractive to some women for the following reasons:
  (a) The responsibility since LMS is vastly increased;
  (b) Curriculum innovation is now so difficult;
  (c) If the woman has children, the hours a head works now makes balancing home/school responsibilities difficult. Governors' meetings and sub-committees are very time consuming.
  (Female Secondary Head) (86)

- All headteachers suffer from piles of paperwork on the desk . . . and that is certainly one of the most distressing things about being a head today . . . there was a time when you could go out of your office thinking you've done a good day's work and everything was right in your world. You can't do that now because there is always something waiting for you on the next day. This will put off women who have families to think about at home. We are perhaps going to get back to the situation of having spinster heads. *(Female Infant School Head) (20)*

- Continuous struggle between school and family . . . my time at home with my family and friends is constantly being eroded . . . I have never begrudged time given for the children and the school but I am becoming more and more resentful that it is my own personal space and time that is being eroded otherwise I am made to feel (by government, Department for Education, media, etc.) that I am failing in my professional duties. This situation is becoming unacceptable to me even though my family is grown up. It must be intolerable for younger teachers with young families. *(Female Primary Head) (49)*

References to the intensification of work pressures and the effects of this upon the personal lives of headteachers could be found in the accounts of both men and women. There was however a qualitative difference in the nature of these responses. For men headteachers, in general, the increased demands of contemporary school leadership were seen to make inroads into the time which they had available to be with their families. This was a situation which they regretted and in some cases felt guilty about. For women headteachers who commented on this issue there was a sense of sharper conflict between the personal and the professional and a sense that a double or cumulative set of responsibilities existed which was becoming impossible to sustain. For these women, if such tendencies continued, then the position of headteacher would become, in effect, only a viable option for single and professional career women.

Evetts (1987), in researching the career strategies of married women who became primary school headteachers in England in the 1960s and 1970s, found that their family responsibilities were always of fundamental importance to them and determined to a great extent their career decisions. Even when they became headteachers, 'they had to continue to meet family and work commitments, balancing one against the other for the whole of their working lives'.[7] The evidence from this study suggests, however, that while it may have been possible for women headteachers to balance their family and professional responsibilities in the 1960s and 1970s, the education reforms of the 1980s and 1990s have, through a process of intensification, brought this social balance to the point of crisis. This does not imply that women will cease to apply for school leadership positions but it does imply that some greater differentiation is likely to take place among women considering career advancement. As one participant observed:

- Headteachers are not a static group—my perception of my role on taking up the post in 1988 was, I think, significantly different from that of a person say in 1986. Governors are appointing all the time and there are . . . 'flavour of the day' heads.
  (Female Secondary Head) (28)

This observation is important not only when considering processes of differentiation which may be occurring among women candidates for school headship but also among male candidates. It prompts the question of what sort of personal and ideological differentiation may be occurring among those teachers aspirant for leadership positions. Are there new model headteachers and school leaders for a transformed schooling culture and, if so, what are the characteristics of such headteachers, especially those appointed after the Education Reform Act of 1988?

Pascall (1986) has argued that:

Educational institutions stand at the junction of private and public worlds, mediating between the family and paid employment . . . There is thus an ambiguity at the heart of girls' education. (p.103)

Such ambiguity may be said to have characterized also women's experience of professional and working life. It seems likely that contemporary education reform and its consequences has sharpened rather than ameliorated these ambiguities for women professionals. It may therefore be the case that only those women who have been able to resolve these ambiguities (by whatever means) are ready to take on the demanding challenges of school leadership.[8]

Women headteachers, along with their male colleagues, have had to negotiate the new power relations of school leadership arising from the empowerment of school governing bodies. It has already been shown that women headteachers had encountered difficulties in the past, especially in junior and secondary schools where male dominated governing bodies held traditional views about strong (male) dominative leadership as an essential prerequisite for headship. However, in the pre-reform period, once a woman was appointed as headteacher she had a relatively autonomous sphere of influence within the schools. After 1988, a continued and negotiated sharing of power and influence in the school was a feature of the new pattern of governance. Women headteachers, in other words, found themselves in a situation in which their conceptions of school leadership had to be made explicit and if necessary justified to male dominated governing bodies on a regular basis.

Deem (1991) has pointed out that the gender relations and consequences of these new forms of power sharing are still in the process of emerging. There was no evidence in the accounts provided by the women headteachers participating in this study, however, that these new relationships were causing any special difficulties for women. Women headteachers were as likely as men headteachers to report that they had 'good' governors or that they felt confident about their ability to manage or lead the governors. What cannot be predicted is how these power relations (for both men and women headteachers) will develop over time. The working relation of largely male Chairs of Governors with women headteachers on important policy issues is likely to be crucial in affecting the power sharing culture of particular schools.

While the new patterns of gender–power relations in school leadership are still emerging in the 1990s, the existence of greater potential contradictions for women in leadership is apparent. Contradictions arise because of the oppositions between two of the major trends in leadership culture and practice. On the one hand, a growing literature of leadership and management studies and of training course and conference discourse celebrates the virtues of consultative, non-hierarchical and participative decision making—in essence, the styles of leadership and management towards which women have particular sensitivities are being held up as models of good practice and efficiency for the future.[9] This major trend could be called the *sharing–consultative model* of educational leadership which was already emergent in the 1970s. On the other hand, however, an oppositional trend towards hierarchy, line-management and executive action can also be discerned. Riley (1994) argues that as practice, rather than simply as discourse, this latter model is in the ascendent and is already working against the interests of women:

Within the UK there is growing evidence to suggest that the characteristics which are associated with successful management of the education service are becoming more, rather than less, associated with male rather than female traits. The increasing emphasis on technical and financial managerial skills and on budgeting controls is reinforcing the tendency for men to be viewed as more suitable candidates for management. The consequence of this is that despite the increase in women in middle management over the last decade, there has been a decrease in the percentage of women appointed as headteachers or deputies (Migniuolo and De Lyon, 1989) . . . a new image of educational leadership is emerging in the UK. Leaders are tough, abrasive financial entrepreneurs managing the new competitive education markets. Managing education organizations is increasingly seen as men's business. (pp.90–1)

This major trend could be called the *masculine–strong leadership model* and it can be seen to have recontextualized earlier masculine cultures of leadership in contemporary forms which seem relevant to market conditions in schooling.

Viewed from the perspectives of education policy scholarship which places contemporary phenomena within a long historical and cultural framework, the existence of such contradictions and oppositional tendencies is hardly surprising. Patriarchal and male power has shaped the construct of leadership, its culture, discourse, imaging and practice for centuries. Alternative conceptions of leadership have to attempt to legitimate themselves against the pervasive influence of these established models. In certain periods of cultural and ideological change and openness, alternative models of leadership, with external political support, can gain ground against the accumulated weight of cultural tradition. However, these advances are always dependent upon the wider socio-political and ideological context. When this context changes, the advances gained in an earlier period can be reversed. In the case of educational leadership and of the scope of women's influence upon it, the 1960s and the 1970s provided the contextual conditions for the 'progress' of women and for any associated models of democratic educational leadership which were gender related. The changed cultural and ideological conditions of the 1980s and 1990s have made that progress much more problematic.

The capacity of patriarchal culture and structures to endure and to be recontextualized in changing conditions has been noted by Goldring and Chen (1994). In their study of the feminization of educational leadership positions in the elementary and secondary schools of Israel, Goldring and Chen observed that as the numbers of women in the principalship increased, the political, professional and bureaucratic power structures within which these women had to operate continued to be male dominated. Thus although women were developing effective leadership styles demonstrating the humane and effective outcomes of sharing/collaborative school cultures, these achievements received little public- or career-related acknowledgment. A major contradiction could therefore be discerned in the education system in Israel whereby:

> ... the resulting structure is a two-tier system in which women principals are highly regarded at the local level, yet isolated from major political and policy decisions.[10]

The women headteachers in this study were similarly operating within political, professional and bureaucratic power structures which were male dominated. However, these 'facts' were so much part of the taken-for-granted working world of these women that virtually none of their accounts make reference to this. For these women educational leaders, this was 'how things are' and their energies had to be devoted not to a critique of male dominance in education but to finding ways in which they could achieve success for their schools despite this male dominance.[11]

In commenting on the new politics of gender which exists in the 1990s, Marshall (1994) has argued that 'it's a long leap from feminist philosophy to the political fray in education and school reform' (p.4).[12] The findings of this study endorse that conclusion. What it also shows however is that faced with serious work intensification most women headteachers have little opportunity for critical engagement with feminist philosophy or for discussing with other women headteachers the shared challenges which they face in educational leadership.

Reviewing the accounts of the twenty-four women headteachers participating in this study, it became apparent that relatively few of them made reference to gender in relation to educational leadership or management. This absence of a specific gender discourse needs to be explained. In earlier chapters, it has been noted that headteacher accounts were relatively silent on other issues, such as racism or the political and ideological character of government education policy. It was suggested that these were topics which either discomforted the headteachers or which they regarded as inappropriate for 'professional' comment. However, as Thomas Cromwell observes in Robert Bolt's play *A Man for All Seasons*, 'silence speaks'. The difficulty is to work out what the silence is saying!

The relative silence of these women headteachers on the gender relations of educational leadership and management could indicate that they did not believe that gender was a relevant issue. However, it is difficult to believe this interpretation in a region where male domination of the leadership of both primary and secondary schools was so visible.[13] To say that gender was not a relevant issue was to fly in the face of statistical and demographic data of the most basic kind. Male domination of school headship was not only an historical fact of the region but a contemporary fact. Of the eighty-seven secondary schools in the sample area, only six had women headteachers at the time of the inquiry. Of the 419 primary schools, only 132 were led by women. It has already been suggested that one of the possible reasons for the silence of the women headteachers in the fact of this massive gender imbalance in the region was that they had come to normalize the situation as 'the way things are'.

There are other possible reasons for silence on gender issues. To construct gender as a central issue can cause difficulties for women school leaders in a number of ways. Once gender is explicitly recognized as a factor in the appointment of headteachers it can imply that a woman, appointed against strong male competition, was not chosen on intrinsic merit but because of a latter-day commitment to equal opportunities. In this sense the professional legitimation of a woman's appointment can be undercut by suggestions that her appointment was necessary for wider political and public relations reasons. Ball (1987) noted in his study of women's careers and the politics of gender, that many women in education who had achieved promotion were quick to deny the existence of discrimination against women. By this overt denial it could be said that they were also covertly implying that there was no equal opportunities bias either. In other words, it could be argued that it is structurally necessary for promoted women in education to insist that professional merit criteria, and not gender, are the gateway to leadership.

Both Hall's (1994) study and this present inquiry have found little evidence of feminist discourse among women headteachers. This is hardly surprising. To utilize Adler *et al.*'s (1993) useful distinction between women in management and feminists in management, it could be said that if the appointment of a woman to a leadership position was exceptional, the appointment of 'a known feminist' would be miraculous, especially in the regional culture under examination.

Marilyn Joyce (1987) has pointed out the difficulties which can arise for women in education if it is known or supposed that they are feminists. In her research in the Inner London Education Authority (ILEA) at a period when political and local education authority support for women (and feminists) was at its strongest, the experience of being a feminist teacher was generally stressful. Joyce concluded that even when the local education state (in this case the ILEA) made anti-sexism a centrepiece of its educational policy, this did not noticeably reduce the pressures upon feminist teachers:

> Even in London, staff who want to work on this issue have to battle, often single-handed, against massive resistance and refusal even to consider the arguments.[14]

In other regions of England where the local education state had not followed the example of the ILEA, the emergence of feminist educators in leadership positions was even more problematic.

The absence of gender discourse and feminist discourse in the accounts of the women headteachers in this study probably arose from this interrelated set of circumstances. Only in the account of one woman primary headteacher was a developed gender discourse apparent. Yet even here the headteacher felt it necessary to distance herself from 'dogmatic' feminist attitudes. All dominant political, social and cultural orders use their control of discourse as part of a strategy for the maintenance of the status quo and for the maintenance of their own hegemony. Thus, those who draw attention to class inequalities in a society can be positioned in a discourse of 'marxism'.[15] Similarly those who draw attention to the existence of racism can be labelled 'extremist' and those who articulate a feminist critique of patriarchy can be said to be 'dogmatic'.[16] In this case, the ideological labelling of feminist positions in education as 'dogmatic' or 'strident' may have caused the women headteachers in this research to distance themselves from any association with feminism. In other words, patriarchal domination of school leadership positions had not been seriously threatened by the promotion of these women headteachers. They had been accommodated in what remained a largely enduring culture of male leadership.[17]

Notes and References

1 Emancipatory praxis is understood to be 'constantly entertaining the possibility that things could be otherwise' . . . 'the development of a critical consciousness is the basis for emancipatory praxis . . . it is not a set of behaviours in which an educational leader can be trained'. See Grundy (1993, pp.171–4).

2 See Chapter 4 for details of research methodology.

3 Hall (1994, p.7).

4 Among these reasons were indicators that many women headteachers had limited opportunities to engage with a critical educational literature which focused upon such questions.

5 A number of the participants were wary of, or even hostile to, educational positions labelled as 'feminist'. An example of this occurred in Account 85, 'I find the abrasiveness of feminism as offensive as male domination and in many instances bearing the same values and attitudes that they, as a group, kick against.'

6 For some women headteachers, the market in education was not a problem and they were ready to operate confidently within it.

7 Evetts (1987, p.27).

8 Mrs Thatcher, as the British Prime Minister throughout the 1980s, had provided a powerful model of a woman leader who had solved the problem of ambiguities. What influence this model may have had upon women headteachers appointed in the 1980s and 1990s awaits research inquiry.

9 Riley (1994) claims that 'through their socialization women are more likely to adopt a cooperative, interactive form of leadership than men' (p.103).

10 Goldring and Chen (1994, p.175).

11 This would include realizing in educational and organizational terms their own constructs of a 'successful' school as indicating a quality of human relationships as well as measurable indicators of academic performance e.g.:

  • I wish wholeheartedly that schools should be fully human communities for people. *(85)*

12 For Marshall a new politics of gender has to be constructed for the 1990s recognizing two major developments, i.e., the limitations of existing liberal approaches to gender equity in education but also the appearance of contemporary ideological trends which are actually hostile to gender equity.

13 Some of the older women headteachers in primary schools frankly admitted that the local culture accepted that the 'natural' realm for women's school leadership was in the infant schools.
14 Joyce (1987, p.69).
15 The classic statement of Dom Helder Camara is very apposite here:

> When I give food to the poor, they call me a saint.
> When I ask why the poor have no food, they call me a communist.

16 It is a particular irony of the dominant discourse that patriarchy which has been *the* source of dogma, should use 'dogmatism' as part of its attack upon feminist positions.
17 For a recent discussion of women headteachers' experiences in male management culture see Evetts (1994, pp.85–94).

Chapter 11

The Past and the Future of Educational Leadership

To this point in the analysis, attempts have been made to illuminate main themes in the study of school leadership with reference to theoretical, historical and cultural sources and insights derived from fieldwork data in a particular setting. What this analysis has made clear is that conceptions of educational leadership are dynamic, contested, historically and culturally situated and at the centre of socio-political and ideological struggles about the future of schooling. Conceptions of educational leadership are not simply technical formulations for making schools effective as organizations, they are also fundamental expressions of cultural and political values. The form and nature of educational leadership has implications for the reproduction, modification or transformation of the wider social, cultural and political features of the society in which it is located. It has implications for the socialization of individuals, the formation of citizens and the structuring of social relations as between different class, race, gender, religious and cultural groups. In its influence upon religious, moral and ethical education, educational leadership is an important constituent of a society's mores and culture. It is in this larger relational context that educational leadership can be seen to be qualitatively different from education management.

Education management is about achieving organizational effectiveness once the major purposes of the organization have been agreed by its members or specified for them by an external agency. Taking an example from Chapter 9, if Catholic educational leadership in America endorses the view that 'a preferential option for the poor' must be the prime mission for the Catholic school in the inner city, then the questions for education management are what financial, logistic, educational and resourcing arrangements must be made to ensure the effective realization of this mission? However, the work of the earlier chapters has also shown that relationships between educational leadership and educational management are not quite as simple as this example implies. There are many complex questions and contradictions to be faced. Among these are questions to do with the source and nature of educational leadership itself,[1] relations between leadership culture and management culture; relations between leadership culture and democratic culture; and questions about how individuals or teams in leadership and management roles actually cope with intensification of work load and the generation of sharper moral, ethical and professional dilemmas in schooling in contemporary conditions.

The most profound of these questions relate to the source and nature of educational leadership and to relations between leadership culture in schooling and democratic culture. This study has shown that English schooling culture has historically been characterized by strong hierarchical and patriarchal leadership. For most of the period under examination, school leadership has been constituted in class dominant, male dominant and authoritarian terms. The cultural epitome of this has been, and is, the headmaster tradition which remains an enduring influence in recontextualized forms even in the late twentieth century. Against this strong cultural practice, which has found new sources of legitimation and life in some formulations of professional autonomy and influence and more recently in a growing management and market culture in schooling, other forms of school leadership have sought to establish an alternative legitimacy and life.

The political, cultural and ideological climate of the 1960s created the conditions in which it was possible to develop forms of school leadership which were more democratic, participative, consultative and power sharing. In conditions of relatively strong schooling autonomy and of strong insulation from the influence of external agents (including the parents) it was possible for innovating headteachers (men and women) to introduce a regime of shared decision making into all types of school culture. An historically dominant concept of 'my' school could by these transformations become a modern practice of 'our' school. By the 1970s, in the HMI report, *Ten Good Schools*, the consultative mode of decision making and the model of the school leader/ headteacher as actively participative rather than hierarchically directive was receiving official commendation as good practice. However, it is possible to overstate the actual range and nature of these transformations in English schooling culture and to suppose, naively, that two decades of new thinking about school leadership could rapidly change one hundred years' practice of hierarchy, patriarchy and authoritarianism.

Transformations of school leadership did occur in the facilitating conditions of the 1960s and 1970s. Hierarchy and authoritarianism in schools were in retreat and the practice of shared decision making and the culture of collegial professional discussion spread in infant, junior and secondary schools in England. As patriarchy weakened in school leadership, women played a more significant and visible role in advancing distinctive perspectives and particular sensitivities as school leaders/headteachers. These changes were real changes in the culture and practice of school leadership in England and many of the experienced headteachers who participated in the fieldwork for this study were proud of the 'modern' and 'progressive' developments that they had facilitated in school governance. As their own personal and professional mission as headteachers, some of them had used the hierarchical power of their leadership position precisely to undermine, or at least modify, the hierarchical and authoritarian features of school culture.

The project for the transformation of school leadership in the 1960s and 1970s was, however, marked by contradictions, limitations and vulnerabilities. Among the contradictions was the fact that, in most cases, the introduction of a more democratic and consultative style of school leadership depended in the first instance upon an exercise of hierarchical initiative by the headteacher. Just as in a later period, the action of a strong state was the necessary preliminary in England for the introduction of market forces in public services, so in these decades the action of strong, hierarchical leadership was often the necessary preliminary for the inauguration of more participative modes of school governance. The paradox arising from this situation was that a form of school leadership which had to be strong enough to bring in a form of progressive change, sometimes against conservative opposition within the school and the community, had at the same time to be strong enough to participate in a reduction of its own manifest leadership role and privileges.[2] Such a change required a particular set of commitments from headteachers and probably an appropriate set of personality dispositions.

It seems likely that these requirements for the transformation of leadership culture limited the range and extent of these changes in the English schooling system. Although detailed research on the actual practice of reformed school leadership in the social democratic period is not extensive, it is probably the case that the dissemination of these new cultural practices was partial and differentiated by school type and school location. Even where transformed models of school leadership involving shared decision making were established at this time, the range of their jurisdiction was sharply limited. The important cultural transition from 'my' school to 'our' school did not, in most cases, carry the radical implications which the language suggests. The dominant professional ideology of the 1960s and 1970s ensured that 'our' school was an extension of manifest jurisdiction from the headteacher alone, to a professional forum comprising all the teachers in the school. Despite the rhetoric of community education and community participation which existed at this time, in only a relatively few locations was serious community participation in school decision making actively practised. Insofar as English schools became more democratic in culture, the model for democracy was Athenian rather than modern.[3] Relatively democratic decision making might include the whole teacher professional group but in general it excluded the parents, the pupils and members of the community in other than a formal sense.

This democracy of the professionals insofar as it developed in the 1960s and 1970s was, when judged against one hundred years of headteacher autocracy, not an inconsiderable achievement. However, even this transformation was a fragile and vulnerable organizational culture. While individual headteachers (with the endorsement of the school governing body) might be prepared to operate relatively egalitarian forms of professional decision making in schools, these democratic forms existed within a set of constraints. External legal and bureaucratic structure continued to operate as if the headteacher was (subject to the formal power of the governors) *the* manifest school leader.

Thus although the professional forum in the school might decide collectively on a particular course of action, it was the headteacher alone who would be held responsible for the consequences of such action. In other words, forms of professional democracy were in a contradictory relation with an external legal and bureaucratic culture shaped by hierarchical assumptions. This situation allowed those headteachers who wished to resist the movement to shared decision making to claim that such arrangements involved 'power without responsibility'.

These constitutional vulnerabilities of more participative school governance were also compounded in some locations by the continued existence of conservative social expectations for strong and decisive leadership from a headteacher. For some schools and for some communities, a 'proper' headteacher was in fact a headmaster, and was evaluated in terms of a personal capacity to make an impact upon the organization. Those headteachers who wished to construct, with others, another form and culture of leadership had to possess the courage and professional integrity to work against the grain of local cultural tradition. As some of the participants in this study indicated, this could be a challenging and difficult enterprise. It could be particularly difficult for women headteachers.

Nevertheless, despite its contradictions, limitations and vulnerabilities, school leadership in England began a cultural transition which can be broadly described as from single leadership autocracy to shared professional decision making. The majority of the participants in this research endorsed such a transition, claimed to practise it and regarded it as part of a modern professional wisdom about how schools should operate.

This study has also shown, however, that the existing professional wisdom of headteachers in England about school leadership and governance and about the ways in which schools should operate has been challenged in the 1980s and 1990s by a series of radical education reforms. These reforms have embodied both the confidence and the contradictions of the New Right ideologies which have in various ways shaped their formation and their implementation. The outcome of these developments, as earlier chapters have indicated, is that contemporary school leadership is locked into a network of contradictory possibilities and shows both confidence and doubt about the future direction of schooling. This network consists of contradictions between the democratic potential of some reforms, for example: empowered school governors; greater accountability to parents; decentralized local management of schools; and, the centralist and controlling tendency of other reforms, e.g., national curriculum and assessment prescriptions, publication of hierarchical league tables of 'results', differential funding according to school status approved by the government.

Other major contradictions have arisen between the values and procedures enshrined in professional culture and those emergent in some forms of the new managerialism in education and in the growing power of market culture and values in schooling. Both of these latter developments in English schooling culture have a potential to reconstitute hierarchy in new forms. The chief executive models of school leadership or the market entrepreneur models do not harmonize easily with democratic or collegial modes of decision making.[4] In many cases, too, the values and priorities arising from a strong managerialist or market culture in schooling stand in a contradictory relation to religious, moral, ethical and value commitments in education. The moral, ethical and professional dilemmas reported by the participants in this inquiry have documented the lived experience of such contradictions among contemporary school leaders.

The critical questions for school leadership in the 1990s and beyond relate to how these contradictions may be resolved. The source and nature of educational leadership has to be clarified. The relationships between leadership culture and democratic culture and between educational leadership and management–market values has to be worked through in particular schools, localities and societies. The rest of this chapter represents a contribution to these debates rather than a prescriptive answer to these questions.

The Source and Nature of Educational Leadership

In English schooling culture, as earlier chapters have shown, educational leadership found its source and legitimation in class hierarchy and class relations. Educational leadership was class leadership in the sense that provided schooling was under the direction and control of the providing classes. This system was maintained by the direct control of governing and managing bodies in schools; by close and detailed surveillance and inspection of school activities; and, by careful selection of key personnel such as headteachers.

Headteachers themselves, within the internal culture of the school, were, in the nineteenth century and in the early decades of the twentieth century, the visible representation, in the lives of the pupils and the teachers, of the reality of social hierarchy. In Bernstein's (1990) terms, headteachers in English schools were a relay for power relations external to the school, in this case the power relations of class and of patriarchy.

The forms of educational leadership which resulted from these originating structures and ideologies reproduced to a greater or lesser extent the characteristics of hierarchy, patriarchy and authoritarian control. The ideal-type headteacher/leader in English schooling culture for over one hundred years was the source of strong leadership. This strong leadership concerned itself first with the establishment of a religious, moral and social order within the school and then such scholarship as was appropriate to the social origins and destinations of the pupils in the school.

The founding conception of educational leadership in English schooling culture, epitomized in the 'headmaster tradition', provided an enduring and pervasive model. It naturalized conceptions of class leadership, of hierarchy and surveillance, of patriarchal domination and of strong authoritarian leadership as taken-for-granted features of the life of schools. In essence both the source and the nature of educational leadership was a confident realization of social hierarchy. The process of schooling under the direction of hierarchical leadership was intended to reproduce a consciousness of the inevitability of hierarchy and an awareness, on the part of the pupil, of his or her place within such hierarchy.

Such was the power and tenacity of this hierarchical school culture in England that it persisted as an organizational form until well into the twentieth century. Even though external political and cultural relations began a transition towards social democracy and modifications of existing class relations and hierarchical forms took place, English schooling culture, insulated by the strong boundaries between school culture and mundane culture, was slow to change. External and formal political leadership became more democratic in constitution but English school leadership did not move in simple correspondence with these developments. The practice of strong, hierarchical leadership persisted in many schools as a natural feature of school life. School culture remained remote from democratic culture.

In the 1960s and 1970s, in changed conditions of strong professional autonomy for headteachers and a ferment of radical ideas about political, cultural, educational and personal relations, new forms of educational leadership could be established by innovative headteachers. The ideal type of headteacher/leader of the social democratic period was innovative in curriculum and pedagogic approaches and operated a consultative and participative culture of shared professional decision making in school. The legitimating source of such educational leadership was to be found in the appointing committees of the local education state and of school governing bodies (using professional merit criteria[5]). The nature of school leadership was, in the main, qualitatively different (in theory at least) from the founding traditions. The new school leadership attempted to ameliorate the hierarchical, patriarchal and authoritarian features of English schooling culture and to constitute in its place, to a greater or lesser extent, more open and consultative regimes of school governance.

The new school leadership of the 1960s and the 1970s, insofar as it was able to establish itself as a dominant cultural practice, had new sources of legitimation when compared with earlier forms of leadership. Its legitimation was to be found not in a direct relation with class hierarchy but in a mediated relation with the formal procedures of social democratic central and local government. Its authority and nature was legitimated by the strong hegemony of professional culture and ideology which had become established in English schooling culture in these decades.

New Right ideological attacks in the 1980s and 1990s upon the legitimacy of the local education state and its formal procedures (denigrated as 'bureaucracy') and upon the legitimacy of professional hegemony in schools (designated as 'producer capture') have thrown this educational settlement into crisis conditions in the 1990s. Government education reforms driven by such ideological positions have begun a process of reconstituting school leadership to operate in radically changed conditions. School leadership must now find its legitimacy not primarily through the formal procedures of the local education state or through the endorsements of collegial professionalism but in a direct social and economic relationship with educational consumers and visible market success. In ideological terms this attempted transformation is expressed as liberating the schools from the shackles of local education bureaucracy and breaking down the barriers of vested interest and professional self-rule, to open the schools to greater democratic accountability. From this perspective schools must be subject to greater democratic control as represented by empowered school governors, empowered school consumers and greater community knowledge of the measurable outcomes of schooling. School leadership must itself, therefore, be brought into a stronger relationship with mechanisms for democratic accountability and become more responsive to consumer culture.

The populist aspects of New Right ideology, by calling for stronger and direct relationships between schooling and 'democratic accountability', targetted the vulnerabilities and contradictions of social democratic education. The insulated tradition of English schooling culture and of English school leadership was vulnerable to charges of relative lack of accountability to parents as a group and to local communities, or at least, to accountability procedures which were formal, tokenistic or nominal rather than real and organic aspects of a working partnership between communities and schools. English schooling culture and its leadership was, as an earlier critique from the Left has pointed out (Education Group, 1981), 'statist'[6] and professional in character rather than democratic, communitarian or popular. New Right popularism was able to appropriate and amplify such critiques in the push to 'roll back the state' and 'free the market for services', thus bringing education, among other things, into a direct relation with the democracy of consumers. In the historical context of English schooling culture such a thesis was radical in conception, plausible in advocacy, and appealing to a significant constituency of voters. It was difficult for most educational leaders, whether national or local politicians, church leaders or headteachers, to oppose directly what appeared to be an important advance in the democratization of schooling.

The headteachers in this study were caught up in these social and political transitions in the nature of schooling culture and with the implications for a changed form of school leadership which flowed from them. Earlier chapters have demonstrated their varied reactions to these transitions. While there were enthusiasts for such changes, the majority of headteachers adopted a cautious, sceptical or defensive stance about the new relationships with the democracy of consumers. The headteacher accounts quoted in previous chapters have illuminated the various grounds for their scepticism and defensiveness. Some of them relate to the confrontational and politically insensitive mode in which such education reforms have been imposed upon headteachers. Others relate to more fundamental concerns about the weakening of important professional and educational values in schooling. The most general ground for their caution, however, arises from the problematic relationship between notions of professional school leadership and notions of democratic accountability and control.

Relationships between leadership culture in English schooling and various realizations of democratic culture historically have been under-developed. The rapid and confrontational educational reforms of the 1980s and 1990s have brought these relationships to the top of the education policy agenda in a sudden and imposed form. Contemporary headteachers now have to work in situations of greater 'democratic accountability' than ever before, although many of them are sceptical about the particular ideological forms in which 'democratic accountability' is being realized. The insulated culture of English schooling has been subjected in the view of many teachers to what Roy (1983) denounced as unacceptable 'political interventionism'.[7] This political interventionism has been expressed in forms which seem to threaten certain essential features of teacher and headteacher professional autonomy. The occupational danger for both teachers and headteachers is that in such a reform context they will become preoccupied with devising strategies for the defence of the old order rather than in exploring the potentialities for progressive change.

It is ironic and contradictory in many ways, that a strong state using a management and market ideology in education should at the same time have precipitated fundamental questions about the relationship between English schooling and notions of democratic accountability, and yet this is what has happened. As an unintended consequence of the radical reforms of the 1980s and 1990s, the historically marginalized issue of schooling and democracy has been brought to centre stage in English culture. It is, therefore, of some importance for the future of educational leadership to go beyond current ideological formulations of what that relationship might be, to attempt a more impartial and analytical examination.

School Leadership Culture and Democratic Culture

In a sustained and scholarly examination of this question Gutmann (1987) has concluded that:

> 'Political education'—the cultivation of the virtues, knowledge and skills necessary for political participation—has moral primacy over other purposes of public education in a democratic society . . . The moral primacy of political education also supports a presumption in favor of more participatory over more disciplinary methods of teaching . . . Democratic education is best viewed as a shared trust of parents, citizens, teachers and public officials. (pp.287–8)

Gutmann's argument is that intelligent and active participation in political and civic life must be the primary aim of schooling in a democratic society. Such participation is crucial to the generation and empowering of particular conceptions of the good life, the just society, the equitable distribution of resources and the nature and provision of public services. It is basic to processes of social reproduction, modification or transformation. For Gutmann, education has failed if it has failed to produce the necessary competences, skills, dispositions and confidence for students to take advantage of their political status of citizens in a democracy. From this perspective, if democratic culture is to be renewed and strengthened, then schooling itself must be permeated by appropriate democratic practice.

While this may have been a powerful constituent of American schooling culture, it has never achieved such status in English schooling. In particular, English school leadership has, in the main, been characterized by class control, autocratic control, statist control and professional control at various historical periods. It has never achieved an organic working relationship with democratic culture or with democratic community. The effect of the radical education reforms of the 1980s and 1990s has broken the leadership settlements of earlier periods. What school leadership could be and should be is now at the centre of a potential educational and cultural transformation. As indicated in previous chapters, there are potentialities for school leadership to be returned[8] to class and patriarchal control (by class and patriarchal domination of governing bodies); there are potentialities for school leadership by headteachers to be continued by manipulation of new arrangements for governance; there are potentialities for the value commitments of educational leadership to be fundamentally changed by management and market values; and there are potentialities for the emergence of new forms of democratically accountable school leadership. Following Gutmann's argument, it could be said that the relationship of school leadership to democratic accountability and to democratic practice in general is the key theoretical and practical issue of the present juncture. It is this issue above all which needs the attention of the reflective practitioner and the reflective community.

At present, a rhetoric of democratic accountability in schooling stands in a contradictory relationship with the actual forms in which it is being realized. Headteachers as school leaders are expected to be accountable to school governing bodies (only partially representative of local communities) and to a constituency of parents rather than a constituency of citizens. In other words, the culture of accountability now empowered in English schooling is corporatist and consumerist rather than democratic. The new order in English schooling is being constructed upon the model of a commercial enterprise with the school governors (as the directors), the headteacher (as chief executive), the parents (as consumers) and the teachers and pupils (as workers).[9] This may be called democratic accountability but it is, in fact, market accountability.

The educational, cultural, and leadership consequences which market accountability seems likely to generate (as earlier chapters have indicated) are not, in essence, democratic but calculative. The organizing concepts of the new regime of English schooling are markets, consumers and strong leadership. These are the concepts which are central to the discourse of radical school reformation. Market forces in education and the empowerment of consumers can produce greater levels of institutional responsiveness in organizations previously insulated from direct public responsibility. They are not, however, the only forms in which greater responsiveness and accountability can be achieved in schooling. As Gutmann (1987) has argued, if democratic education is taken seriously as a prime commitment of the schooling system, then greater responsiveness and accountability can be found by a closer articulation of schooling culture with democratic culture and with concepts of local democracy. Democratic accountability in schooling, when taken seriously, is a far more radical conception than market accountability. Its organizing concepts are communities, citizens and democratic leadership and the model for the school is not that of the commercial enterprise but that of democratic community itself.

Part of the difficulty which arises in even conceptualizing these possibilities in English schooling culture is related to the hegemony of particular versions of strong leadership in education. Strong leadership both in its historical and cultural formation and in its present manifestations in New Right ideology individualizes leadership potential or at least restricts it as the legitimate function of a small, controlling group. If schooling requires strong leadership (and it is generally thought that it does) then such leadership is looked for in exceptional individuals or in limited constituencies of 'responsible' citizens.

It is possible to argue, against these traditional forms, for another conception of strong leadership in education. This would be a leadership which was strong enough to open up the schooling process to the scrutiny and the participation of all citizens in the locality. Such wider democratic involvement would require imaginative and hospitable settings and user-friendly means of communication and dialogue if it was not to collapse into formal tokenism. The notion of the Community Forum[10], as first articulated in the education reforms of the fourth Labour government in New Zealand, provides a model for realizing such wider democratic accountability in schooling (Grace, 1990). Within the school itself an alternative conception of strong leadership could be realized in a leadership which was strong enough to facilitate internal, democratic accountability in other than nominal forms. Pat White's 'unashamedly radical' thesis (1983) could be acted upon:

> In a participatory democracy there would be training for the whole staff in school organization and the role of the 'head' would be radically different. (p.118)

The headteacher, elected by an appropriate constituency for a particular period of office, would constitute a strong form of democratic accountability in schooling. It would also assist in the transformation of the school's hidden curriculum of hierarchy into a visible curriculum of democratic practice.[11]

Democratic culture within the school could be strengthened further if pupils and students elected by their peers were represented in decision-making bodies and school governing bodies. The idea that school pupils and students are too immature to participate in responsible decision making in schools or aspects of school governance is a useful argument for the maintenance of adult and professional hegemony. There is now evidence, however, to suggest that children and young people have greater political and organizational intelligence than the ideology of immaturity has projected.[12] With suitable preparation, there is no reason to suppose that elected representatives of the learning community in the school would be other than valuable participants in the exercise of greater democratic accountability within schooling.

There are, of course, many impediments to the effective realization of democratic school leadership. The most obvious of these is the existence of external political, economic and ideological conditions which are inimical to the serious development of democratic education as opposed to limited realizations of it. Similarly, if legal and bureaucratic structures relating to education remain hierarchical in their conceptions of authority and institutional responsibility, then any democratization of school culture is heading for inevitable conflict. Within English schooling culture, in particular, there is no obvious reason why formerly autonomous and empowered headteachers should welcome a democratization process which will inevitably constrain their own professional and leadership autonomy. The fieldwork accounts of this study have demonstrated that the number of committed headteacher–democrats is very small. After a long historical struggle to establish the domain of teacher and headteacher autonomy in English schooling, it is not surprising that most of the headteacher participants in this research were cautious about the implications of 'democratic accountability'. This cannot be dismissed as mere vested interest or as the innate conservatism of English headteachers in a situation of radical change. It represents a more profound and considered caution about getting the balance right between the legitimate sphere of professional autonomy and leadership in schooling and the legitimate sphere for the authority and practice of democratic culture.

In the shaping of any democratic settlement of schooling, it seems clear that the partnership of governance or 'shared trust' (in Gutmann's terms) has to produce an equitable and effective representation of the interests of the central and the local state, the interests of the education professional and the students, and the interests of local, democratic community. A major problem in accomplishing such a settlement lies in the sheer difficulty of achieving such a balance, which is, in the last analysis, a balance of power. It could be said that the history of all hitherto existing educational settlements in England has been a history of power domination rather than of power sharing. A democratic school settlement has yet to emerge.

For all these difficulties, there remain powerful arguments for the necessity of a more democratic school culture and a more democratic school leadership in the future. Not to proceed in this direction entails a major contradiction between education for democracy as a formal aim of the schooling system and the actual experience of non-democratic socialization which is the hidden curriculum of most schools. English political life has been histor-ically characterized by an early achievement of formal democratic rights for citizens but also by schooling cultures which have failed to take education for democratic citizenship seriously. A more visibly democratic practice of school leadership and governance could strengthen responsible political education in schools.

More democratic and inclusive forms of school leadership and governance would also have the advantage of sharing the work intensification and 'moral maze' complexities which face contemporary school leaders. This study has shown that contemporary headteachers, even with the support of school governors, senior management teams and professional support groups, have experienced work intensification which has had deleterious effects upon both their professional and their personal lives. It has also shown the range and complexity of the moral, ethical and professional dilemmas which headteachers encounter in their work. The culture of individual school leadership, as practised by the headteacher, is breaking under the impact of work intensification and moral dilemma intensification. There are, therefore, strong functional and instrumental arguments for saying that this intensification and organizational pressure in schools should be more democratically shared with school gov-ernors, with teachers and students, and with members of the local commun-ity. Headteachers, as leading professionals, might continue to take the initiative in the resolution of difficult policy issues in schooling but responsibility for final decision making could be located more explicitly and more visibly in wider democratic structures.

It would be naive to suppose, however, that such a transition could be smoothly accomplished even if both the external and internal conditions for change seemed right. There remains an intrinsic tension between notions of professional school leadership and notions of democratic school governance. Lynn Davies (1990) argues that the very concept of leadership, even of demo-cratic leadership, should become redundant in the future of school governance:

> Put simply then, to achieve equity and efficiency, out go coercion, streaming, hierarchies and leadership; and in come federalism, power-sharing, organizational responsiveness . . . (p.210)

The concept of leadership from this perspective preserves the concept of 'headship', which in turn preserves the culture of hierarchy and therefore subverts the growth of democratic practice in education. This is a powerful argument but given the undeveloped state of democratic culture and practice both in external political relations and in the internal culture of schools, the excision of leadership from either the consciousness or the discourse of edu-cation seems improbable. In fact, as this study has shown, moves, both to a market culture in schooling and to autonomous, opted-out school status, have been generative of a new discourse of strong leadership.

The challenge, at this present juncture in education policy and practice, is to construct balanced and representative forms of democratic school leadership. Such leadership could go beyond education management. It could go beyond the market to the community. It could go beyond consumer culture to a greater realization of democratic culture. It could go beyond existing conceptions of strong leadership to demonstrate that it is possible to be strong in participative leadership. Such work can begin, even in present structural and ideological circumstances, because potentiality for such changes exists in the contradictions of contemporary education reforms.

Notes and References

1 In the example quoted, the question is, what constitutes 'Catholic educational leadership'? The answer to this question is no longer as clear cut as it once was.
2 To introduce more participative governance might be a stimulating and rewarding leadership experience. To live with its day-to-day reality might be a different experience. *Praxis* in other words might be harder to live with.
3 Schools premised on a model of Athenian democracy allow 'citizenship' rights for teachers but not for pupils, other school staff or parents and community members.
4 Part of the reason for this is that executive and entrepreneurial modes of leadership tend to place a premium on rapid decision making and an 'action this day' imperative. Democratic and professional modes generally involve longer discussion, consultation and reflection requirements.
5 Professional merit criteria were the formal categories for regulating the activity of appointing committees in the social democratic period. In practice, unofficial criteria, relating to the political or religious affiliation of candidates or to their race or gender continued to have an influence. Participants in this inquiry mentioned the importance of political networks and of gender as gateway mechanisms in access to headteacher positions in the region.
6 See Education Group (1981, pp.36–46) for a discussion of statism in social democracy. One of its interpretations is that the local education state may claim to act for the popular or community interest but as a result of its own bureaucratic procedures may not be in an organic relationship with community members. Statism then becomes action for the people rather than action by the people.
7 This account by a practising headteacher and leading member of the National Union of Teachers represents a strong defence of teachers' professional autonomy in the face of political interventionism by the state.
8 In one sense, it can be argued that school leadership cannot be 'returned' to patriarchal control because, in England at any rate, it has remained under patriarchal control.
9 It can be noted that the undermining of teachers' professional status and their terms and conditions of service which has occurred during the 1980s in England has given much credence to earlier predictions that a process of proletarianization of teaching is taking place; see Ozga (1988) and Grace (1991).
10 The Community Education Forum was intended to be a setting in which all interested citizens in a locality could express their views on significant issues of education policy. For details see *Tomorrow's Schools: the Reform of Educational Administration in New Zealand (the Picot Report)* Wellington, New Zealand, Government Printer, 1988.
11 There are many difficult questions to be resolved here. What would be the appropriate constituency for the election of a headteacher? What would be an appropriate

term of office and what salary and status safeguards would be equitable when headship was a rotational office rather than a permanent one? The notion of rotational or elective headship is not, however, without precedents. Knox (1953, p.40) records the practice in nineteenth-century Scottish education, and in more recent times elected Chairpersons have replaced permanent Heads of Department in many higher education institutions. For a discussion of the changing leadership culture of higher education institutions see Middlehurst (1993).

12 See, for instance, the work of Cullingford (1992).

Chapter 12

Politics, Markets and Democratic Schools

The whole world is being swept by a realization that markets have tremendous advantages over central control and bureaucracy. (Chubb and Moe, 1992, p.46)

In reporting to Americans on *A Lesson in School Reform From Great Britain*, Chubb and Moe (1992) are convinced that the radical education reforms of the 1980s and 1990s have much to teach the American educational system about decentralization, competition and choice. From this perspective, direct democratic control of schooling in America exercised by communities, state legislatures and school boards has simply resulted in bureaucratic domination rather than democratic responsiveness or effective scholarly performance. For Chubb and Moe, constitutional democracy as a system of governance for schools has failed. The salvation of America's schools in the future will be found, not in the culture and procedures of constitutional democracy, but in the culture and dynamics of market democracy. Market democracy by the empowerment of parents and students through resource-related choices in education has the potential, according to Chubb and Moe, to produce greater responsiveness and academic effectiveness.

British educational reform, and in particular the strong contemporary emphasis upon choice in an educational market, is seen to be the way forward for American reform. Britain has 'boldly' implemented a market democracy in education through various mechanisms for the empowerment of choice within government guidelines:

Choice is not a free market system. Its educational markets operate within an institutional framework and the government's job is to design the framework . . . If this framework is designed with care and concern, markets can be allowed to work their wonders within it— for everyone's benefit.[1]

This 1992 report to the American people, reinforced by interviews with a small and unrepresentative sample of English headteachers,[2] gives the impression that market democracy in schooling is already 'working its wonders' for the transformation of English schooling culture. This being so, Americans are encouraged not to be left behind:

In fundamental respects then Britain is not unique. What is happening there is happening in the United States: the problems, the reforms, the conflicts, and the alliances are all roughly the same. The only real difference is that Britain, owing to its parliamentary form of government, has been able to move further and faster toward a radical overhaul of its educational system—and is far more likely to succeed.[3]

This present essay cannot conclude in the same terms of high ideological confidence and triumphalism. It is far from obvious that English schooling culture is being swept by the realization that market democracy has tremendous advantages. The majority of the headteacher participants in this study had experienced a much more complex and contradictory matrix of changes which had involved the simultaneous impact of increased central control and bureaucracy, on the one hand, with moves towards a deregulated education market, on the other.

What this study has demonstrated is that English headteachers, as school leaders, have deplored the action of a strong state in attempting 'bold and rapid' transformation of schooling culture without due processes of professional and democratic consultation. It has also shown that while the majority of headteachers have welcomed the greater freedom for manouevre involved in local management of schools, they have wished to operate that freedom in a responsible relation with reformed local democracy in education. The strong form of market democracy in schooling has been represented by Chubb and Moe (1990) in these terms:

> Schools would be legally autonomous; free to govern themselves as they want, specify their own goals and programs and methods, design their own organizations, select their own student bodies and make their own personnel decisions. Parents and students would be legally empowered to choose among alternative schools . . . (p.226)

Thus the vision for the future has been a scenario of varied and freestanding schools, characterized by strong leadership at the individual-site level and responsive to the market democracy of consumer choice. It would be a misrepresentation of the present state of schooling culture in England, however, to imply that such a vision had been endorsed by the majority of English school leaders (governors and headteachers) or by a majority of parents and community members.[4]

It is possible to represent the resistance to market democracy shown by most of the headteachers in this study as professional conservatism, vested interest and 'fear of freedom'. On the other hand, it is possible to interpret it as an informed professional judgment about its limitations. Whatever interpretation is adopted, it cannot be denied that the autonomous tradition of English school headship does not articulate easily with either constitutional democratic control (as realized in the local education authority, empowered governing bodies or community forum) or with market democratic control (as realized in greater inter-school competitiveness and empowered educational consumers).

What this study has demonstrated is that English school leadership is at a major cultural turning point. The established cultural practices and the old leadership settlements are breaking up and new patterns are emerging. The critical question is, what will shape these new patterns and what form will they take?

English school leadership has moved historically from being the property of a dominant class to being the practice of a dominant leader. It has moved again from being the practice of a dominant leader to being a shared enterprise with teachers and school governors. Now, in an era of democratic account-ability in schooling, it has to construct new relationships and a new sense of vision. Although, as the headteacher accounts of this study have shown, there will be attempts to preserve the old relationships, these can only be short-term tactical manouevres. If headteachers are, as educational leaders, the providers of strategic vision and the articulators of fundamental principles, then it is clear that they have a crucial role in the transition of English schooling to greater democratic accountability in some form. At this present juncture, the strategic choice appears to be a democratic accountability mediated by a relationship with an educational market or a democratic accountability mediated by a relationship with democratic community. Chubb and Moe (1990) have argued that 'there are many paths to democracy and public education' (p.229) and this claim can be accepted. The question for educational judgment and for educational leadership is, which is the best path?

The headteachers in this study were cautious about taking the path of market democracy in education. Their professional caution, as educational leaders, arose in most cases because they believed that market forces and market values in education would be inimical to educational and professional values. Democratic accountability to the market had, in their view, the po-tential to distort values and relationships and the nature of education itself. How could education—which has at its heart a concern for religious, moral, ethical and value issues and for the equitable nurture of all children and young people—become accountable to market democracy which cannot give a special place to any of these considerations?

The majority of headteachers in this study did not believe that markets would 'work wonders—for everyone's benefit'. They recognized that markets might work wonders for a minority of schools but to the disadvantage of other schools and communities. Observing the potential effects of market accountability from a professional standpoint which endorsed the serious pursuit of equality of educational opportunity, most of the participants in this research did not believe that this constituted the best path for progress.

Some of them were critical of the claim that market accountability was in fact a form of democratic accountability. To be more accountable to par-ents and school governors was an advance in the culture of English schooling, but parents and governors were only a sector of the local community. How representative were they?

Most of these English headteachers were cautious about the combined effects of managerial and market culture upon the nature of educational leadership itself. The incremental progression from scholar/professional/teacher to manager/executive/entrepreneur was being experienced as a profound cultural transformation. There was considerable uncertainty, in most cases, as to the long-term effects of these changes upon relationships with curriculum and pedagogy and with social and educational relationships with teachers and pupils.

If these headteachers were cautious about the path of market accountability and market democracy, they were also cautious about the path of greater community accountability. Relatively few of them welcomed the new partnerships with empowered school governors as providing the first stage towards a fuller realization of community involvement in educational decision making. Their caution in this case arose primarily because they still conceived of such involvement as 'interference' in the realm of professional jurisdiction rather than as partnership in a shared enterprise of schooling. A long historical concern to protect the proper sphere of professional autonomy in education resulted in a generally defensive stance to ideas for greater community involvement in the setting of the educational mission.

The dilemma for English headteachers as school leaders is, should they take the path of market accountability in schooling, or should they take the path of community accountability?[5] The first option claims the legitimacy of responding to the democracy of consumers. The second option involves responding to the democracy of citizens (including the pupils). Stated in this form, of course, the leadership dilemma is oversimplified. In the first place, the 'options' are heavily constrained by government empowerment of, and advocacy for, market accountability. This, in political terms, is the real option. As this study has demonstrated, once a group of school leaders begins to operate upon market principles in their locality, it becomes difficult for other adjacent schools to opt-out of competitive marketing relationships. This means that despite professional reservations about market accountability, the responsibility of educational leaders to ensure institutional survival in competitive conditions removes the notion that there is a policy option. English headteachers are not unfamiliar with a political discourse which simultaneously articulates 'choice' and the injunction 'there is no alternative'.[6]

For those headteachers who are attracted to market accountability, generally from the base of a strongly resourced school, new forms of executive and entrepreneurial leadership have their rewards. These rewards may be immediate and tangible in salary and status enhancements or micro-political in strengthening the power relations of executive school leadership. In other words, democratic accountability to an external market need not result in greater internal democracy in a school but rather to a renaissance, in modern form, of strong leadership.

Against such structural empowerment, external pressures and internal inducements to take the path of market accountability in schooling, the 'option' for greater democratic accountability to the community seems theoretical—a construct of the educational seminar rather than of the culture of practical school leadership. Such a view arises, however, only if school leaders in England remain parochial in outlook. There are models of democratic accountability in schooling and of democratic leadership and practice in education from which English schooling could learn. But, as with all learning, the critical issue is motivation to learn. If English headteachers wish to resist the marketization of schooling then they will have to learn more about the democratization of schooling. If Gutmann's (1987) argument for the moral primacy of democratic education is accepted, then the moral primacy of accountability to the community rather than to the market can be asserted. From this perspective 'democratic community' is the larger and morally prior concept, which subsumes market relations as one sector of its activities and field of operation. Education's responsibilities are, therefore, primarily to the democracy of citizens rather than to the democracy of consumers.

It is, however, one thing to claim moral primacy for an educative relationship. It is quite another thing to show that such a relationship can be realized in practice. It is here that the comparative study of already existing forms of democratic education and of democratic educational leadership assumes importance. Although different models of educational practice cannot be simplistically transposed from one cultural setting to another, the examination of such models can provide the basis for appropriate cultural adaptation. If educational leadership in England, for instance, is to make any serious move in the direction of greater democratic accountability, then lessons must be learned from other historical and cultural settings—and there are models from which to learn.

Chubb and Moe (1990 and 1992) have suggested that constitutional democratic control has been the pattern of American schooling and that it has clearly failed. They have encouraged American policy makers and citizens to look to Britain's example in moving towards forms of market accountability in schooling. However, it is by no means obvious that the assertions of Chubb and Moe represent a consensus of American educators or of American citizens. There are other claims, that the schooling system of the USA demonstrates various types of democratic control and leadership and that some of these types are associated with greater responsiveness and greater educational effectiveness.[7] In other words, the suggestion that America can learn from Britain about educational markets, rather than Britain learning from America about educational democracy in action, seems premature. The schooling system of the USA has been historically a vast and complex setting for the realization of forms of democratic leadership in education. There is much to be learned from this democratic culture of schooling.

In Europe, the Laboratory of Democratic Educational Research at the Royal Danish School of Educational Studies in Copenhagen has disseminated examples of the process of democratization in schools. There are examples of power sharing in education to be studied[8] in Denmark (school democratization), in Germany (Oberstufen-Kolleg, Bielefeld), in France (The Villeneuve Project), in the Netherlands (The Kinkerhoek Project), in Portugal (democratic school management) and in Spain (elected headteachers).[9] Deem (1994) has noted that in Catalunya, an autonomous region of Spain:

> What is striking . . . both in the ideological rhetoric of the education system and in the structures adopted, is the strong belief in democratic participation in the school for its own sake. (p.34)

As Soutendijk (1989) argues, 'democracy can't work without publicity' (p.190). In the struggle to shape schooling systems and forms of educational leadership for the future it is remarkable how much publicity has been given to market reforms of schooling in the USA and Britain and how little publicity has been given to democratic reforms in Europe. Reviewing various moves towards greater democratization of schooling in Europe, Jensen and Walker (1989) accept that democratization of education is a process and a struggle in many national contexts rather than an accomplishment. Nevertheless at whatever level the process is operative, the constant factor throughout is a commitment to power sharing in education and to the idea that education is the central responsibility of democratic community. Simons (1987), in arguing for greater democratic involvement in the evaluation of school achievements and outcomes, recognizes that:

> It will take time and patience and planning to achieve at the local level any form of democratization that has a chance of empowering the traditionally powerless both within the classroom and within the community. (p.250)

Such proposals for democratic involvement, not only in the setting of the educational mission of the school but in the evaluation of its outcomes, are imaginative and radical. These ideas need as much publicity, for public deliberation, as propositions that market forces will 'work wonders' in education.

In the debates which must take place about the future of education and of educational leadership, existing school leaders have a particular responsibility. In England, for instance, school governors and headteachers are strategically placed to be the providers of a vision for the future. It is important that they resist complete *immersion*[10] in day-to-day management concerns to find the spaces and the settings for the exercise of reflective leadership. Reflective leadership has to evaluate the claims that market accountability is the best path for schooling and society against the claims that community accountability is the best path. It is not possible to be neutral in this debate. As this study has shown, powerful interests and ideological agencies are working to empower the market solution for educational provision and leadership. The commodification of education and the corporatization of educational leadership is already in progress in a number of societies. The only agency which has both the legitimacy and the capacity to resist these developments (if it chooses to do so) is democratic community, fully informed and fully active.[11]

Greenfield (1986) has argued that 'organizations are built on the unification of people around values' (p. 166). The responsibilities of educational leadership are to build educational institutions around central values. The great issue for the 1990s and beyond is, are those central values to be those of market culture or of democratic culture?

Notes and References

1 Chubb and Moe (1992, pp. 10–11).
2 The number of headteachers interviewed by Chubb and Moe (1992) is not stated but appears to be between six and ten, most of whom were heads of grant-maintained schools.
3 Ibid., p. 50.
4 Despite massive government publicity in favour of the grant-maintained school, for instance, only 1,000 schools have opted for this relatively autonomous status. As a proportion of Britain's 25,000 schools this suggests that English parents are not endorsing the break-up of the local education community service in favour of individual school advantage.
5 In formal terms, this is a decision for school governing bodies, insofar as they have any discretion within the strong parameters of government policy. However, it is posed as a dilemma for headteachers because in most cases school governing bodies are still likely to look to the professional leader for guidance on this issue.
6 One of the contradictions of English political and policy discourse is that 'choice' is celebrated while at the same time there is an approved 'right answer'.
7 See, for instance, Rollow and Bryk (1994).
8 See Jensen and Walker (1989).
9 The system of elected headteachers in Spain is part of a wider process for the democratization of the Spanish educational system.
10 Immersion refers to the process of becoming absorbed by day-to-day organizational 'busyness' with the result that no opportunities exist to reflect critically upon the purposes of such busyness. Immersion is a growing organizational phenomenon and it arises from work intensification.
11 See the quotation from Thomas Jefferson used as a preface in the *Picot Report*, 1988:

> I know of no safe depository of the ultimate power of the society but the people themselves and if we think them not enlightened enough to exercise their control with a wholesome discretion, the remedy is not to take it from them but to inform their discretion.

Bibliography

ADLER, S., LANEY, J. and PACKER, M. (1993) *Managing Women: Feminism and Power in Educational Management*. Buckingham, Open University Press.

AL-KHALIFA, E. (1989) 'Management by halves: Women teachers and school management', in H. DE LYON and F. MIGNIUOLO (Eds) *Women Teachers: Issues and Experiences*, Milton Keynes, Open University Press.

ALLEN, B. (1968) (Ed.) *Headship in the 1970s*, Oxford, Basil Blackwell.

ANGUS, L.B. (1988) *Continuity and Change in Catholic Schooling*, London, Falmer Press.

APPLE, M. (1988) 'Work, class and teaching', in J. OZGA (Ed.) *SchoolWork: Approaches to the Labour Process in Teaching*, Milton Keynes, Open University Press.

APPLE, M. (1989) 'Critical introduction: ideology and the state in educational policy', in R. DALE (Ed.) *The State and Education Policy*, Milton Keynes, Open University Press.

ARNOT, M. (1994) 'Male hegemony, social class and women's education', in L. STONE (Ed.) *The Education Feminist Reader*, London, Routledge.

ARNOTT, M., BULLOCK, A. and THOMAS, H. (1992) *The Impact of Local Management on Schools: A Source Book: The First Report of the 'Impact' Project*, Birmingham, School of Education.

ARTHUR, J. (1994a) 'Catholic responses to the 1988 Education Reform Act: problems of authority and ethos', in L. FRANCIS and D.W. LANKSHEAR (Eds) *Christian Perspectives on Church Schools*, Leominster, Fowler Wright Books.

ARTHUR, J. (1994b) 'Parental involvement in Catholic schools: A case of increasing conflict', *British Journal of Educational Studies*, XXXXII, 2, June, pp.179–90.

BACON, A.W. (1978) *Public Accountability and the Schooling System*, London, Harper and Row.

BALL, S.J. (1987) *The Micropolitics of the School*, London, Routledge.

BALL, S.J. (1990) *Politics and Policy Making in Education: Explorations in Policy Sociology*, London, Routledge.

BALL, S.J. (1994) *Education Reform: A Critical and Past-Structural Approach*, Milton Keynes, Open University Press.

BARNARD, C. (1972) *The Functions of the Executive*, Cambridge, Mass., Harvard University Press.

BARNES, C. (1993) *Practical Marketing for Schools*, Oxford, Blackwell Business.

BARON, G. (1970) 'Some aspects of the headmaster tradition', in P.W. MUSGRAVE (Ed.) *Sociology, History and Education*, London, Methuen.

BARRY, C. and TYE, F. (1972) *Running a School*, London, Temple Smith.

BATES, R. (1992) 'Leadership and School Culture', paper presented at the University of Seville, December 1992, Faculty of Education, Deakin University, Australia.

BEARE, H., CALDWELL, B. and MILLIKAN, R. (1993) 'Leadership', in M. PREEDY (Ed.) *Managing the Effective School*, London, Paul Chapman.

BECK, L. and MURPHY, J. (1993) *Understanding the Principalship: Metaphorical Themes, 1920s–1990s*, New York, Teachers College Press.

BELL, L. (1989) *Management Skills in Primary Schools*, London, Routledge.

BELL, L. (1992) *Managing Teams in Secondary Schools*, London, Routledge.

BENNIS, W. (1959) 'Leadership theory and administrative behaviour', *Administrative Science Quarterly*, 4, pp.259–301.

BERNBAUM, G. (1973) 'Countesthorpe College, Leicester United Kingdom, in *Case Studies of Educational Innovation III, Centre for Educational Research and Innovation*, Paris, OECD.

BERNBAUM, G. (1976) 'The role of the head', in R.S. PETERS (Ed.) *The Role of the Head*, London, Routledge.

BERNSTEIN, B. (1977) 'Aspects of the relations between education and production', in B. BERNSTEIN *Class, Codes and Control: Vol.3. Towards a Theory of Educational Transmissions* (2nd edn), London, Routledge.

BERNSTEIN, B. (1990) *The Structuring of Pedagogic Discourse: Vol.IV. Class, Codes and Control*, London, Routledge.

BLACKMORE, J. (1989) 'Educational leadership: A feminist critique and reconstruction', in J. SMYTH (Ed.) *Critical Perspectives on Educational Leadership*, London, Falmer Press.

BOTTERY, M. (1990) *The Morality of the School*, London, Cassell.

BOTTERY, M. (1993) *The Ethics of Educational Management*, London, Cassell.

BOURDIEU, P. and PASSERON, J.C. (1977) *Reproduction: In Education, Society and Culture*, London, Sage.

BOWE, R. and BALL, S.J. with GOLD, A. (1992) *Reforming Education and Changing Schools: Case Studies in Policy Sociology*, London, Routledge.

BROADFOOT, P., POLLARD, A., CROLL, P., OSBORN, M. and ABBOTT, D. 'National Assessment: who calls the shots?' paper presented at AERA Conference, New Orleans, April 1994.

BRIAULT, E. and WEST, N. (1990) (Eds) *Primary School Management: Learning from Experience*, London, Routledge.

BRYK, A., LEE, V. and HOLLAND, P. (1993) *Catholic Schools and the Common Good*, Cambridge, Mass., Harvard University Press.

BUCKLEY, J. (1985) *The Training of Secondary School Heads in Western Europe*, Windsor, NFER-Nelson.

BURNHAM, P.S. (1968) 'The deputy head', in B. ALLEN (Ed.) *Headship in the 1970s*, Oxford, Basil Blackwell.

BUSH, T. *et al.* (1980) (Eds) *Approaches to School Management*, London, Harper and Row.

CAINES, J. (1992) 'Improving education through better management: A view from the DES', in T. SIMKINS, L. ELLISON and V. GARRETT (Eds) *Implementing Educational Reform: The Early Lessons*, Harlow, Longman.

CALDWELL, B. and SPINKS, J. (1988) *The Self-Managing School*, London, Falmer Press.

CALDWELL, B. and SPINKS, J. (1992) *Leading the Self-Managing School*, London, Falmer Press.

CALLAHAN, R.E. (1964) *Changing Conceptions of the Superintendent in Public Education 1865–1964*, Cambridge Mass., Harvard Graduate School of Education.

CAMPBELL, J. and EMERY, H. (1994) 'Curriculum policy for key stage 2: possibilities, contradictions and constraints', in A. POLLARD (Ed.) *Look Before You Leap: Research Evidence for the Curriculum at Key Stage Two*, London, Tufnell Press.

CARRINGTON, B. and TYMMS, P. (1994) 'Headteachers' perspectives on policy changes in primary education: a national survey', in I. REID, H. CONSTABLE and P. GRIFFITHS (Eds) *Teacher Education Reform: The Research Evidence*, London, Paul Chapman.

CAVE, E. and WILKINSON, C. (1990) (Eds) *Local Management of Schools: Some Practical Issues*, London, Routledge.

CHITTY, C. (1989) *Towards a New Education System: The Victory of the New Right?* London, Falmer Press.

CHITTY, C. (1992) *The Education System Transformed*, Manchester, Baseline Books.

CHUBB, J. and MOE, T. (1990) *Politics, Markets and America's Schools*, Washington, The Brookings Institute.

CHUBB, J. and MOE, T. (1992) *A Lesson in School Reform from Great Britain*, Washington, The Brookings Institute.

CODD, J. (1989) 'Educational leadership as reflective action', in J. SMYTH (Ed.) *Critical Perspectives in Educational Leadership*, London, Falmer Press.

COFFIELD, F. (1994) 'The stoned age', *Times Educational Supplement*, 4068, 17 June, p.21.

CORDINGLEY, P. and KOGAN, M. (1993) *In Support of Education: Governing the Reformed System*, London, Jessica Kingsley.

CRAIG, I. (1989) (Ed.) *Primary Headship in the 1990s*, Harlow, Longman.

CROLL, P., ABBOTT, D., POLLARD, A., BROADFOOT, P. and OSBORN, M. (1994) 'Coercion or compromise: How schools react to imposed change', paper presented at AERA Conference, New Orleans.

CROUCH, C. and HELLER, F. (1983) (Eds) *International Yearbook of Organizational Democracy*, New York, John Wiley.

CULLINGFORD, C. (1992) *Children and Society: Children's Attitudes to Politics and Power*, London, Cassell.

CUMPER, P. (1994) 'Racism, parental choice and the law', in M. HALSTEAD (Ed.) *Parental Choice and Education*, London, Kogan Page.

DALE, R. (1989) *The State and Education Policy*, Milton Keynes, Open University Press.

DALE, R. (1992) 'Review essay: Whither the state and education policy? Recent work in Australia and New Zealand', *British Journal of Sociology of Education*, 13, 3, pp.387–95.

DAVIES, B. and ANDERSON, L. (1992) *Opting out for self-management: The Early Experiences of Grant-maintained Schools*, London, Routledge.

DAVIES, B. and ELLISON, L. (1991) *Marketing the Secondary School*, Harlow, Longman.

DAVIES, J. (1993) (Ed.) *God and the Market Place: Essays in the Morality of Wealth Creation*, London, Institute of Economic Affairs.

DAVIES, L. (1987) 'The role of the primary school head', *Educational Management and Administration*, 15, pp.43–7.

DAVIES, L. (1990) *Equity and Efficiency? School Management in an International Context*, London, Falmer Press.

DEAN, J. (1987) *Managing the Primary School*, London, Routledge.

DEEM, R. (1990) 'The reform of school governing bodies: The power of the consumer over the producer?', in M. FLUDE and M. HAMMER (Eds) *The Education Reform Act 1988: Its Origins and Implications*, London, Falmer Press.

DEEM, R. (1991) 'Governing by Gender? school governing bodies after the Education Reform Act', in P. ABBOTT and C. WALLACE (Eds) *Gender, Power and Sexuality*, London, Macmillan.

DEEM, R. (1993) 'Educational Reform and School Governing Bodies in England 1986–92: old dogs, new tricks or new dogs, new tricks?', in M. PREEDY (Ed.) *Managing the Effective School*, London, Paul Chapman.

DEEM, R. (1994) 'Free marketeers or good citizens? Educational policy and lay participation in the administration of schools', *British Journal of Educational Studies*, XXXXII, 1, March 1994, pp.23–37.

DEEM, R. and BREHONY, K. (1992) 'Consumers and education professionals in the organisation and administration of schools: partnership or conflict?' paper presented to AERA Conference, San Francisco.

DELYON, H. and MIGNIUOLO, F. (1989) (Eds) *Women Teachers: Issues and Experiences*, Milton Keynes, Open University.

DEPARTMENT FOR EDUCATION (1992) *Choice and Diversity: A New Framework for Schools*, (July 1992) Cm.2021. London, HMSO.

EARLEY, P., BAKER, L. and WEINDLING, D. (1990) *'Keeping the Raft Afloat': Secondary Headship Five Years On*, Slough, NFER.

EDUCATION GROUP (CCCS) (1981) *Unpopular Education: Schooling and Social Democracy in England since 1944*, London, Hutchinson.

EDUCATION GROUP II (1991) *Education Limited: Schooling and Training and the New Right since 1979*, London, Unwin Hyman.

EGAN, J. (1988) *Opting Out: Catholic Schools Today*, Leominster, Fowler Wright Books.

EVERARD, B. and MORRIS, G. (1990) *Effective School Management*, London, Paul Chapman.

EVETTS, J. (1987) 'Becoming Career Ambitious: the career strategies of married women who became primary headteachers in the 1960s and 1970s', *Educational Review*, 39, 1, pp.15–29.

EVETTS, J. (1994) *Becoming A Secondary Headteacher*, London, Cassell.

FAY, B. (1975) *Social Theory and Political Practice*, London, Allen and Unwin.

FAY, B. (1987) *Critical Social Science*, Cambridge, Polity Press.

FISCHER, F. and SIRIAANI, C. (1984) *Critical Studies in Organisation and Bureaucracy*, Philadelphia, Temple University Press.

FLEW, A. (1991) 'Educational Services: Independent competition or maintained monopoly?', in D. GREEN (Ed.) *Empowering the Parents: How to Break the Schools' Monopoly*, London, Institute of Economic Affairs.

FLYNN, M. (1985) *The Effectiveness of Catholic Schools*, Homebush, St Paul Publications.

FOSKETT, N. (1992) (Ed.) *Managing External Relations in Schools: A Practical Guide*, London, Routledge.

FOSTER, W. (1989) 'Towards a critical practice of leadership', in J. SMYTH (Ed.) *Critical Perspectives on Educational Leadership*, London, Falmer Press.

FULLAN, M. (1993) *Change Forces: Probing the Depths of Educational Reform*, London, Falmer Press.

GALBRAITH, J.K. (1992) *The Culture of Contentment*, London, Sinclair-Stevenson.

GALTON, M., SIMON, B. and CROLL, P. (1980) *Inside the Primary Classroom*, London, Routledge and Kegan Paul.

GILLBORN, D. (1989) 'Talking heads: Reflection on secondary headship at a time of rapid educational change', *School Organisation*, 9, 1, pp.65–83.

GLATTER, R. (1972) *Management Development for the Education Profession*, London, Harrap.

GOLDRING, E. and CHEN, M. (1994) 'The feminization of the principalship in Israel: The trade-off between political power and cooperative leadership', in C. MARSHALL, (Ed.) *The New Politics of Race and Gender*, London, Falmer Press.

GORDON, P. (1974) *The Victorian School Manager*, London, Woburn Press.

GRACE, G. (1978) *Teachers, Ideology and Control: A Study in Urban Education*, London, Routledge and Kegan Paul.

GRACE, G. (1984) (Ed.) *Education and the City: Theory, History and Contemporary Practice*, London, Routledge and Kegan Paul.

GRACE, G. (1987) 'Teachers and the state: A changing relation', in M. LAWN, and G. GRACE (Eds) *Teachers: The Culture and Politics of Work*, London, Falmer Press.

GRACE, G. (1989) 'Education: Commodity or public good?', *British Journal of Educational Studies*, XXXVII, 3, pp.207–21.

GRACE, G. (1990) 'Labour and education: The crises and settlements of education policy', in M. HOLLAND and J. BOSTON (Eds) *The Fourth Labour Government*, Auckland, Oxford University Press.

GRACE, G. (1991) 'The state and the teachers: Problems in teacher supply, retention and morale', in G. GRACE and M. LAWN (Eds) *Teacher Supply and Teacher Quality: Issues for the 1990s*, Clevedon, Multilingual Matters.

GRACE, G. (1994) 'Education is a public good: On the need to resist the domination of economic science', in D. BRIDGES and T. MCLAUGHLIN (Eds) *Education and the Market Place*, London, Falmer Press.

GRACE, G. (1995) 'Theorising social relations within urban schooling: A socio-historical analysis', in P. ATKINSON, B. DAVIES and S. DELAMONT (Eds) *Discourse and Reproduction*, New York, Hampton Press.

GRAY, J. (1992) *The Moral Foundations of Market Institutions*, London, Institute of Economic Affairs.

GRAY, L. (1991) *Marketing Education*, Milton Keynes, Open University Press.

GREEN, A. (1991) 'The peculiarities of English education', in Education Group II (Ed.) *Education Limited: Schooling and Training and the New Right since 1979*, London, Unwin Hyman.

GREENFIELD, T. (1986) 'The decline and fall of science in educational administration', re-printed in T. GREENFIELD and P. RIBBINS (1993) *Greenfield on Educational Administration: Towards a Humane Science*, London, Routledge.

GREENFIELD, T. and RIBBINS, P. (1993) (Eds) *Greenfield on Educational Administration: Towards a Humane Science*, London, Routledge.

GRIGGS, C. (1989) 'The new right and English secondary education', in R. LOWE (Ed.) *The Changing Secondary School*, London, Falmer Press.

GRUNDY, S. (1993) 'Educational leadership as emancipatory praxis', in J. BLACKMORE and J. KENWAY (Eds) *Gender Matters in Educational Administration and Policy: A Feminist Introduction*, London, Falmer Press.

GUTMANN, A. (1987) *Democratic Education*, Princeton, Princeton University Press.

HALDANE, J. (1993) 'A prolegomenon to an unwritten philosophy of education: Catholic social teaching and the common good', paper presented to the 'Contemporary Catholic School and the Common Good' Conference, St Edmund's College, Cambridge, July 1993.

HALL, V. (1993) 'Women in educational management: A review of research in Britain', in J. OUSTON (Ed.) *Women in Education Management*, Harlow, Longman.

HALL, V. (1994) 'Making it happen: A study of women headteachers of primary and secondary schools in England and Wales', paper presented at AERA Conference, New Orleans, April 1994.

HALL, V., MACKAY, H. and MORGAN, C. (1986) *Headteachers at Work*, Milton Keynes, Open University Press.

HALPIN, D., POWER, S. and FITZ, J. (1993) 'Opting into state control? Headteachers and the paradoxes of grant-maintained status', *International Studies in Sociology of Education*, 3, 1, pp.3–23.

HARDIE, B. (1991) *Marketing the Primary School*, Plymouth, Northcote House.

HARGREAVES, A. (1994) *Changing Teachers, Changing Times: Teachers' Work and Culture in the Postmodern Age*, London, Cassell.

HARGREAVES, D.H. (1982) *The Challenge for the Comprehensive School: Culture, Curriculum and Community*, London, Routledge.

HARVEY, D. (1989) *The Condition of Postmodernity*, Cambridge, Polity Press.

HEGARTY, S. (1983) (Ed.) *Training for Management in Schools*, Windsor, NFER-Nelson.

HMI/DES (1977) *Ten Good Schools: A Secondary School Enquiry*, London, DES.

HODGKINSON, C. (1978a) 'The failure of organisation and administrative theory', *McGill Journal of Education*, 13, 3, pp.271–8.

HODGKINSON, C. (1978b) *Towards a Philosophy of Administration*, Oxford, Basil Blackwell.

HODGKINSON, C. (1983) *The Philosophy of Leadership*, Oxford, Basil Blackwell.

HODGKINSON, C. (1991) *Educational Leadership: The Moral Art*, Albany, State University of New York Press.

HORNSBY-SMITH, M. (1978) *Catholic Education: The Unobtrusive Partner*, London, Sheed and Ward.

HOYLE, E. (1986) *The Politics of School Management*, London, Hodder and Stoughton.

HUGHES, M. (1985) 'Leadership in professionally staffed organisations', in M. HUGHES et al. (Eds) *Managing Education: The System and the Institution*, London, Cassell.

HUMES, W. (1986) *The Leadership Class in Scottish Education*, Edinburgh, John Donald.

JENSEN, K. and WALKER, S. (Eds) (1989) *Towards Democratic Schooling: European Experiences*, Milton Keynes, Open University Press.

JOHNSON, R. (1970) 'Educational policy and social control in early Victorian England', *Past and Present*, 49, pp.96–119.

JOHNSON, R. (1991) 'A new road to Serfdom? A critical history of the 1988 Act', in Education Group II, *Education Limited, Schooling and Training and the New Right since 1979*, London, Unwin Hyman.

JONES, A. (1987) *Leadership for Tomorrow's Schools*, Oxford, Basil Blackwell.

JONES, K. (1983) *Beyond Progressive Education*, London, Macmillan.

JONES, K. (1989) *Right Turn: The Conservative Revolution in Education*, London, Hutchinson.

JOYCE, M. (1987) 'Being a feminist teacher', in M. LAWN and G. GRACE (Eds) *Teachers: The Culture and Politics of Work*, London, Falmer Press.

KEDDIE, N. (1971) 'Classroom knowledge', in YOUNG, M.F.D. (Ed.) *Knowledge and Control: New Directions for the Sociology of Education*, London, Collier-Macmillan.

KNOX, H.M. (1953) *Two Hundred and Fifty Years of Scottish Education, 1696–1946*, Edinburgh, Oliver and Boyd.

KOGAN, M., JOHNSON, D., PACKWOOD, T. and WHITAKER, T. (1984) *School Governing Bodies*, London, Heinemann.

LEVACIC, R. (1991) (Ed.) *Financial Management in Education*, Milton Keynes, Open University Press.

LONDON FEMINIST HISTORY GROUP (1983) *The Sexual Dynamics of History*, London, Pluto Press.

LOWE, R. (1989) (Ed.) *The Changing Secondary School*, London, Falmer Press.

MARSHALL, C. (1994) (Ed.) *The New Politics of Race and Gender*, Washington DC, Falmer Press.

McLAREN, P. (1993) *Schooling as a Ritual Performance: Towards a Political Economy of Educational Symbols and Gestures*, London, Routledge.

McLAUGHLIN, T. (1994) 'Politics, markets and schools: The central issues', in D. BRIDGES and T. McLAUGHLIN (Eds) *Education and the Market Place*, London, Falmer Press.

McNAMEE, C. (1993) 'Catholic Schools in the US: Perspectives and Developments', paper presented to the 'Contemporary Catholic School and the Common Good' Conference, St Edmund's College, Cambridge, July 1993.

MICHELS, R. (1958) *Political Parties*, Chicago, Free Press.

MIDDLEHURST, R. (1993) *Leading Academics*, Buckingham, SRHE/Open University Press.

MONCK, E. and KELLY, A. (with EVANS, J. and LUNT, I.) (1992) *Managing Effective Schools: Local Management and its Reform*, London, Institute for Public Policy Research.

MORGAN, C. and HALL, V. (1982) 'The post project: What is the job of the secondary school head?', *Education*, 159, 25, i–iv, 18 June.

MORTIMORE, P. and MORTIMORE, J. (1991a) (Eds) *The Secondary Head: Roles, Responsibilities and Reflections*, London, Paul Chapman.

MORTIMORE, P. and MORTIMORE, J. (1991b) (Eds) *The Primary Head: Roles, Responsibilities and Reflections*, London, Paul Chapman.

MUKHERJEE, T. (1984) 'I'm not blaming you—an antiracist analysis', *Multicultural Teaching*, 2, pp.5–8.

MUSGRAVE, P.W. (Ed.) (1970) *Sociology, History and Education*, London, Methuen.

MUSGROVE, F. (1971) *Patterns of Power and Authority in English Education*, London, Methuen.

NEWCASTLE COMMISSION (1861) *Report to the Popular Education Commission*, Vol.2, London, HMSO.

O'KEEFE, J. (1993) 'Catholic schools for the poor: rationale and current status', paper presented to the 'Contemporary Catholic School and the Common Good' Conference, St Edmund's College, Cambridge, July 1993. (Boston, Boston College.)

O'KEEFFE, B. (1992) 'Catholic schools in an open society: The English challenge', in V.A. McCLELLAND (Ed.) *The Catholic School and the European Context*, Hull, University of Hull.

OZGA, J. (1988) (Ed.) *Schoolwork: Approaches to the Labour Process of Teaching*, Milton Keynes, Open University Press.

OZGA, J. (1993) (Ed.) *Women in Educational Management*, Buckingham, Open University Press.

PASCALL, G. (1986) *Social Policy: A Feminist Analysis*, London, Tavistock.

PETERS, R.S. (1976) (Ed.) *The Role of the Head*, London, Routledge.

POLLARD, A. (1985) *The Social World of the Primary School*, London Holt, Rinehart and Winston.

POLLARD, A. (1994) (Ed.) *Look Before You Leap: Research Evidence for the Curriculum at Key Stage Two*, London, Tufnell Press.

POSTER, C. (1968) 'The head and the community school', in B. ALLEN (Ed.) *Headship in the 1970s*, Oxford, Basil Blackwell.

POSTER, C. (1976) *School Decision-Making*, London, Heinemann.

PREEDY, M. (1993) (Ed.) *Managing the Effective School*, London, Paul Chapman.

PRING, R. (1993) 'Markets, education and Catholic schools', paper presented to the 'Contemporary Catholic School and the Common Good' Conference, Cambridge, July 1993. (Oxford, Department of Educational Studies).

RANSON, S. (1993) 'Markets or democracy for education', *British Journal of Educational Studies*, XXXXI, 4, pp.333–52.

RIBBINS, P. (1989) 'Managing secondary schools after the act: Participation and partnership?', in R. LOWE (Ed.) *The Changing Secondary School*, London, Falmer Press.

RILEY, K. (1994) *Quality and Equality: Promoting Opportunities in Schools*, London, Cassell.

RISEBOROUGH, G. (1993) 'Primary headship, state policy and the challenge of the 1990s: An exceptional story that disproves total hegemonic rule', *Journal of Education Policy*, 8, 2, pp.155–73.

RIZVI, F. (1989) 'In defence of organizational democracy', in SMYTH, J. (Ed.) *Critical Perspectives on Educational Leadership*, London, Falmer Press.

ROLLOW, S. and BRYK, A. (1994) 'Democratic politics and school improvement: The potential of Chicago school reform', in C. MARSHALL (Ed.) *The New Politics of Race and Gender*, London, Falmer Press.

ROY, W. (1983) *Teaching Under Attack*, London, Croom Helm.

SCHÖN, D. (1983) *The Reflective Practitioner: How Professionals Think in Action*, New York, Basic Books.

SERGIOVANNI, T. (1992) *Moral Leadership: Getting to the Heart of School Improvement*, San Francisco, Jossey-Bass.

SHAKESHAFT, C. (1989) *Women in Educational Administration*, Newbury Park, Corwin Press.

SIMKINS, T., ELLISON, L. and GARRETT, V. (1992) (Eds) *Implementing Educational Reform: The Early Lessons*, Harlow, Longmans.

SIMON, B. and CHITTY, C. (1993) *SOS: Save Our Schools*, London, Lawrence and Wishart.

SIMON, H. (1945) *Administrative Behaviour: A Study of Decision-making Process in Administrative Organisation*, New York, Free Press.

SIMONS, H. (1987) *Getting to Know Schools in a Democracy: The Politics and Process of Evaluation*, London, Falmer Press.

SOUTENDIJK, S. (1989) 'Democratization and educational theory', in K. JENSEN and S. WALKER (Eds) *Towards Democratic Schooling: European Experiences*, Milton Keynes, Open University Press.

SOUTHWORTH, G. (1988) 'Looking at leadership: English primary school headteachers at work', *Education* 3–13, 16, pp.53–6.

SMYTH, J. (1989) (Ed.) *Critical Perspectives on Educational Leadership*, London, Falmer Press.

SMYTH, J. (1993) (Ed.) *A Socially Critical View of the Self-Managing School*, London, Falmer Press.

TAYLOR, W. (1968) 'Training the head', in B. ALLEN (Ed.) *Headship in the 1970s*, Oxford, Basil Blackwell.

TAYLOR, W. (1976) 'The head as manager: Some criticisms', in R.S. PETERS (Ed.) *The Role of the Head*, London, Routledge.

THOMAS, H. (1988) 'Financial delegation: Its effect on the school and the role of the head', *School Organisation*, 8, 2, pp.177–83.

THOMAS, H. (1990) 'From local financial management to local management of schools', in M. FLUDE and M. HAMMER (Eds) *The Education Reform Act 1988: Its Origins and Implications*, London, Falmer Press.

TOMLINSON, J. (1993) *The Control of Education*, London, Cassell.

TOOLEY, J. (1992) 'The "Pink Tank" on the Education Reform Act', *British Journal of Educational Studies*, XXXX, 4, p.335.

TOOLEY, J. (1993) *A Market-led Alternative for the Curriculum: Breaking the Code*, London, Institute of Education.

TROPP, A. (1959) *The Schoolteachers*, London, Heinemann.

TROYNA, B. (1993) *Racism and Education*, Buckingham, Open University Press.

WALLACE, M. and HALL, V. (1994) 'Team Approaches to Leadership in Secondary Schools', paper presented at the AERA Meeting, New Orleans, April 4–8.

WALLER, W. (1965) *The Sociology of Teaching*, New York, Wiley.

WATKINS, P. (1989) 'Leadership, power and symbols in educational administration', in J. SMYTH (Ed.) *Critical Perspectives on Educational Leadership*, London, Falmer Press.

WATTS, J. (1976) 'Sharing it out: the role of the Head in participatory government', in R.S. PETERS (Ed.) *The Role of the Head*, London, Routledge.

WATTS, J. (Ed.) (1977) *The Countesthorpe Experience*, London, Allen and Unwin.

WEBER, M. (1947) *From Max Weber: Essays in Sociology*, GERTH, H. and WRIGHT MILLS, C. (Eds) London, Routledge.

WEST, N. (1989) 'The professional development of headteachers: The wider view', in I. CRAIG (Ed.) *Primary Headship in the 1990s*, Harlow, Longman.

WHITE, J. (1990) *Education and the Good Life*, London, Kogan Page.

WHITE, P. (1982) 'Democratic perspectives on the training of headteachers', *Oxford Review of Education*, 8, 1, pp.69–82.

WHITE, P. (1983) *Beyond Domination: An Essay in the Political Philosophy of Education*, London, Routledge and Kegan Paul.

WILKINSON, R. (1964) *The Prefects: British Leadership and the Public School Tradition*, Oxford, Oxford University Press.

WRIGHT MILLS, C. (1973) *The Sociological Imagination*, Harmondsworth, Penguin.

YATES, L. (1993) 'The theory-practice relationship in schooling: Academia and feminist theory', in J. BLACKMORE, and J. KENWAY (Eds) *Gender Matters in Educational Administration and Policy*, London, Falmer Press.

YOUNG, M.F.D. (1971) (Ed.) *Knowledge and Control: New Directions for the Sociology of Education*, London, Collier Macmillan.

YOUNG, M.F.D. (1976) *Some Thoughts on Collaborative Research with Teachers*, London, Institute of Education.

Author Index

Subject Index